SETTING GLOBAL TELECOMMUNICATION STANDARDS

The Artech House Telecommunication Library

SETTING GLOBAL TELECOMMUNICATION STANDARDS

GERD WALLENSTEIN

Artech House

Library of Congress Cataloging-in-Publication Data

Wallenstein, Gerd D.
　　Setting global telecommunications standards : the stakes, the
　players, and the process / Gerd Wallenstein.
　　　　p.　　cm.
　　Includes bibliographical references (p.　).
　　ISBN 0-89006-390-7
　　1. Telecommunication--Standards. 2. Telecommunication--
　International cooperation. I. Title.
　TK5102.5.W35　1989　　　　　　　　　　　　　　　89-27445
　384'.0218--dc20　　　　　　　　　　　　　　　　　　CIP

British Library Cataloguing in Publication Data

Wallenstein, Gerd　1913-
　　Setting global telecommunications standards
　　1. Telecommunication systems
　　I. Title
　　621.38

　　ISBN　0-89006-390-7

Copyright © 1990

ARTECH HOUSE, INC.
685 Canton Street
Norwood, MA　02062

International Standard Book Number: 0-89006-390-7
Library of Congress Catalog Card Number: 89-27445

10　9　8　7　6　5　4　3　2　1

to

Nicole, David, and Ethan

Contents

Foreword

We are witnessing dramatic changes in telecommunication all over the world: new technologies are implemented at a breathtaking speed; more and more new services and applications are offered to the customers almost every day. In addition, the regulatory environment is changing from long-standing monopolistic structures toward liberal, competitive marketplaces. Key words like deregulation, privatization, and liberalization of telecommunication networks and services are the signposts marking this new road. Also, there is no common approach to the best resolution of all these technical and regulatory challenges: each country is struggling with these problems in a different way, based on its own national telecommunication policy.

Looking at this worldwide scenario, what is evident is that standardization in telecommunication was never more crucial than today and will be even more so in the future. Telecommunication standards are the bridges providing interconnectivity and interoperability of national telecommunication networks and services.

For many years, the International Telecommunication Union (ITU) through its Consultative Committees, CCITT and CCIR, has drawn up international telecommunication standards in the form of nonbinding "Recommendations."

Yet ITU's almost exclusive role in worldwide standardization is more and more challenged—the changing environment in telecommunication worldwide is now disturbing and reforming the standardization scenario as well. As a consequence, new standardization organizations have entered the scene, such as the regional committee for North America known as T1, for Japan known as TTC and for Europe under the name of ETSI. The users, too, are flexing their muscles; they are forming user associations as third parties, ready to participate in the "standardization club" previously constituted of network and service providers and the manufacturing industry. The upcoming information technologies are blurring the borderlines between computer and telecommunication technologies; thus, ISO and IEC are moving closer to what was regarded as the domain of CCITT. Finally, regulators and politicians are more and more recognizing the need for, and the importance of, telecommunication standards as strategic tools for their national economies in securing future markets for their telecommunication products and services. Creation of ETSI, largely initiated by the European Community, is just one example of political forces influencing the standardization process.

Even for a professional telecommunication standardizer, to know who is doing what in which sector of telecommunications, is sometimes difficult as is knowing who are the main players in the international standardization puzzle.

Gerd Wallenstein, for many years a leading expert in standardization and active participant in many ITU standardization activities, has undertaken the difficult task of illuminating the current scene of international telecommunication standardization. The results of his work are now compiled in this book; it provides a comprehensive overview on the current situation of standardization worldwide. Wallenstein documents how this situation is changing under legal and political influences in regions and individual countries, and he presents the major players and forces on stage as well as behind the scenes. Although the material has been researched thoroughly and many details are given, the book addresses not only the expert, but everybody who needs to know more of the complicated web of worldwide telecommunication standardization. In the presence of numerous publications in this field, this book truly fills a gap. I am convinced that it will meet the author's objective; that is, to create a broad readership's awareness of the changing methods of international telecommunication standardization and its pivotal importance for worldwide trade and development.

Theodor Irmer
Director
CCITT

Preface

On this page, dear reader, I can address you in the first person. It gives me a time-honored, priceless opportunity for reaching out, a chance to lay bare my objectives and motivation for this effort.

A quick perusal of the Table of Contents might reveal this book's ambitious scope. The impression would be correct. I attempt to combine here four approaches to presentation of a complex subject, approaches traditionally kept separate in different publications. The four are:

- Reporting newsworthy developments;
- Analysis of these developments;
- Synthesis of decisions and events occurring over widely dispersed areas; and
- Author's judgment and opinions about the significance of these events.

Worldwide enthronement of standards policies is seen here as the most decisive phenomenon of telecommunication development. This book brings together dispersed manifestations of this phenomenon and analytically relates them to models of standardization carried forward from more serene times. This, then, concisely said, is my objective in combining reporting with synthesis and analysis.

Now, let us speak of motivation, the mainspring of my thrust into the turbulent arena, where judgment and opinion are exposed.

Thirty years ago, I attended a CCITT study group meeting for the first time. It had been called for a working party focused on a single question (number 43) in one study group. The question concerned CCITT's possible standardization of data modems "for transmission of accounting data over the telephone network." The meeting was attended by more than one hundred people, many representing companies in the data processing industry. They had no prior experience with CCITT. The meeting, CCITT's largest up to that time, turned into a somewhat theatrical clash of two cultures—if that hallowed term is not debased by the metaphor. Yet when the one-week meeting came to a close, a formula for peaceful coexistence, even collaboration, had been found. Within a year, a first set of basic data transmission characteristics was ready for approval by the 1960 Plenary Assembly. The spectacular growth of CCITT Recommendations in data modems and comprehensive data communication networks, assembled during the ensuing twenty-eight years, is already history. Collaboration between mutually distrustful bedfellows was born at one meeting's peak experience and has blossomed forth beyond any original participant's expectations.

My participation in that memorable meeting solidified a motivation that I had dimly felt until then. I became driven forward to ever widening involvement in CCITT and some CCIR work, sensing a clearly emerging power, capable of overcoming deeply entrenched nationalistic or business-competitive obstructions. From 1966 onward, I volunteered for the new handbook-writing groups, requested by developing countries. While the group composing an engineering handbook was scrupulously to stay out of preparing any new standards, the effort proved an acid test for the intelligibility and usefulness of existing CCITT Recommendations. I am confident that handbook writers (and their home offices) gained as much as, if not more than, readers in developing countries from the extraordinary experience in pooling their best expertise.

Sharing is the keynote for all international committee activities. Sharing perspectives over the effects of these activities on the telecommunication sector has motivated me to put together this new book. Now, it is the readers' turn to share.

Gerd Wallenstein   *Atherton, CA*
May 1989

ACKNOWLEDGMENTS

Much information used in this work was contributed by colleagues whose names are here recorded in gratitude.

Henry Marchese and Jeanne Smith, Bedminster, NJ; Gerhard Stürmer, Berlin; Heinrich Venhaus and Gert Hausmann, Bonn; George Lajtha, Budapest; Günther Zedler, Darmstadt; David Cairns and Ann Recktenwald, Mountain View, CA; Michel Toutan and Germain Delmas, Paris; Don Ashford, San Francisco; Diodato Gagliardi, Sophia-Antipolis; and Don Dunn, Stanford University.

Permission to use copyrighted material, granted by AT&T, Bellcore, IEEE, and Rand McNally & Company is hereby gratefully acknowledged.

Finally, I thank Vinton Cerf and Mark Walsh for valuable critique, and Mako Bockholt for patiently producing clean copy of the catalytic, first part of the manuscript.

G.W.

Introduction

Gerd Wallenstein's book is published at a very crucial point in the story of world telecommunications. Deregulation and re-regulation, open network architecture and open network provision, the installation of ISDN narrow-band and broad-band, the rapid opening of the supranational markets, the strong pressures for speeding up the standards-making process, the confirmation of the increasing power of the world regional bodies for standardization are clear indications of the deep and rapid changes in the telecommunications area.

Gerd Wallenstein has perfectly sensed these changes in the world of telecommunications; his wide experience, gained by working for many years with manufacturers, universities, and International regulatory bodies, enables him to have a clear vision of the reasons for and the outcome of the evolutionary tendencies.

He rightly stresses that the evolution in the world of telecommunications has made the need for standards extremely important, standards which are, in some ways, the architect of the evolution itself. Gerd Wallenstein's book puts an emphasis on the increasing power of telecommunications standards and analyzes the evolution of the phenomenon, taking into account the situation in many countries and regions of the world. I am quite convinced that the analysis carried out by Gerd Wallenstein provides a better comprehension of the present situation and of the future goals in telecommunications.

I have had the honor to work for many years with Gerd Wallenstein within CCITT, and, can guarantee that his great enthusiasm and ability, perspicacity, and intuition make his book a most important contribution to the world of telecommunications.

Professor Diodato Gagliardi
Director
ETSI

Sophia Antipolis,
France
November 1989

Chapter One
Introduction

A new world power is in the making—not a superpower, but a true suprapower. Its realm is the transnational structure of standards. It has no sovereign territory, no capital city, no currency, no police or military force. Its leaders owe allegiance to regional or global organizations; their broad mandates provide only for coordination of the work of others, not line management authority. Decisions are made by autonomous committees, whose members fight internecine battles that end in peace agreements published as standards. This suprapower's diffused activities proceed far from public awareness, and farther still from critical debate in the media or government circles. Yet the published output has heavy economic and political significance. Many standards acquire the force of law worldwide or regionally. They control widely used products and services, and thereby the success or failure of major businesses. However, high-level managers, business elite's "decision-makers," have little influence on standards and must accept them as decided by people at lower levels of their own organizations. Indeed, both development and administration of standards is left to experts with little management responsibility. Coming together from competing companies and diverse countries, these standards-makers form a small, transnational subculture held together by technical expertise and a specialized language of their own making.

Thus, the much hailed information age builds its own controlling structure that transcends the powers of national governments. Yet delegates designated by nations have created the standards in the first place. Once adopted internationally, a standard is supreme reference, beyond challenge by lawyers and courts. It can be unmade or modified only through the same international process. Like the law that governs in all civil law countries, a standard is of anonymous parentage. As it does not perpetuate names of its protagonists nor of any other collaborating decision-makers, it stands on its own, a presumably fair, equitable, and common property of mankind.

What may be most perplexing to actors in industries controlled by standards is their seemingly passive, self-regulating enforcement. A provider of products or services is free to ignore the applicable standards at the risk of losing customers.

However, if the provider promises to meet the standard, he must be prepared to have conformance verified down to picayune details. Thus, procurement and supply in a standards-controlled industry tend to rely on detailed specifications and customer acceptance tests characteristic of dealings with the military.

In summary, standards for the information infrastructure exert great power over service and equipment providers as well as the end users. Their power becomes more pervasive and more absolute with time in response to legal and political pressures from outside the information industries. This development takes standardization far beyond the objectives set for it by the policy-makers of cognizant organizations, on record as recently as the early 1980s. The long-term effect of standarization's trend toward status as an independent suprapower needs yet to be recognized. This book's purpose is to analyze the trend in depth.

Overview of the Chapters to Follow

The next chapter documents the significance of enforceable standards in servicing a society dependent on exchange of information. Telecommunication network performance and interworking were early targets of voluntary standardization among a few, authorized service providers. Our analysis shows why, how, and when entire groups of network standards progressed from "recommended" to "mandatory" status. A rapid, expansive evolution of telecommunication offerings stimulated a hardening of interworking requirements, voluntarily adopted by the industries' collaborating service providers. Characteristic of this trend is *"a priori"* standardization of a major product or service innovation yet to prove its worth in the marketplace. Examples document this approach.

Chapter Three, titled "Stratification and Arbitration of Standards," may be read as a tutorial. Included are definitions of standardization at different levels of governmental and nongovernmental decision making. Structure and working methods of the standardizing organizations are illustrated and explained.

Chapter Four examines the outside forces bearing down on the information industries—demanding, imposing, or enforcing standards. Legalistic decision making in favor of rigorous competition in the public service sector has been the driving force in the United States. In Western Europe, the Common Market bureaucracy of the European Communities asserts its power through political pressure. Implementation of all procompetitive measures demands pervasive standards.

Chapter Five reports on the consequences already in full view and others yet to take shape. The thesis of a standards suprapower at work is confirmed by a thoroughly documented look at new forces, intent on control of worldwide telecommunication markets. Regional committees are claiming this power, delegated to them by the respective national governments.

The evolving effect of these developments is analyzed in the final chapter. Highlighted are trends for worldwide competition, effects on developing countries' aspirations, and a need for recognizing standards activities as a critical preoccupation for competing organizations.

Chapter Two
The Industry's Own Drive to Standards

2.1 STANDARDS IN THE INFORMATION SOCIETY

Over half of the people employed in remunerative work in the United States are estimated to be engaged in processing information [1]. If we add to that the family household's increasing dependence on wired services and media, information may be seen as dominating life of the modern society. The United States and Canada appear as avant-garde in this development, a continental sized laboratory as it were; but Japan and most of Europe are duplicating it. Significantly, these other industrialized countries are no longer emulating a trend first set in North America. In fact, some, more centrally directed societies have initiated programs in the early 1970s with the purpose of leading their respective nations smoothly toward becoming full-blown "information societies."

Such long-range, ambitious plans have blossomed in Japan, where model communities have been built around a "total" computer-telecommunication infrastructure [2]. The long-time head of Nippon Electric (NEC), Dr. Koji Kobayashi, has acquired world class stature as an advocate of these concepts [3]. In France, then President Valéry Giscard d'Estaing brilliantly analyzed the changes facing French society in an information-dominated age and outlined appropriate steps for the government to take [4]. The mass introduction of a videotex type of service, named Minitel, initially subsidized by government, was a *tour de force* justified under Giscard d'Estaing's comprehensive vision. Indeed, Minitel's popular success has pushed France to the forefront of Western countries [5].

The information society functions through a pervasive telecommunication-cum-computer infrastructure, composed of networks and terminal stations. The role of standards needs to be considered separately for networks and terminals, respectively. In the following, we shall concentrate on network standards.

2.2 NEED FOR NETWORK STANDARDS

Networks differ by geographical coverage and diversity of applications. A *local area network* (LAN) may serve only a small cluster of buildings; a national telephone monopoly's network covers that country's territory from border to border. In diverse applications, one network may provide primarily speech telephone, another may offer packet switched data service. The variety of possible options has encouraged installation of narrow-purpose or single-user networks in countries where government policy permits. Economic advantages claimed for such choices frequently cite attractively amortized first costs. However, annual charges needed for maintenance and future replacement of equipment may have been ignored. Also, when users invest in their own network systems, they risk having outmoded equipment of limited flexibility on hand when the public service providers move on to improved and augmented features in step with future innovations. Moreover, decisions favoring user-independence or an upstart, nonconformist service provider may sidestep the dominant industry standards that ensure national and international through-connection.

In an information-driven society, no man or woman, no office, no home is an island; interdependence has become axiomatic. Today's one-location LAN will need to perform properly tomorrow on long-distance interconnections, lest it cause its users lost opportunities rather than promised savings. What matters most is not to decide who owns what network, but whether a network—any network—meets prevailing standards.

The make-or-break power of international network standards, as postulated here, did not originate with the link-up of computers and telecommunication. However, it extends now over myriad end-user applications, whereas previously it affected only the service providers and their suppliers. The progression of network standards from minimal, voluntary performance objectives to very detailed, binding specifications has been gradual, but relentless. It was driven by user service expectations as much as by technology and operating economics. More users accessing public telecommunication networks expected to reach more destinations with certainty, immediacy, high-quality connection, and at reasonable price. Therefore, tighter and more detailed agreements were needed among network operators of different countries. To meet these user requirements and to stimulate exploitation of available facilities, the functions of network response to call origination were progressively automated. Many monitoring and discretionary decision functions previously performed by humans were thus relegated to machines. Making machines at some distance from each other perform intricate steps in response to a few coded signals requires a very high degree of standardization. How this standardization has been accomplished is discussed in the following two sections.

2.3 LAYING THE FOUNDATIONS

The process of standardizing equipment and operating practices (i.e., software) went into high gear after World War II. Standards making began within national networks, but some international standards were soon developed for Europe, where a minimal groundwork had been laid as far back as the late 1920s [6]. Europe's national service providers, called "Administrations" in the parlance of the ITU (International Telecommunication Union; see Figure 2.1), operated as monopolies, making standardization strictly an internal affair. Decision making was coordinated, though not necessarily shared, with the respective country's leading suppliers. In North America, the dominant monopoly service providers undertook similar internal standardization. In the 1950s, what was then known as *Bell System Practices* may be said to have provided a more sophisticated and comprehensive rule book in the United States and Canada than had been assembled by European countries (see examples in Boxes 2.1 and 2.2). One incentive for standardization by the two North American Bell Systems (AT&T and Bell Canada) may be found in the necessity to serve a continental sized territory in cooperation with many independent, less sophisticated, small service providers. In this respect, the network situation in the United States and Canada presented a model of international interworking, with the difference that the many minority participants did not have the separate authority of sovereign nations. In a truly international setting, acceptance of standards must be negotiated among nominally equals. In North America, the nondominant independents accepted Bell standards for the good of interconnection; they had no influence on them.

The two North American Bell System network organizations had an additional incentive for wide ranging, meticulous technical standards: they owned the equipment manufacturers, too. Total integration of network service with the planning, design, and production of the required equipment provides a unique opportunity for maximizing the benefits of standardization. Particularly in the design and trial installation phases, technical characteristics may be distributed between transmission lines, switching and transmission equipment, customer station equipment, or even network supervisory and maintenance practices. The result of trade-offs for a given development is then codified in a family of standards, which may regulate each piece of hardware and human intervention associated with the particular system.

By comparison with network policies in other parts of the world, the North American integration of responsibilities and thus standards appears unique only because of ownership and top management being concentrated in one company. Europe's and Japan's network operators have never owned suppliers of equipment. In these countries, however, a cartel type of relationship with leading suppliers has been established for many years. The governmental or privatized-yet-monopolistic network providers maintain close watch on every equipment development, with particular emphasis on the standards that it must meet. In the standards-making study groups of ITU's CCITT (International Telegraph and Telephone Consultative Com-

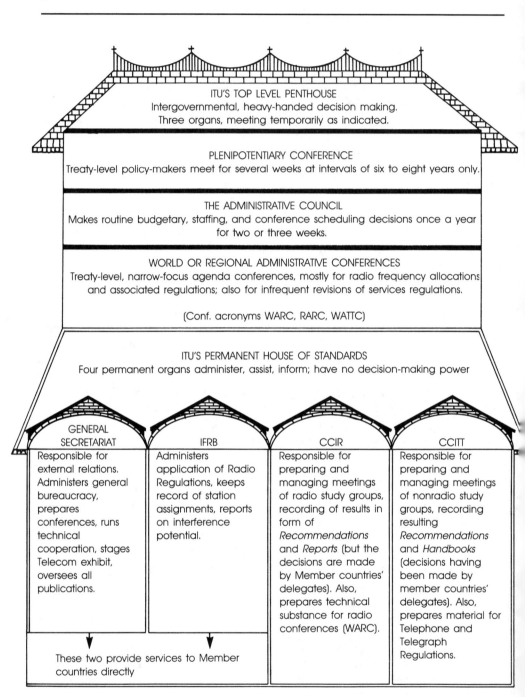

Figure 2.1 ITU's House of Seven Organs.

Box. 2.1

Typical Bell System Practice (BSP) of 1934 Vintage

(Front Page Reproduced Only)

BELL SYSTEM PRACTICES
Toll Test Room Operation
Service Maintenance and Plant
Operation Routines

SECTION E24.151
Issue 1, April, 1934
Standard

NOISE AND CROSSTALK TESTS ON CARRIER TELEPHONE SYSTEMS

1. GENERAL

1.01 This section covers noise and crosstalk tests on carrier telephone systems.

1.02 The information included in this section is outlined as follows:

Subject	Page
1. GENERAL	1
2. NOISE TESTS	1
(A) Where carrier telephone systems are added	1
(B) Where type B carrier telegraph systems are added .	1
3. CROSSTALK TESTS	2
(A) General	2
(B) Testing Procedure	3
(C) Crosstalk coupling performance values	4
(D) Staggered crosstalk performance values	5

1.03 The noise and crosstalk values given in this section are intended for use as performance guides and not as maintenance requirements. As such they are intended to indicate whether or not the carrier facilities, both equipment and connecting facilities, meet the noise and crosstalk standards for which they were designed. In applying the crosstalk coupling performance values of Tables IV and V, particularly those values for the shorter lengths of parallel, appreciably less than 1,000 crosstalk units for the K-8, K-10 and Type D designs and 1,500 crosstalk units for the Alternate Arm design, judgment should be exercised in deciding the extent to which remedial measures should be applied. In such cases, however, where the measured values (corrected in the usual manner) approach the values given above, steps should be taken to clear the trouble. Where the noise values of Table II and the staggered crosstalk values of Table VI are exceeded, steps should also be taken to clear the trouble.

1.04 The tests should be made on a voice frequency basis between the carrier terminals of the overall carrier systems as soon as practicable after installation in order that any troubles which may exist may be cleared before circuits are assigned to the system.

1.05 These tests should also be made where existing systems are reassigned to other open wire pairs or where major changes in assignments are made in toll entrance cables.

1.06 Where systems have been turned down for a period of time exceeding six months these noise and crosstalk tests should be made before the system is again placed in service. On systems turned down for periods of less than six months noise and crosstalk tests should be made only when monitoring observations during the service test period indicate excessive noise or crosstalk.

1.07 The tests outlined below assume that the open wire facilities have been thoroughly checked for irregularities which may affect noise or crosstalk.

1.08 All tests should be made under normal operating conditions of the various systems involved.

1.09 The testing procedure and the crosstalk values given in this section assume in general that the carrier systems on which measurements are to be made have the same direction of transmission (that is, the low groups of systems transit from east to west and the high groups from west to east). Where reversed direction of frequencies is involved special consideration needs to be given. The particular channels to be tested and the values to be met in the latter cases should be those which are specified locally for such systems.

2. NOISE TESTS

(A) Where Carrier Telephone Systems are Added

2.01 Noise tests should be made on each channel of the new carrier telephone system at each of the carrier terminals during the relatively busy traffic periods.

(B) Where Type B Carrier Telegraph Systems are Added

2.02 Where Type B carrier telegraph facilities are operated on open wire lines on which carrier telephone systems operate, noise measurements should be made on the carrier telephone systems, with the carrier telegraph channels in the marking conditions, as indicated below, during the relatively busy traffic periods. The particular telephone channels to be involved in these tests may be obtained from Table I.

Page 1

Box. 2.2
An Irreverent Spoof that Captures the Spirit

BULL SYSTEM PRACTICES
Special Engineering
Extraordinary Services

SECTION Z999,998
Issue 1, 4-26-37
Provisional Standard

NUMBER 2-B REGRETTOR
DESCRIPTION AND PROCEDURES
For People Who Think They Think

1. GENERAL

1.11 The No. 2-B Regrettor is a light weight, compact unit, recently developed specifically for use by persons whose capacities for regretting are below normal, or who, due to various activities have more to regret than can be conveniently handled without artificial aid.

1.12 Through the use of this device it is possible for the user to have his bad moments regretted for him, and he is meanwhile left free to engage in activities which may be regretted later.

1.13 This device may be absolutely depended upon to faithfully regret in accordance with the wishes of even the most talented of bunglers. It is guaranteed to bend every effort to perform its duties, being equipped with a dynamically stabilized micro-synchronous effort bender of the cantilever type.

1.14 By means of a simple change-over switch, the No. 2-B Regrettor can be made to rue. Days are the least difficult of all items to rue. To "rue the day" it is necessary merely to set the machine up in accordance with the simple instructions given under OPERATION.

   a. In case there is doubt as to the simplicity of the instructions, see Part 4.

1.15 Provision has been made for the use of the No. D-9445 Anticipatory Converter Attachment in connection with the No. 2-B Regrettor. The combined action of these two units operating in conjunction is such that the Regrettor functions in a negative sense. The net result is essentially that of an Anticipator. The advantages attendant upon such flexibility hardly require pointing out.

   a. This singular effect is explained in Part 3 under CONVERTER ATTACHMENT.

1.16 The No. 2-B Regrettor may be adjusted to give down pangs of regret if such are desired. All frequencies up to 20 pangs per second are obtainable under control of the operator. When the Pang Frequency Control

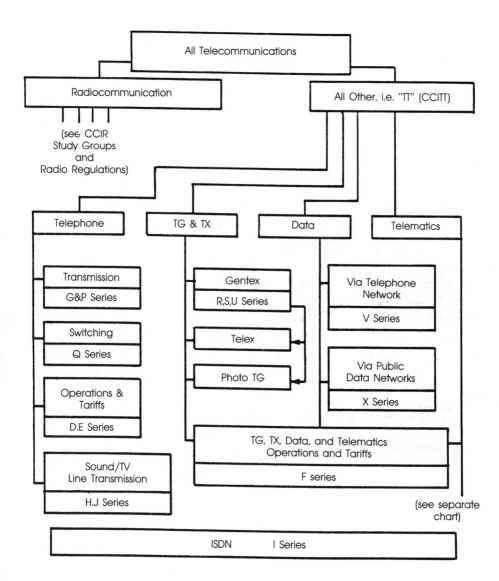

Figure 2.2(a) ITU's Realm of Telecommunication.

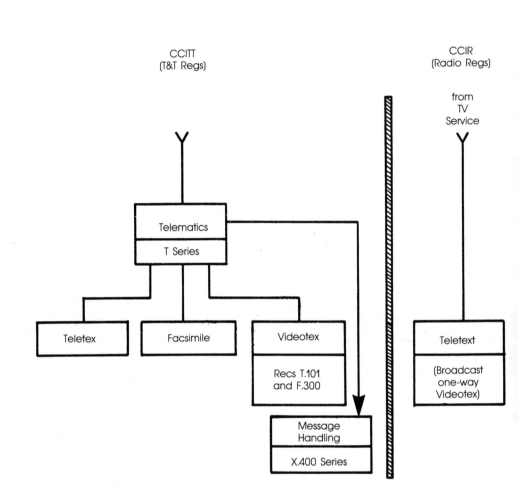

Figure 2.2(b) Telematic Services Defined by the ITU. (See detail in Box 2.3.)

mittee), spokespersons for the respective country's Administration nowadays have their counterparts from the country's suppliers' industry participating in deliberation and decision. On many "nuts-and-bolts" standard preparations, industry's specialists assume complete control, as if they were under the Administration's direction and on its payroll. We need to understand, then, that the making of network standards is perceived as a collaborative, joint responsibility of network operators and equipment suppliers everywhere in the world. The structure of ITU with its two technical committees CCITT and CCIR (International Radio Consultative Committee) is illustrated in Figure 2.2 and Boxes 2.3 and 2.4.

Box 2.3
CCITT Definitions Relating to Telegraph, Telematic, and Data Transmission Services
(Excerpts from Supplement No. 1 to Series F Recommendations)

---

1. General Definitions

    1.1 Telematic Services
        1.1.1 Telematic Services
        1.1.2 Teletex Service
        1.1.3 Public Facsimile Service
        1.1.4 Videotex Service
        1.1.5 Message Handling Services

1.1.1 Telematic services

   International telecommunication services, excluding telephone, telegraph and data transmission services, offered by Administrations and defined by CCITT for the purpose of exchange of information via telecommunication networks.
   Note 1—The definition of service covers the full range of functions according to the Open System Interconnection (OSI) model.
   Note 2—Examples of telematic services are teletex service, facsimile service and Videotex service.
   Note 3—The term "Teleservice" belongs to the concept of ISDN. Telematic services provided on an ISDN may be considered as Teleservices.

1.1.2 Teletex service

   An international telematic service offered by Administrations enabling subscribers to exchange correspondence via telecommunication networks.

1.1.3 Public facsimile service

   An international telematic service offered by Administrations for the purpose of transmitting documents between facsimile terminals via telecommunication networks.

Box 2.3 (continued)

1.1.4 Videotex service

A Videotex service is an interactive service which provides, through appropriate access by standardized procedures, for users of Videotex terminals to communicate with data bases via telecommunication networks.

Note—The Videotex service includes the following set of characteristics:

1) information is generally in an alpha-numeric and/or pictorial form;
2) information is stored in a data base;
3) information is transmitted between the data base and users by telecommunication networks;
4) displayable information is presented on a suitably modified television receiver or other visual display device;
5) access is under the user's direct or indirect control;
6) the service is easily operated by the general public as well as specialist users, i.e., the service is user-friendly;
7) the service provides facilities for users to create and modify information in the data bases;
8) the service provides data base management facilities which allow information providers to create, maintain and manage data bases and to manage closed user group facilities.

1.1.5 Message handling services

Service provided by means of Message Handling Systems.

Note 1—Service may be provided through Administration Management Domains or Private Management Domains.

Note 2—Examples of Message Handling Services are:
—Interpersonal Messaging Service (IPM) Service;
—Message Transfer Service (MT Service).

NB: The 1989 edition of this Supplement, in the *CCITT Blue Book,* carries this footnote: "The definition of Message Handling Service as a telematic service and the use of the term public in the definitions of telematic services is for further study.

In the United States, divestiture decreed in 1982 [7] and its aftermath have changed the collaboration from one company's built-in strength to a diffuse, contentious burden on potentially hostile actors seeking pieces of the same pie. For the time being, AT&T's inherited dominance in long-distance and international networking, with ownership of Bell Laboratories and Western Electric (AT&T Technologies) intact, perpetuates a segment of predivestiture in-house collaboration of standards. However, jealous competitors, a watchful federal judge responsible only

Box 2.4
List of CCIR Study Groups

Number	Title
1	Spectrum Utilization and Monitoring
2	Space Research and Radioastronomy Services
3	Fixed Service at Frequencies Below About 30 MHz
4	Fixed Satellite Service
5	Propagation in Non-Ionized Media
6	Propagation in Ionized Media
7	Standard Frequency and Time-Signal Services
8	Mobile, Radiodetermination, and Amateur Services
9	Fixed Service Using Radio-Relay Systems
10	Broadcasting Service (Sound)
11	Broadcasting Service (Television)
CMTT*	CCIR–CCITT Joint Study Group for Television and Sound Transmission
CMV*	CCIR–CCITT Joint Study Group for Vocabulary

Numbers and names of study groups as of the XVIth Plenary Assembly, Dubrovmik, 1986. Note that this structure of CCIR has been carried over for many years, while CCITT has undergone substantial changes.

*CM = Commission Mixte, French for "Joint Study Group."

to himself and his perceived mandate, and the regulatory agency FCC (Federal Communications Commission), contrive that every technical modification or innovation offered for the long-distance network may be examined as much for its effect on competitor's market position as for contribution to end-user service. Certainly, the position of a US delegation to international study group meetings is weakened by openly antagonistic currents within it.

2.4 THE MULTIFACETED EVOLUTION OF STANDARDS

Growth of international telecommunication standards in sheer numbers has been widely noted. However, simultaneous expansion in several dimensions has been less understood. Failure to recognize the results of this expansion carries a heavy penalty for all those wishing to participate in the information markets. Today's standards affect so many aspects of products and services that a supplier's freedom to adapt and to experiment is greatly curtailed. This represents a dramatic change of ground rules in a relatively few years; yet, it came about gradually, as an evolution. Indeed, contrary to often repeated slogans of a "telecommunications revolution," changes in this information infrastructure business have come steadily, step by step, standard by standard, and not abruptly at all. As behooves an evolutionary process, companies do best that have influenced the changes, rolling forward with them, rather than having them imposed by revolution from outside their ranks.

In the years since 1960, standards have grown and expanded in several dimensions, highlighted by the examples in this and the following chapter.

2.4.1 Assuring Transmission Performance

The earliest CCITT Recommendations (taken over from predecessor organizations, CCIF and CCIT, founded in the 1920s) were content with providing a framework for delivering adequate speech volume on long European connections. Today's worldwide requirements for end-user transmission performance occupy several hundred pages in several volumes of the CCITT book [8]. Maintaining and delivering an adequate signal level is now the least critical concern. The thrust of CCITT Recommendations (RECs.) is directed toward eleven other characteristics that can cause transmission impairments. Noteworthy among them are relative "newcomers" that owe their importance to innovative systems, for example:

- Satellite systems introduce much longer transmission delays than terrestrial systems, giving rise to the impairments of echo and double-talk;
- Wide scale use for data transmission of circuits primarily intended for telephony puts the focus on group delay and nonlinear distortions, in particular; and
- Digital transmission systems can experience quantizing distortion and phase jitter, potential impairments unknown to the traditional analogue transmission systems plant.

Control of these and other possible impairments is the aim of transmission plans and system Recommendations. Meeting objectives over a great variety of random connections makes necessary the apportionment of permissible maxima. Apportionment has spread outward from strictly international circuits to the national networks and, finally, to local connections serving the subscribers. These particular international standards are still labelled "Recommendations," reminiscent of the era when acceptance was voluntary and degree of implementation was discretionary. Nevertheless, most service provider organizations have integrated CCITT performance standards into their internal rule books and hold their suppliers responsible for meeting apportioned contribution limits to overall performance. Box 2.5 lists the most significant Recommendations in this category.

As a result, transmission quality standards have become codified at rigorous test values stipulated for worldwide, random dial-up services. Some observers see this codification as an obstacle to innovation. Others demand relief from tight standards for telecommunication development in poor countries so that lower cost systems may be used. However, when and where substantial exceptions to CCITT performance standards are taken, the systems so designed are likely to serve restricted local purposes. Such an installation's useful life span may be limited to the date when connection to national and international networks is required.

Box 2.5 (a)
CCITT Service Quality and Maintenance Recommendations (Not an Exhaustive List)

Rec. Series	Title and Remarks
E.420 to E.428	Checking the Quality of Telephone Service.
E.800 (entire series)	Quality of Services, Concepts, Models, Objectives, Dependability Planning. (Focused on telephone service.)
G.100 (entire series)	General Characteristics of International Telephone Connections and Circuits. Includes models of calls and connections; transmission performance objectives and their apportionment to national sections; terms and definitions related to quality of service, availability, and reliability.
G.800	Quality of Service, Performance, and Maintenance of Digital Networks.
I.350*ff*	ISDN Quality of Service Objectives.
M (entire series)	Maintenance. Four fascicles with 900 pages. Comprehensive coverage of maintenance associated with most telecommunication services, except data networks. Includes, *inter alia*, Rec. M.21, "Principles of a telecommunication management network"; see figure reproduced on next page.
P (entire series)	Telephone Transmission Quality. Rec. P.11, "Effect of transmission impairments" explains thirteen different impairments and provides guidelines for their assessment.
X.134 to X.140	Packet Switched Public Data Networks Performance Parameters and Criteria.

Box 2.5 (b)
Figure 1 of Rec. M.21: Performance Concepts

Relationship between Quality of Service factors which are relevant to maintenance
Figure 1/M.2b indicates the relationship between the availability performance of individual items (e.g., terminal equipment, networks, *et cetera*) which are used in the operation of a service and the [serviceability] performance of that service. This relationship is such that, given satisfactory trafficability and propagation performances, then the availability performance of each item is the means by which satisfactory [serviceability] of a service is obtained.

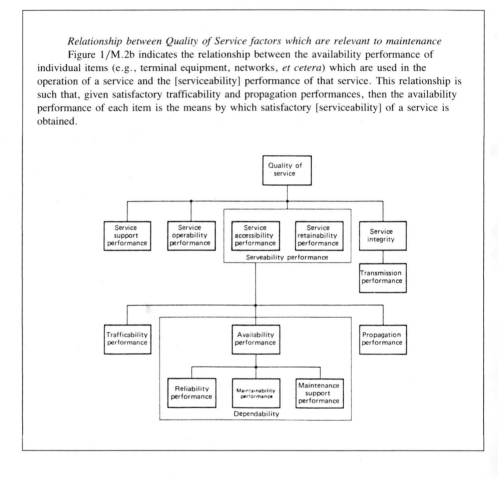

2.4.2 Specifications for Mandatory End-to-End Compatability

The requirements of worldwide, random access over fully automated networks and end office facilities have led to detailed, rigorous specifications for the necessary electronic systems. Already, in the 1960s, an entire family of Recommendations for signalling systems was placed in the mandatory specification category. This is expressed in a Preliminary Note that has been retained ever since, now reading as follows:

The strict observance of the specifications for standardized international signalling and switching equipment is of the utmost importance in the manufacture and operation of the equipment. Hence, these clauses are obligatory except where it is explicitly stipulated to the contrary. The values given below are imperative and must be met under normal service conditions. [9]

Lest such language in CCITT Recommendations be attributed to a dominating European tradition, note that chairmanship of the cognizant Study Group XI passed from a member of the French Ministry of Posts, Telephone and Telegraph (PT&T) to Mr. Ryan, an expert of AT&T Bell Laboratories, (US), in 1972. This same person has been reconfirmed as chairman four times, and now remains in charge until 1992. Moreover, Canadian, Australian, and Japanese specialists have made important contributions to the more recent international signalling systems. We shall revisit this truly global scope collaboration under the separate heading of *a priori* standards (Section 2.5).

Similarly explicit, mandatory Recommendations cover echo suppressors and echo cancellers. These devices have become *sine qua non* requirement at the terminations of satellite derived circuits. Without them, the delayed return of his or her own words to the telephone speaker's ears can make international conversation all but impossible. Here is another example of the innovation itself driving toward more rigorous and more rigid standardization. Yet innovation and standardization are popularly described as natural antagonists. The truth makes less popular reading. In reality, today's innovation is posed as the enemy of yesterday's standards, while its advocates press hard to have it installed as a henceforth untouchable successor. It is a case of "the King is dead, long live the King!" The CCITT books are handy references to prove the point.

In the fields of record transmission (i.e., conventional telegraph, telex, facsimile, and data transmission), rigorous international compatibility requirements have a longer tradition than in telephone service. Machines are less tolerant than humans in making allowance for errors or omissions. Moreover, information exchange for business purposes carries the risk of lost transactions and opportunities; therefore, users demand a very high reliability of the networks as well as terminal equipment on their premises.

The particularly rapid and diversified development of data communication has put a premium on timely standards for interworking of computers and communication networks. International organizations have chosen to set standards before many incompatible solutions have established their respective markets.

2.5 THE WAVE OF *A PRIORI* STANDARDS

In the past, before the European Administrations banded together in CEPT (Conférence Européenne des Postes et Télécommunications) [10], international standards evolved from experience with services and systems already introduced in one or several countries. Clearly, agreement on a single world standard may be harder to achieve when some versions of the system or service under study are already in the marketplace. Nevertheless, first user reactions and supplier's real life experience with technical problems help set realistic targets for standards. European and North American attitudes also differ on the best timing for standardization. Europeans are generally more averse to risk than Americans. Telecommunication administrations and their suppliers serve limited, government-policy-controlled markets. Therefore, new services and equipments are adopted only after careful study of all technical and economic questions. The greater the leap forward, the more numerous are the uncertainties, hence the more procrastination prior to a decision. In such an environment of caution, *a priori* standardization before formal introduction of a product or service will be much preferred. By extension, the only choice is to avoid false starts and heavy economic losses when a single European standard is desired at the outset.

In the United States, government and industry leaders tend to look to the marketplace for a shakedown of competing products. In theory, a standard is to emerge from vigorous competition. In practice, it is sometimes a single company's victorious system, or more often a negotiated compromise among several companies' entries. In the field of telecommunication, US practice was an approximation to European policies. During the many years when the AT&T Bell System held the long-distance service monopoly in addition to operating some 80% of the national network, new systems or services were *de facto* standardized by Bell Laboratories, Western Electric, or the AT&T engineering department, respectively. While their standards were strictly established for intra-Bell System application, adoption by connecting service providers was promoted. More significantly for the present analysis, the AT&T-*qua*-US delegates to CCITT study group meetings would submit their standard as the logical applicant for international adoption. This approach placed the US representation squarely in the middle between European and US preferences. The Europeans saw it as an attempt to steal the "*a priori*" initiative for which they were only in preparation. For US non-Bell System competitors, it satisfied the notion of safe criteria proven in the marketplace, although these criteria were made standard by unilateral decision.

2.5.1 Digital Transmission Systems

For a historic perspective still very much acute in the late 1980s, the case of Bell Laboratories' (i.e., AT&T's) initiative for digital transmission systems may be cited. The critical engineering choices were made in the latter half of the 1950s [11]. Thirty years later, these system standards govern networks in all of North America, regardless of which company is the service provider or system hardware supplier. Similar digital systems have become the norm for networks worldwide, but outside North

America only Japan seems to have adopted the same standard. The European CEPT organization ensured that some twenty competing European proposals, all *a priori* at the time, were reduced to one. The standard was made final in the 1968–1972 CCITT study period, and was since adopted by most other countries around the world. As can be expected from a large, time-consuming effort superimposed on an existing model, the European choice claims some advantages over its American counterpart, which was put on the market about ten years prior.

The European Administrations doubtless had more than the principle of an *a priori* standard in mind. They were under pressure from the Council of the European Community (EC) to lower barriers to telecommunication procurement within the Community (see Chapter Four). Only if all administrations were to buy equipment of the same standards could this objective be realized. Work on a digital transmission system gave the first opportunity for a large-scale procurement item that might remain standard for many years—as, in fact, it has done so far. In the presence of fully developed production lines and application experience in the United States for a similar system, the Europeans would not buy from American suppliers before their own national manufacturers were ready. Thus, disagreement about the particular choice of standard characteristics was a necessary ploy for safeguarding European commercial interests.

A chronological overview of the rise and spread of digital systems is given in Box 2.6. In Box 2.7, we reproduce the first three pages of AT&T's current Standard Practice, describing the T1 digital line. This case teaches an important lesson. If a single world standard is the objective, all major competitors must have a chance for contribution to the end result. That chance is lost whenever one competitor already has put its product in service, in large quantities and with commitments to adhere to it as the standard. Consequently, *a priori* standardization by international agreement emerges as the only equitable solution. The European Common Market demands this approach, and its precedent-setting weight may carry North America along.

2.5.2 Signalling Systems

Collaborative *a priori* standardization has become the rule concerning international signalling systems [12] and data communication networks [13]. In all of this CCITT study group work, delegates from North America and other non-European countries have collaborated harmoniously from the outset. In other words, the concept of standardizing major systems and even wholly new networks has been well received by representatives of the competitive, open-market persuasion as well as those bound to entrenched governmental monopolies.

Fruits of this collaboration have been two new complex signalling systems, known as CCITT Number 6 and Number 7, respectively. Box 2.8 gives an elementary summary of functions to be performed by signalling. System Number 6 was

Box 2.6
Thirty Years of Digital Systems Evolution:
From Proprietary Development to Everybody's Standard Information Pathways

1939–1940	Reeves of ITT (UK) files basic patents for PCM system [a].
1947	Watershed paper, "The Philosophy of PCM," by Bell Laboratories' luminaries Oliver, Pierce, and Shannon [b].
1956	Bell Laboratories develop first block of PCM carrier *T* family, the 24-channel PCM carrier, *short-haul* system, type *T-1*. However, release for manufacture is put off by several years. Technical problems are overshadowed by difficulties with meeting the ambitious low-cost objective. System is to prove in over cable pair installations below 10 miles [c].
1957	President of Bell Laboratories highlights "the potential economy of the pulse code carrier method and its large technical advantages especially for data and other record transmission provide large incentives for its universal use in exchange plant transmission" [d].
1960 to 1964	CCITT Plenary Assembly (P.A.) adopts study of digital transmission systems, under Question 33 of Study Group XV. Next P.A. continues this study for another four years. Progress slowed by profusion of competing proposals.
1962	Bell System's T-1 ready for mass production, at costs close to objectives. Bell Operating Companies (BOCs) buy large quantities [e], [f].
1962 to 1968	Service providers and manufacturers outside the North American Bell Systems' coordinated circle, worldwide, do not follow AT&T's lead. Europeans cannot justify immediate large quantities for their networks and insist on developing their own systems, while actual need will have time to mature. However, UK and Japan develop and place into service modest quantities of a PCM system that could be made T-1 compatible. During this period, some 20 different system designs are proposed to CCITT [g].
1968 (Oct.)	CCITT Fourth P.A. adopts a concise *Recommendation* of provisional intent. It gives essential characteristics of two mutually incompatible systems: T-1 and a European compromise, *CEPT approved* system. The latter has laboratory status only. Hope for a single world standard is expressed and carried forward to the 1969–1972 study period. Study of all digital systems is assigned to a new *Special Study Group D*, chaired by R. Boyd of Bell Laboratories. Question No. 1/Sp D "Planning of Digital Systems," already aims at eventual integrated services digital network (ISDN).
1972	CCITT Fifth P.A. adopts, with finality, the two noncompatible system standards. Chair of group Sp.D, renamed XVIII, passes to T. Irmer of Germany.
1973 through present	Two different PCM hierarchies are developed under CCITT aegis. Study of Digital Switching and Signalling is pursued intensely, in a close-knit circle of experts. Three special "languages" become *Recommendations* in a new, letter "Z" family. CCITT's separately pursued, voluminous output on Data Communication Networks enjoys good coordination with digital system studies.
1980	Seventh P.A. adopts concept of *telematic services*, gives responsibility to one, enhanced scope study group (VIII). Telematics are recognized as prime beneficiaries of future ISDN.

Box 2.6 (continued)

1984	CCITT Eighth P.A. approves coherent package of ISDN *Recommendations,* culminating fifteen years of piecemeal, though coordinated, studies. T. Irmer, chairman of digital systems Study Group XVIII since 1972, is elected Director of CCITT. His worldwide popularity is due, in part, to personal identification with development of digital network standards, holding promise for developing countries. New *Recommendations* in G.600 and G.900 series focus on digital transmission over optical fiber cables.
1985	Proliferation of competing suppliers and consultants, offering *T-1 Technology* for the burgeoning LAN (Local Area Network) market in US. Spreading installations of optical fiber cables rely completely on T-1 based digital multiplexing, from user-owned LAN to transcontinental common carrier [h], [i].
1988	TAT-8, first transatlantic cable using optical fiber and digital transmission technology, is placed in service by year-end. Its capacity is 40,000 voice grade channels. This cable links Europe's CEPT and North America's *T* standard digital networks [j].

ANNOTATED REFERENCES TO BOX 2.6

[a] The inventor's own historical evaluation is presented in E. M. Deloraine and Alec H. Reeves, "The 25th Anniversary of Pulse Code Modulation," *IEEE Spectrum,* Vol. 2, No. 5 (May 1965); pp. 56–63; with 39 references.
[b] B. M. Oliver, J. R. Pierce, and C. E. Shannon, "The Philosophy of PCM," *Proceedings of the IRE,* Vol. 36, No. 11, November 1948; pp. 1324–1331. The three Bell Laboratories authors are representative of the vision and competence that gave the Bell System undisputed world leadership. Mr. Oliver left Bell Laboratories to become Vice-President of Engineering of Hewlett-Packard. In later years, he took initiative for the scientific fantasy project *Search for Extraterrestrial Intelligence.* John Pierce has been honored internationally, particularly for his role in early satellite communication development. Claude Shannon, an IRE Fellow at age 34, published his pathbreaking *Mathematical Theory of Communication* that same year. The unit of logarithmic relationship of two information events is named after him.
[c] As recorded in this author's trip report, published for internal company use, of visit with Bell Telephone Laboratories at North Andover, MA, and Murray Hill, NJ, October 1956.
[d] Mervin Kelly, president of Bell Laboratories: "The Trends of Telecommunication as Affected by Solid State Instrumentation," *Alta Frequenza,* Vol. XXVI, No. 5, October 1957, pp. 342–344.
[e] G. Davis, "An Experimental Pulse Code Modulation System for Short-Haul Trunks," *BSTJ* (now *AT&T Technical Journal*), Vol. 41, No. 1, January 1962; pp. 1–24; four related articles in the same issue.
[f] Statistics provided at the time by William Bloecker. AT&T international systems engineer, in a paper titled, "The Future of Telecommunication on Metallic Paths." Paper given at a conference at Rome, Italy, in early 1964, and distributed at CCITT Third Plenary Assembly, Geneva, June 1964.

Box 2.6 (continued)

[g] For a partial overview of contending European proposals, see H. Geissler, "Beitrag zur Planung von Pulscode Modulations-Systemen" (in German), *NTZ,* Vol. 20, No. 11 (1967); pp. 667–682.

[h] *IEEE Communications Magazine,* Entire issue devoted to LAN, Vol. 22, No. 8 (August 1984).

[i] See the periodical, *LAN, The Local Area Network Magazine.* Premier issue dated October 1986.

[j] *Associated Press* (AP) release, published December 1988, in newspapers affiliated with AP service. *Source*: *Peninsula Times Tribune,* Palo Alto, California, December 17, 1988.

Box 2.7 T1 Digital Line—General Description for Digital Transmission Systems (Standard No. 365-200-100. Copyright © 1987 AT&T. All Rights Reserved. Reprinted with Permission of AT&T.)

AT&T PRACTICE
Standard

AT&T 365-200-100
Issue 9, May 1987

T1 DIGITAL LINE

GENERAL DESCRIPTION

DIGITAL TRANSMISSION SYSTEMS

Box 2.7 (continued)

Box 2.7 (continued)

ISS 9, AT&T 365-200-100

1. GENERAL

1.01 This practice contains a general description of the T1 digital line and associated equipment. It is confined to metropolitan T1 equipment and does not include modifications for special applications. The application schematics which give broad schematic coverage are SD-3C252-02 (T1C/T1 ORB), SD-97080-01 (201 ORB), and SD-97080-02 (206 ORB).

1.02 This practice is being reissued to add information on the following:

(a) Full Cable Fill

(b) DC-DC Converters

(c) Intra-Office Repeater (IOR) Shelf

(d) Fault Locate Filters

(e) Switch Options

(f) J98725 P, R, and S Office Repeater Bays

(g) Small Cross-Section Office Repeater Shelf (SXSS)

(h) 800-Series DSX Frame System.

Change arrows have been used to emphasize the more significant changes.

1.03 The T1 digital line is a zero-loss facility for digital transmission between digital terminal locations. The rate of bipolar digital transmission using time-division multiplex pulse code modulation on the T1 digital line is 1.544 megabits per second (Mb/s) which in the digital signal hierarchy is called DS1 rate or signal.

Box 2.7 (continued)

1.04 A T1 digital line uses 4-wire transmission; a separate cable pair is required for each direction of transmission. The T1 digital lines consist of office repeater bays, cross-connect bays, and line repeaters placed in cable pairs to regenerate the signal after it traverses a section of cable. T1 lines can be aerial, buried, or ducted, and repeater locations can be in manholes or above ground. Line repeaters and cables are arranged to form spans (paragraph 2.01). The office repeaters, except 201-type and 208-type repeaters, contain a single regenerator. Line repeaters contain two separate regenerators and a common power supply. Power is supplied to the repeaters over the cable pairs via a simplex circuit.

1.05 The different codes of repeaters used for T1 digital lines are shown in Table A. The repeaters are used as line repeaters, office repeaters, and bridging repeaters. They are described in AT&T Practice 365-200-101.

1.06 The T1 digital line is designed for use on paired metropolitan area trunk (MAT*) cable and intercity outstate trunk (ICOT™) cable. The repeater section loss used in engineering the T1 system is 31 dB and corresponds to the average value of insertion loss for a 6000-foot section of 22-gauge high capacitance cable at 772 kHz. Because the repeater sections adjacent to central offices (COs) are subjected to impulse noise originating in the central offices, these sections are usually shorter than a normal repeater section. The end sections may be of any length up to 4500 feet of 22-gauge cable and are built out to the nominal repeater section loss of 31 dB. Extensive details for engineering a T1 line are given in AT&T Practice 855-351-101.

2. SPAN CONCEPT

2.01 The sum of all paralled span lines between two CO buildings is called a *span*. A *span line* is a string of regenerators in tandem from the digital

Box 2.8
Elementary Functions Performed by Automated Signalling

Signalling Systems must perform these two functions:

1. Supervision and control;
2. Register signalling.

Supervision and control follow the calling subscriber's "make busy" of a line, through intervening switches, lines, transmission systems, so as to cause the intended response at called party's station.
The function continues to monitor status of the call to its eventual termination at both ends.

Register signalling accepts, processes, and records for charging purposes, as required, the subscriber numbers involved in the call.

Fully automated systems meet the following needs:

1. Human-machine interaction, i.e., human initiative;
2. Machine-machine interaction;
3. Machine-human communication, at machine's initiative.

first introduced during the 1968–1972 study period. A digital version was subsequently prepared, again by international design. Nevertheless, Number 6 found only limited acceptance around the world. The effort might have paid off more as a learning process for the daring proposition that an entire, complicated electronic system may be designed by committee, whose members reside in New Jersey, Tokyo, Paris, London, Munich, and other distant places.

As it happened, prior investment in separate regional systems held its own for several more years. At the same time that Number 6 was adopted, North America's well entrenched in-band, tone-pulse system was fully described for CCITT purposes and given the identification "R1"; i.e., Regional System Number 1. This instantaneous making of an international standard, for the record, came about as a defensive move against the demand for CCITT recognition of a significantly different European design, adopted by Latin American countries as their regional signalling system. The United States saw operational limitations in this competing approach, particularly in its reliance on round-trip signal confirmation before a dialed call request would be completed. On a geopolitical level, the Latin American decision to reject Western Hemisphere integration of telecommunication networks was a severe blow to North American aspirations. The system adopted by Latin American and some European countries became standardized as *CCITT R2*. Thus, the CCITT books introduced two regional standard systems, at the very time when global cooperation had developed more advanced systems that assured smooth through-connection among all countries. Box 2.9 reproduces the official record of the CCITT Fourth Plenary Assembly session, meeting at Mar del Plata in October 1968, at which the two regional systems were adopted by action from the floor. This occurrence was contrary to CCITT policy of collaborative study prior to acceptance of a standard.

The newest, *CCITT Number 7* (see Box 2.10), is designed to perform all functions that may be needed in a fully implemented ISDN (integrated services digital network). ISDN has been conceived as the multipurpose telecommunication user offering of the future. Its *a priori* development under the aegis of CCITT will be considered in the next section.

Signalling System Number 7 (SS 7) made its debut in CCITT Q-Series Recommendations at the Eighth Plenary Assembly (P.A.), 1984. Considerably expanded in scope and technical detail, its specification in the CCITT *Blue Book* of 1988 spreads over three fascicles with a total of 1540 pages. Additional Recommendations supporting the design and application of digital signalling in general are found in other fascicles of the Volume VI set. Still more associated Recommendations are found in the Z-Series published in Volume X, which encompasses the programming languages developed specifically for intricate automatic functions such as are handled by SS 7. The *a priori* creation of these languages through international collaboration used to be carried on in the same CCITT Study Group XI, responsible for switching and signalling. However, since the P.A. of 1984, a new study group of specialists was created for this purpose. The volume of output may be judged by the spread of

Box 2.9
Extract from the Minutes of the Plenary Meetings (CCITT IVth Plenary Assembly, Mar del Plata, October 1968)

SIXTH PLENARY MEETING

Monday, 21 October 1968, 9.30 a.m.

Chairman: Lieutenant-Colonel R. R. ALBARIÑO (Argentina)

Subjects discussed	*Document Nos.*
1. Report of Study Group IX	AP IV/14, 17 and 90
2. Report of Study Group X	AP IV/31, 34 and 102
3. Report of Study Group VIII	AP IV/18, 35 and 98
4. Report of Study Group XI	AP IV/32, 52, 59, 95, 104 and 108

The CHAIRMAN presented the draft programme of work for the week from 21 to 25 October which had been prepared by the meeting of Chairmen and Vice-Chairmen. The Assembly *approved* the programme and, on the proposal of the delegate of the UNITED KINGDOM, *appointed* Mr. VAN LOMMEL as Chairman of the Working Party on Books.

Mr. TOBIN (United Kingdom), Chairman, presented the Study Group's report contained in documents AP IV/32 (preliminary report), AP IV/52 (Specifications for signalling system No. 5 *bis*), AP IV/59 (Specifications for signalling system No. 6), AP IV/95 (final report), AP IV/104 (final report of the Joint Working Party of Study Groups IV and XI on ATME No. 2) and AP IV/108 (Proposal for the study of the MFC (Bern) signalling system with a view to its standardization).

The Assembly unanimously *adopted* the specifications of signalling systems Nos. 5 *bis* and 6.

The delegate of BRAZIL, seconded by the delegate of ARGENTINA, proposed amending the text of new Question F/XI on study by the C.C.I.T.T. of the standardization of the MFC band system, so that the end of the sentence would read "with a view to its adoption on a regional basis as a C.C.I.T.T. Standardized System".

The Brazilian proposal was supported by the delegates of the following countries: PHILIPPINES, FEDERAL REPUBLIC OF GERMANY, FRANCE, CENTRAL AFRICAN REPUBLIC, ITALY, AUSTRIA, PARAGUAY, FRENCH OVERSEAS TERRITORIES, POLAND, SWITZERLAND, SPAIN AND CONGO (BRAZZAVILLE).

The delegate of BELGIUM also supported the Brazilian proposal but, considering that the system already existed, was working and that its specifications were clearly established, he proposed that the Assembly approve it directly without setting it for study.

The DIRECTOR OF THE C.C.I.T.T. observed that the Assembly was sovereign and while the procedure proposed by Belgium was admittedly unusual, it was not irregular. If the Assembly found the procedure unacceptable, there was another procedure open to it, namely, to appoint a special working party to study the MFC (Bern) system and prepare the necessary provisional recommendation, assuming that the idea of accepting provisional recommendations would be generally accepted by the Assembly. In his opinion, the standardization could in that way already become a fact in 1969.

Box 2.9 (continued)

The delegate of JAPAN was in favour of setting the system for study.

The delegate of BELGIUM, considering that study of the system could in no case change it, saw no point whatever in studying it and again requested the immediate approval of the system by the Assembly. He was supported by the delegates of ARGENTINA, BRAZIL, SPAIN, PARAGUAY and URUGUAY.

The delegate of the UNITED STATES OF AMERICA, supported by the delegate of CANADA, did not think that the Assembly could approve the standardization of the MFC (Bern) system without prior study. He asked that the North American system which was also used by several countries on a regional basis be studied as well.

The DIRECTOR OF THE C.C.I.T.T. then suggested that the Assembly standardize the *regional* use of the MFC (Bern) system and of the North American system without undertaking their study since they were perfectly well known to everybody. His suggestion was supported by the delegates of FRANCE, CANADA, UNITED STATES OF AMERICA, LEBANON, MALAYSIA and ITALY.

The delegate of the UNITED KINGDOM suggested that the introduction of two new signalling systems, each used on a regional basis by agreement between the countries concerned, raised the problem of defining their sphere of application and their interworking with existing standardized systems. It could be settled by preparing a new draft recommendation on the lines of Recommendation Q.7.

Mr. TOBIN having asked who would provide the C.C.I.T.T. Secretariat with specifications of these systems with a view to their publication in the *White Book*, the delegate of the UNITED STATES OF AMERICA said that the A.T. & T. would send the specifications of the North American system within three months and the delegate of SWITZERLAND announced that he would similarly send the specifications of the MFC (Bern) system which were the joint work of a number of European administrations.

The Plenary Assembly then *decided* unanimously to standardize the MFC (Bern) system and the North American system on a regional basis. The changes to be made in Recommendation Q.7 to take account of that fact would be prepared by the Drafting Group of Volume VI of the *White Book*. Questions F/XI and G/XI were therefore withdrawn from the programme of studies submitted by Study Group XI.

Mr. Tobin completed the presentation of the report of Study Group XI which was *approved* unanimously by the Assembly.

The CHAIRMAN associated himself with the thanks that Mr. Tobin had addressed to Working Party XI/1 and to its Chairmen, Mr. McGuire and Mr. Jouty, and to Mr. Bernard's drafting group for the enormous amount of work that they had done. He asked the Assembly to join with him in thanking and congratulating Mr. Tobin who was due to retire.

[Prolonged applause.]

Box 2.10

CCITT Rec. Q.700

Signalling System Number 7

INTRODUCTION TO CCITT SIGNALLING SYSTEM No. 7

1   General

This Recommendation provides an overview of the Signalling System by describing the various functional elements of CCITT No. 7 and the relationship between these functional elements. This Recommendation provides a general description of functions and capabilities of the Message Transfer Part (MTP), Signalling Connection Control Part (SCCP), Telephone User Part, ISDN User Part (ISDN-UP), Transaction Capabilities (TC), and the Operations, Maintenance and Administration Part (OMAP) which are covered elsewhere in the Q.7xx series of Recommendations. However, in the case of contradiction between the specifications and Q.700, the Q.7xx specification shall apply.

Supplementary Services in CCITT S.S. No.7 ISDN applications are described in the Q.73x series of Recommendations.

In addition to these functions in the CCITT No. 7 signalling system, the Q.7xx series of Recommendations describes the CCITT No. 7 network structure, and also specifies the Tests and Measurements applicable to CCITT No. 7.

This Recommendation is also a specification of those aspects such as CCITT S.S. No. 7 Architecture, Flow Control and general compatibility rule which are not specified in separate Recommendations, and are applicable to the overall scope of S.S. No. 7.

The remainder of this Recommendation describes:

—   § 2: Signalling network concepts components and modes;

—   § 3: The functional blocks within CCITT Signalling System No. 7 and the services provided by them;

—   § 4: CCITT Signalling System No. 7 protocol layering and its relationship to OSI modelling;

—   § 5: Node, application entity and user part addressing;

—   § 6: Operations, administration and maintenance aspects of CCITT S.S. No. 7;

—   § 7: Performance aspects of the functional blocks within CCITT S.S. No. 7;

—   § 8: Flow control for both the signalling network and within nodes;

—   § 9: Rules for evolving CCITT S.S. No. 7 protocols while preserving compatibility with earlier versions;

—   § 10: A cross-reference to a glossary of terms.

1.1   *Objectives and fields of application*

The overall objective of Signalling System No. 7 is to provide an internationally standardised general purpose common channel signalling (CCS) system:

—   optimised for operation in digital telecommunications networks in conjunction with stored program controlled exchanges;

—   that can meet present and future requirements of information transfer for inter-processor transactions within telecommunications networks for call control, remote control, and management and maintenance signalling;

—   that provides a reliable means for transfer of information in correct sequence and without loss or duplication.

The signalling system meets requirements of call control signalling for telecommunication services such as the telephone, ISDN and circuit switched data transmission services. It can also be used as a reliable transport system for other types of information transfer between exchanges and specialised centres in telecommunications networks (e.g. for management and maintenance purposes). The system is thus applicable for multipurpose uses in networks that are dedicated for particular services and in multiservices networks. The signalling system is intended to be be applicable in international and national networks.

Box 2.10 (continued)

The scope of CCITT S.S. No. 7 encompasses both circuit related and non-circuit related signalling.

Examples of applications supported by CCITT S.S. No. 7 are:

- PSTN,
- ISDN,
- Interaction with Network Databases, Service Control Points for service control,
- Mobiles (Public Land Mobile Network),
- Operations Administration and Maintenance of Networks.

The signalling system is optimized for operation over 64-kbit/s digital channels. It is also suitable for operation over analogue channels and at lower speeds. The system is suitable for use on point-to-point terrestrial and satellite links. It does not include the special features required for use in point-to-multipoint operation but can, if required, be extended to cover such an application.

1.2   *General characteristics*

Common channel signalling is a signalling method in which a single channel conveys, by means of labelled messages, signalling information relating to, for example, a multiplicity of circuits, or other information such as that used for network management. Common channel signalling can be regarded as a form of data communication that is specialised for various types of signalling and information transfer between processors in telecommunications networks.

The signalling system uses signalling links for transfer of signalling messages between exchanges or other nodes in the telecommunication network served by the system. Arrangements are provided to ensure reliable transfer of signalling information in the presence of transmission disturbances or network failures. These include error detection and correction on each signalling link. The system is normally applied with redundancy of signalling links and it includes functions for automatic diversion of signalling traffic to alternative paths in case of link failures. The capacity and reliability for signalling may thus be dimensioned by provision of a multiplicity of signalling links according to the requirements of each application.

1.3   *Components of CCITT S.S. No. 7*

CCITT S.S. No. 7 consists of a number of components or functions which are defined as a series of Q.7xx Recommendations.

CCITT S.S. No. 7 function	*Recommendations*
Message Transfer Part (MTP)	Q.701-Q.704, Q.706, Q.707
Telephone User Part (TUP) (including supplementary services)	Q.721-Q.725
Supplementary services	Q.730
Data User Part (DUP)	Q.741 (note 1)
ISDN User Part (ISDN-UP)	Q.761-Q.764, Q.766
Signalling Connection Control Part (SCCP)	Q.711-Q.714, Q.716
Transaction Capabilities (TC)	Q.771-Q.775
Operations Maintenance and Administration Part (OMAP)	Q.795

Note 1 — Functions of the DUP are fully specified in Recommendation X.61.

these Z-Series Recommendations, over seven fascicles, as of the Ninth P.A., approved at Melbourne, November 1988.

Remarkably, the universal scope CCITT SS 7 has already penetrated national and local service networks, where previously CCITT's international application systems have found little acceptance. In early 1989, both the long-distance carrier US Sprint and GTE companies serving local areas reported installations of the SS 7 system. Sprint claimed considerable cost savings due to speedier processing of calls and auxiliary functions made available by SS 7 [14]. GTE praises the system's ability to offer many enhanced user's service options that were not practicable before [15]. The central standards engineering organization of the seven Regional Bell Operating Companies (RBOCs), Bell Communications Research (Bellcore), has offered its US-adapted specification for this CCITT system since 1985 [16].

2.5.3 ISDN

The acronym ISDN denotes *integrated services digital network*. The concept of the integrated services digital network has been so well promoted for so long that its gradual implementation, during the last years of the 1980s, must appear anticlimactic to many potential users. The groundwork was laid in 1972, when the CCITT central organization at Geneva took the bold step of inviting the chairmen and key members of several study groups to combine fields of competence for a preview of future all-purpose digital systems. The resultant, special meeting produced a document for consideration by the next Plenary Assembly, scheduled for the end of December 1972; it substantiated the desirability of placing the question for study. However, the attached contributions from national service providers showed, at the time, a wide disparity of ideas and intentions with respect to realizing an ISDN, when technically practical, in their respective countries. France, for example, favored an early, purposeful start in that direction. By contrast, the United States, speaking for the formal administration rather than AT&T and other Recognized Private Operating Agencies (RPOAs), stressed the obstacle of separate and different tasks of the services that would need to be integrated, particularly with regard to US regulatory barriers erected between the telephone and record carries. See Box 2.11 for the report of this watershed CCITT meeting.

The mixed perspective of 1972 is worth recalling here as part of an explanation for the passage of fifteen years before ISDN became a reality in most of the industrialized world. Another, substantial part of that delay is, of course, attributable to the need for very detailed standards work, without which one venturesome designer's ISDN equipment will be incommunicado with that from another supplier.

Thus, ISDN became a model of *a priori* planning. Decisions on design features, offerings to users, planned interworking with data networks, all needed to be developed by worldwide participation before any definite product would have created

Box 2.11
Watershed 1972 Preparatory Meeting for ISDN (CCITT Vth Plenary Assembly, Geneva, 1972)

International Telegraph and Telephone Consultative Committee (C.C.I.T.T.)

Document AP V-No. 119-E
Published on 4 December 1972

Vth Plenary Assembly

Geneva, 1972

Original : English

This document is the same as :
COM X   -No. 59-E
COM XI   -No. 161-E
COM Sp.A-No. 283-E
COM Sp.D-No. 158-E
GM/NRD   -No. 110-E

Vth PLENARY ASSEMBLY - DOCUMENT No. 119

STUDY GROUP X - CONTRIBUTION No. 59
STUDY GROUP XI - CONTRIBUTION No. 161
SPECIAL STUDY GROUP A - CONTRIBUTION No. 283
SPECIAL STUDY GROUP D - CONTRIBUTION No. 158
JOINT WORKING PARTY NRD - CONTRIBUTION No. 110
==

SOURCE : JOINT MEETING OF SELECTED REPRESENTATIVES[*] OF STUDY GROUPS X, XI, SPECIAL A, SPECIAL D, AND JOINT WORKING PARTY NRD, ON THE INTEGRATED SERVICES DIGITAL NETWORK

TITLE : OPTIONS TO BE TAKEN BY THE Vth PLENARY ASSEMBLY FOR STUDIES IN 1973-1976 ON THE INTEGRATED SERVICES DIGITAL NETWORK

SUMMARY

PART I   - General

PART II   - Conclusions of the Joint Meeting

                     Annex 1 - New Question G/XI
                               proposed by Study Group XI

                     Annex 2 - Question 1/D

PART III   - Reports submitted by various I.T.U.
                     Members on the Question

[*] Delegates of Administrations and Recognized Private Operating Agencies

Box 2.11 (continued)

PART I

GENERAL

1.　　　　The Joint Meeting convened by C.C.I.T.T. Circular Letter No. 199 of 28 August 1972 took place at the I.T.U. Headquarters on Tuesday, 28 November 1972. According to an agreement between the Chairmen of the various Study Groups concerned, Mr. R. Boyd (U.S.A.), Chairman of Special Study Group D, took the chair.

2.　　　　The terms of reference of the Joint Meeting were stated in the Circular Letter No. 199 as follows :

> "To make proposals to the Vth Plenary Assembly to determine how studies of digital networks (until now considered independently by different Study Groups) should be conducted during the period 1973-1976 and to consider whether there should be a special organization (ad hoc group or special cooperative arrangements) to coordinate these studies."

3.　　　　Three possibilities for conducting the studies were mentioned in Circular Letter No. 199 :

a) <u>Service integrated digital network</u>

Should the international digital network be used in the future for telephony, telex and data?

b) <u>Specialized digital networks</u>

Should the digital networks be specialized, i.e. should there be one digital network for telephony and another digital network for specific data transmission requirements?

c) <u>Two specialized networks with limited interconnection</u>

If the two specialized networks in b) are provided, should limited interconnection be permitted between the two networks? (If so, studies will have to determine to what extent.)

and the Joint Meeting had to express its opinion on the option to be taken by the Plenary Assembly.

Box 2.11 (continued)

4.   Contributions were received from :

Australia

Japan

Netherlands

Federal Republic of Germany

Spain (C.T.N.E.)

Scandinavian Administrations (Denmark, Finland, Norway, Sweden)

Italy

United States of America

France

United Kingdom (United Kingdom Post Office)

Switzerland

and are reproduced in Part III of this Report.

5.   The conclusions of the Joint Meeting are given in Part II of this Report.

PART II

CONCLUSIONS OF THE JOINT MEETING

1.   The Joint Meeting noted a general consensus that an Integrated Services Digital Network (hereafter quoted as "ISDN network") might be the ideal global communication network for the future. However, studies would be needed regarding :

  i) the conditions,

 ii) the degree of integration,

iii) the services integrated,

 iv) the time scale,

according to which integration of services would be economically advantageous.

2.   The studies of digital networks for various telecommunicatio services (telephone, telex, data ...) could not presently be based on the assumption of a single integrated services digital network with a common signalling system for the following reasons :

Box 2.11 (continued)

2.1   The requirements for the various services are different.

2.2   If the requirements for telephony are well defined, it is not yet the case for the future data network which is planned.

3.   For these reasons and other considerations (economic, geographic, etc.) the Joint Meeting concluded that the present studies for questions under consideration by :

- Study Group X (telex),

- Study Group XI (telephone) (see in Annex 1 the new Question G/XI proposed by Study Group XI at its February 1972 meeting),

- Joint Working Party NRD (data),

- Special Study Group D (digital transmission and switching),

for digital networks should continue during the next study period 1973-1976.

These studies on specialized digital networks should be carried out during this period with a view to possible integration in a ISDN network.

4.   To ensure compatibility between the results obtained

- by Joint Working Party NRD, for the digital <u>data</u> network

- by Study Group X, for the digital <u>telex</u> network

- by Study Group XI, for the digital <u>telephone</u> network

and commonality in system philosophy and system design where this is possible and advantageous, the Joint Meeting proposed that the feasibility of the integration of services on the digital network should be considered by Special Study Group D in the context of the present Question 1/D (see Annex 2) and in particular Point B of Note 1.

The Joint Meeting considered that Special Study Group D should include in its future work programme an appropriate question relating to integrated service.

The following basic points indicate, in the opinion of the Joint Meeting, the type of studies which are desirable :

1) How shall the integrated switching and transmission digital technique be realized and how shall it be incorporated in the existing network? How should

Box 2.11 (continued)

the present network gradually develop towards a
digital network?

2) Under what conditions, to which degree, for what
    services and in which time scale is an <u>integration
    of services</u> economically advantageous?

5.   The Chairmen of the three Study Groups (X, XI and Special D)
and Joint Working Party NRD shall be responsible for coordinating the
studies of their Group concerning this problem of integration of
services, with the Chairman of Special Study Group D acting as a
convener for this coordination.

SOURCE : UNITED STATES OF AMERICA

TITLE : INTEGRATED SERVICES DIGITAL NETWORK

        In response to C.C.I.T.T. Secretariat Circular No. 199, dated
28 August 1972, the United States of America wishes to express its opinion
that the future studies of digital networks for various telecommunications
services such as telephone, telex and data should not be based on the
assumption of a single integrated services digital network with a
common signalling system.

        This opinion is a result of the following considerations :

1) Requirements and characteristics for the two types of services
    (i.e., telephone and data) are sufficiently diverse that
    efforts to arrive at a common solution would be likely to cause
    unacceptable delays in establishing either type of service.
    These requirements and characteristics include, among others,
    set up times, supervisory signalling, billing, calling,
    calling patterns, error protection, etc.

2) Economic, geographic and other considerations for
    implementation may differ for each type of service, an integrated
    services digital network approach would again be likely to
    delay implementation of either type of service in such cases.

3) Telephone traffic is still expected to constitute the bulk of
    the telecommunication transfer for the immediate future. An
    integrated services digital network approach could well be
    a major delaying factor in establishing efficient data
    network(s) in countries which do not plan substantial
    implementation of digital telephony in the near future.

Box 2.11 (continued)

4) A priory assumption of a single integrated services digital
network could well lead to inefficiencies in any or all types
of services, leading to increased user costs, lesser quality
of service, or both.

The above position does not preclude the sharing of facilities
between networks where this presents an advantage to both.

It is also considered desirable to permit interconnection of
the networks to the maximum extent compatible with the characteristics
of each network.

SOURCE : FRENCH P.T.T.

TITLE   : INTEGRATED NETWORKS (REFERENCE : CIRCULAR LETTER No. 199)

French P.T.T. favours full integration both of transmission
and switching and also of services, chiefly because of the savings it
will permit on customer loops and central networks and flexibility of
services. This is obviously a matter for the future but every effort
should be made now in order not to prejudice this future stage but
rather to render it feasible.

Signalling would then be conducted in the central part of the
network via a separate common channel (S C C) according to appropriate
schemes designed for flexibility.

Special attention should be paid to local networks to enable
them to be maximally transparent to new services — these being handled
in the central part of the network - in such a manner that the local
telephone network would become, so to speak, the harvester of the crop
of networks for other services.

a *fait accompli* situation. We should not be surprised to learn that meetings of Study
Group XVIII, responsible for ISDN, were among the most heavily attended in CCITT
history (e.g., about 500 participants at Hamburg in 1987).

The first set of Recommendations was published after the Eighth P.A. in 1984.
By the time of the following P.A., November 1988 at Melbourne, a complete structure of ISDN Recommendations (I-Series) had been fleshed out. The I-Series takes
up three fascicles in *Blue Book* Volume III, totaling 750 pages (see Box 2.12 for an
overview). Yet all of this is only the beginning for future, general-purpose, "work-

Box 2.12

CCITT Rec. I.110 for ISDN (VIIIth Plenary Assembly, Geneva, 1984)

---

1.   <u>Recommendation I.110</u>

PREAMBLE AND

GENERAL STRUCTURE OF THE I-SERIES RECOMMENDATIONS

FOR THE

INTEGRATED SERVICES DIGITAL NETWORK (ISDN)

PREAMBLE

<u>Introduction</u>

An ISDN is a network, in general evolving from telephony Integrated Digital Network (IDN), that provides end-to-end digital connectivity to support a wide range of services, including voice and non-voice services, to which users have access by a limited set of standard multi-purpose user network interfaces.

This concept requires a family of CCITT Recommendations.

The I-Series Recommendations will provide principles and guidelines on the ISDN concept, as well as a detailed specification of the User-Network and Internetwork interfaces. They will further contain suitable references so that the detailed Recommendations on specific elements within the network can continue to be developed in the appropriate Recommendation series.

Figure 1 produces a broad outline of the structure of the I-Series of Recommendations and their relationship to other Recommendations.

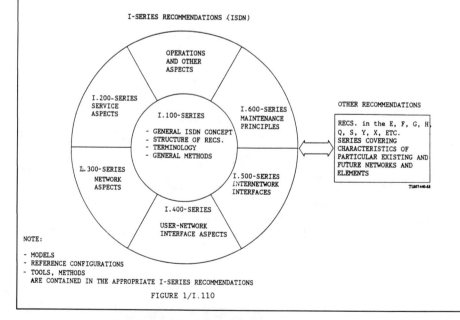

FIGURE 1/I.110

Box **2.12** (continued)

FIGURE 1/I.110

Structure of I-Series Recommendations and their
relationship with other Recommendations

As shown in Figure 1 above, the current structure of the I-Series
documentation is subdivided into seven major parts. Other I-Series documents may
be added as the need arises. In addition, to support the implementation of the
ISDN concepts, Recommendations have been produced and others will be produced in
other Series by the appropriate specialist group (see Recommendation I.111)

Basis of the I-Series approach

In order to standardize all necessary aspects of ISDN the CCITT has
divided the issues into a number of distinctive (but obviously related)   areas
(see Figure 2). Three of these areas are the following:

1)   Services (I.200-Series of Recommendations);

2)   Network aspects (I.300-Series of Recommendations);

3)   User-network access and interfaces (I.400-Series of
Recommendations).

Network aspects are further supported by other Recommendations both
inside and outside the I-Series.

The I-Series Recommendations are directed at the following principles:

a)   the standardization of services offered to subscribers, so as to
enable services to be internationally compatible;

b)   the standardization of user-network interfaces, so as to enable
terminal equipment to be portable (and to assist in a));

c)   the standardization of network capabilities to the degree
necessary to allow user-to-network and network-to-network
interworking, so as to achieve a) and b) above.

The distinction that has been made in this approach between services
and network capabilities is perhaps the most important. In the past, each
service which was a candidate for standardization was treated in isolation and
the necessary standards developed. For the ISDN, a wide range of services has to
be considered in a coordinated manner. In addition, there has not been a
conscious decision in the past to separate the definition of standards required
for services from the definition of the standards for the network capabilities
to support these services.

The approach, in the development of the I-Series, has been, firstly, to
establish the broad concepts of the two areas of standards, secondly, to
uniquely define these two concepts, and thirdly, to show the relationship
between them.

Box 2.12 (continued)

The fourth area shown in Figure 2, is user equipment. The I-Series includes reference configurations which identify key functional groupings and their physical relationship. The interfaces with the network are explicitly defined, however the I-Series does not provide a detailed description of any specific terminal element.

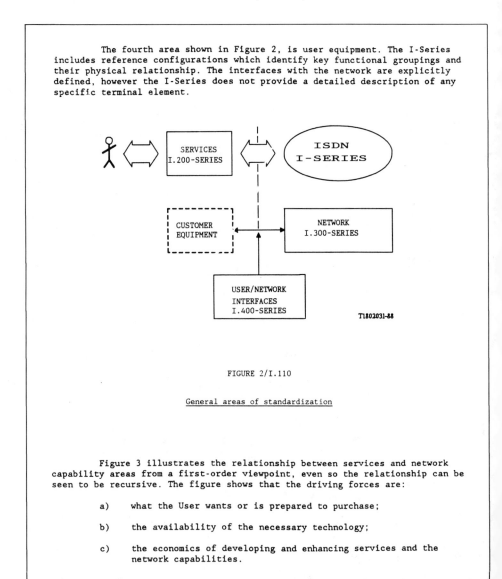

FIGURE 2/I.110

General areas of standardization

Figure 3 illustrates the relationship between services and network capability areas from a first-order viewpoint, even so the relationship can be seen to be recursive. The figure shows that the driving forces are:

a)   what the User wants or is prepared to purchase;

b)   the availability of the necessary technology;

c)   the economics of developing and enhancing services and the network capabilities.

Box 2.12 (continued)

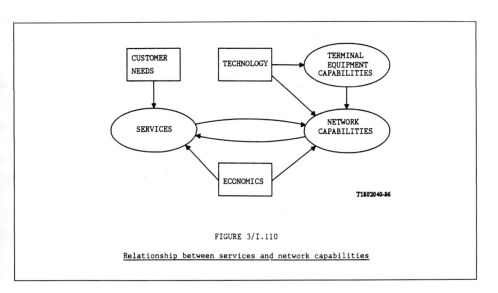

FIGURE 3/I.110

Relationship between services and network capabilities

horse" networks. More international standardization needs to be accomplished for the introduction of *broadband ISDN* (B-ISDN). Only that evolving system approach can carry full television channels, in addition to a "menu" of video display, data, facsimile, and voice in any desired combination (Box 2.13). The vehicle of transmission will be optical fiber cable. Because this latter facility has developed technically and economically so far so fast, its presence is likely to precede availability of Broadband ISDN equipment. Therefore, this next phase of ISDN may ease into the market by trial and feedback of design information. This dynamic process will provide market testing of applicants for *a priori* decision. Thus, the development of final B-ISDN Recommendations may be accelerated.

2.5.4 Public Data Networks

Most widely recognized *a priori* standards are those presented in six out of seven volumes concerned with data communication. Only the standard Modems for Data Transmission over the Public Telephone Network, given in the first fascicle of the *Blue Books'* Volume VIII set, had been developed after interaction with the marketplace. However, the quest for public data networks that would be optimized for transmission of data, not speech, created a Special Working Party of CCITT, active in the 1969-1972 study period. Its documentary output was voluminous, and worldwide interest ran high. Consequently, a new study group (Study Group VII) was

Box 2.13

CCITT Rec. I.121 for B-ISDN (VIIIth Plenary Assembly, Geneva, 1984)

5.   Recommendation I.121

                    BROADBAND ASPECTS OF ISDN

Foreword

         This Recommendation should be interpreted as a guideline to the
objective of providing more detailed Recommendations on all broadband aspects of
ISDN (B-ISDN) during the next study period (1989-1992).

         The Recommendation was elaborated taking into account the following:

-    the emerging demand for broadband services;

-    the availability of high speed transmission, switching and signal
     processing technologies;

-    the need for covering broadband aspects of ISDN, in CCITT
     Recommendations;

-    the need to integrate both interactive and distribution services;

-    the need to integrate both circuit and packet transfer modes into
     one universal broadband network;

-    the need to provide flexibility to both user and operator.

1.   Principles and concept

1.1   Principles of B-ISDN

         The main feature of the ISDN concept is the support of a wide range of
audio, video and data applications in the same network. A key element of service
integration for an ISDN is the provision of a range of services using a limited
set of connection types and multipurpose user-network interfaces.

         In the context of this Recommendation, the term B-ISDN is used for
convenience in order to refer to and emphasize the broadband aspects of ISDN.
The intent, however, is that there is one comprehensive notion of an ISDN which
provides broadband and other ISDN services.

         B-ISDNs support both switched and non-switched connections. Connections
in a B-ISDN support both circuit-mode and packet-mode services.

         A B-ISDN will contain intelligence for the purpose of providing service
features, maintenance and network management functions. This intelligence may
not be sufficient for some new services and may have to be supplemented by
either additional intelligence within the network, or possibly compatible
intelligence in the user terminals.

         A layered structure should be used for the specification of the access
protocol to a B-ISDN.

         It is recognized that ISDNs may be implemented in a variety of
configurations according to specific national situations.

Box 2.13 (continued)

1.2   Evolution to B-ISDN

1.2.1   Target transfer mode

        Asynchronous transfer mode (ATM) is the target transfer mode solution
for implementing a B-ISDN. It will influence the standardization of digital
hierarchies and multiplexing structures, switching and interfaces for broadband
signals.

Asynchronous transfer mode

        ATM is used in this Recommendation as addressing a specific packet
oriented transfer mode using asynchronous time division multiplexing technique:
the multiplexed information flow is organized in fixed size blocks, called
cells. A cell consists of a user information field and a header; the primary
role of the header is to identify cells belonging to the same virtual channel on
an asynchronous time division multiplex. Cells are assigned on demand, depending
on the source activity and the available resources. Cell sequence integrity on a
virtual channel is preserved by the ATM layer.

        ATM is a connection-oriented technique. Header values are assigned to
each section of a connection when required and released when no longer needed.
The connections identified by the headers remain unchanged during the lifetime
of a call. Signalling and user information are carried on separate virtual
channels.

        ATM will offer a flexible transfer capability common to all services,
including connectionless services.

1.2.2   Evolution steps

        B-ISDN will be based on the concepts developed for ISDN and may evolve
by progressively incorporating additional functions and services (e.g. high
quality video applications).

        The deployment of B-ISDN may require a period of time extending over
one or more decades. Thus arrangements must be developed for the interworking of
services on B-ISDN and services on other networks.

        In the evolution towards a B-ISDN, digital end-to-end connectivity will
be obtained in part via plant and equipment used in existing and planned
networks, such as digital transmission and switching. Relevant Recommendations
for these constituent elements of a B-ISDN are contained in the appropriate
series of Recommendations of CCITT and of CCIR.

        In the early stages of the evolution of B-ISDN, some interim user-
network arrangements (e.g. combinations of Synchronous Transfer Mode (STM) and
ATM techniques) may need to be adopted in certain countries to facilitate early
penetration of digital service capabilities.

2.   Service aspects of B-ISDN

2.1   General

        The principles of services supported by an ISDN are described in the
I.200-Series Recommendations. The description of B-ISDN services is based on the
principles of the existing I-Series Recommendations.

Box 2.13 (continued)

This section describes the classification of broadband services, the definition of those service classes, and gives examples of services in each service class proposed to be supported by the ISDN.

This classification does not take into account the location of the implementation of the functions either in the network or in the terminals. This classification is primarily from the point of view of the network and not from the user point of view.

Depending on their communication functions and applications, the services to be supported by the B-ISDN may be internationally standardized and offered by the administration as bearer services or teleservices.

2.2   Service classes

Depending on the different forms of the broadband communication and their applications, two main service categories have been identified: interactive services and distribution services. The interactive services are subdivided into three classes of services, viz., the conversational services, the messaging services, and the retrieval services. The distribution services are represented by the class of distribution services without user individual presentation control and the class of distribution services with user individual presentation control.

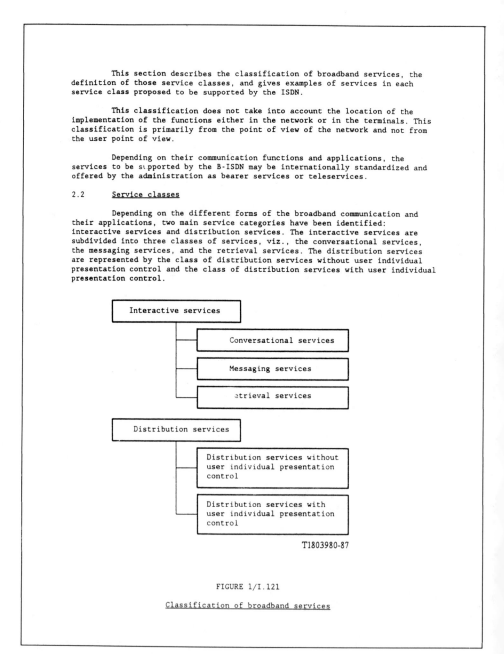

T1803980-87

FIGURE 1/I.121

Classification of broadband services

Box 2.13 (continued)

2.3   Definition of service classes

2.3.1   Conversational services

Conversational services in general provide the means for bidirectional dialogue communication with real-time (no store-and-forward) end-to-end information transfer from user to user or between user and host (e.g. for data processing). The flow of the user information may be bidirectional symmetric, bidirectional asymmetric and in some specific cases (e.g. such as video surveillance), the flow of information may be unidirectional. The information is generated by the sending user or users, and is dedicated to one or more individual communication partners at the receiving site.

Examples of broadband conversational services are videotelephony, video conference and high speed data transmission.

2.3.2   Messaging services

Messaging services offer user-to-user communication between individual users via storage units with store-and-forward, mailbox and/or message handling (e.g. information editing, processing and conversion) functions.

Examples of broadband messaging services are message handling services and mail services for moving pictures (films), high resolution images and audio information.

2.3.3   Retrieval services

The user of retrieval services can retrieve information stored in information centres and in general provided for public use. This information will be sent to the user on his demand only. The information can be retrieved on an individual basis. Moreover, the time at which an information sequence is to start is under the control of the user.

Examples are broadband retrieval services for   lm, high resolution image, audio information, and archive information.

2.3.4   Distribution services without user individual presentation control

These services include broadcast services. They provide a continuous flow of information which is distributed from a central source to an unlimited number of authorized receivers connected to the network. The user can access this flow of information without the ability to determine at which instant the distribution of a string of information will be started. The user cannot control the start and order of the presentation of the broadcast information. Depending on the point of time of the user's access, the information will not be presented from its beginning.

Examples are broadcast services for television and audio-programmes.

2.3.5   Distribution services with user individual presentation control

Services of this class also distribute information from a central source to a large number of users. However, the information is provided as a sequence of information entities (e.g. frames) with cyclical repetition. So, the user has the ability of individual access to the cyclical distributed

Box 2.13 (continued)

information and can control the start and order of presentation. Due to the
cyclical repetition, the information entities selected by the user will always
be presented from its beginning.

One example of such a service is full channel broadcast videography.

2.4   Examples of broadband services

Table 1 of Annex 1 contains examples of possible services, their
applications and some possible attribute values describing the main
characteristics of the services.

Guideline prose definitions, service attributes and attribute values
for describing a number of possible broadband services are presented in Annex 2.
Services described include:

-     broadband unrestricted bearer services;

-     high quality broadband video telephony;

-     high quality broadband video conference;

-     existing quality and high definition TV distribution;

-     broadband Videotex.

2.5   User-network interface from service point of view

2.5.1   Need for simultaneous services

The user-network interface will be required to support a varying
mixture of services to broadband network users. The simultaneous services
required at the interface will vary between customers, e.g., the requirements
for residential customers may differ from those of business customers. The
capacity of the interface, the mix of simultaneous services, and the bit rate
required for each service are all inter-related.

The user-network interface must be able to accommodate at least an H_4
user rate (see note), (or an equivalent mix of services whose aggregate bit rate
may be up to that of an H_4 user rate), plus some additional narrow-band services
and signalling. Moreover, there may be a need to carry a greater volume of
services and to provide the capability of supporting services whose rates exceed
the H_4 user rate.

The study of simultaneous service requirements is important and will
impact broadband aspects of ISDN such as bit rates, user interfaces, protocol
processing, etc. Urgent further study is required.

Note - The term H_4-user rate is used here to give an indication of the range of
bit rates available to the user (see § 5). No implications for channel provision
are intended.

2.5.2   Flexibility of the user-network interface

Not only will ISDNs in different environments need to support a large
variety of customer requirements for different services, but also the access
requirements of a given customer may often change from time to time.

Box 2.13 (continued)

ANNEX 1

(to Recommendation I.121)

Examples of broadband services

Table 1 contains examples of possible services, their applications and some possible attribute values describing the main characteristics of the services.

TABLE 1

Possible broadband services in ISDN

Service classes	Type of information	Examples of Broadband services	Applications	Some possible Attribute Values[7,8]
Conversational services	Moving pictures (video) and sound	Broadband[2] Note 3) Video-telephony	Communication for the transfer of voice (sound), moving pictures, and video scanned still images and documents between two locations (person-to-person)[3] Tele-education. Tele-shopping Tele-advertising	- Demand/reserved/ permanent - Point-to-point/ multipoint - Bidirectional symmetric/bidirectional asymmetric - (Value for information transfer rate is under study)
		Broadband[2] Note 3) Videoconference	Multipoint communication for the transfer of voice (sound), moving pictures, and video scanned still images and documents between two or more locations (person-to-group, group-to-group)[3] Tele-education Tele-shopping Tele-advertising	- Demand/reserved/ permanent - Point-to-point/ multipoint - Bidirectional symmetric/bidirectional asymmetric
		Video-surveillance	- Building security - Traffic monitoring	- Demand/reserved/ permanent - Point-to-point/ multipoint - Bidirectional asymmetric/unidirectional
		Video/audio information transmission service	- TV signal transfer - Video/audio dialogue - Contribution	- Demand/reserved/ permanent - Point-to-point/ multipoint - Bidirectional symmetric/bidirectional asymmetric

Box 2.13 (continued)

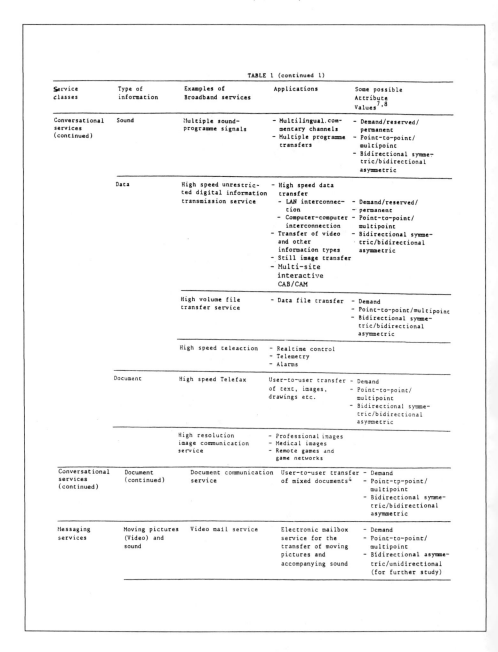

TABLE 1 (continued 1)

Service classes	Type of information	Examples of Broadband services	Applications	Some possible Attribute Values[7,8]
Conversational services (continued)	Sound	Multiple sound-programme signals	- Multilingual. commentary channels - Multiple programme transfers	- Demand/reserved/ permanent - Point-to-point/ multipoint - Bidirectional symmetric/bidirectional asymmetric

	Data	High speed unrestricted digital information transmission service	- High speed data transfer
			  - LAN interconnection
			  - Computer-computer interconnection
			- Transfer of video and other information types
			- Still image transfer
			- Multi-site interactive CAB/CAM
				- Demand/reserved/ permanent
				- Point-to-point/ multipoint
				- Bidirectional symmetric/bidirectional asymmetric

		High volume file transfer service	- Data file transfer	- Demand - Point-to-point/multipoint - Bidirectional symmetric/bidirectional asymmetric
		High speed teleaction	- Realtime control - Telemetry - Alarms	
	Document	High speed Telefax	User-to-user transfer of text, images, drawings etc.	- Demand - Point-to-point/ multipoint - Bidirectional symmetric/bidirectional asymmetric
		High resolution image communication service	- Professional images - Medical images - Remote games and game networks	
Conversational services (continued)	Document (continued)	Document communication service	User-to-user transfer of mixed documents[4]	- Demand - Point-tp-point/ multipoint - Bidirectional symmetric/bidirectional asymmetric
Messaging services	Moving pictures (Video) and sound	Video mail service	Electronic mailbox service for the transfer of moving pictures and accompanying sound	- Demand - Point-to-point/ multipoint - Bidirectional asymmetric/unidirectional (for further study)

Box 2.13 (continued)

TABLE 1 (continued 2)

Service classes	Type of information	Examples of Broadband services	Applications	Some possible Attribute Values[7,8]
	Document	Document mail service	Electronic mailbox service for "mixed" documents[4]	- Demand - Point-to-point/multipoint - Bidirectional asymmetric/unidirectional (for further study)
Retrieval services	Text, data, graphics, sound, still images, moving pictures	Broadband Videotex	- Videotex incl. moving pictures - Remote education and training - Telesoftware - Teleshopping - Advertising - News retrieval	- Demand - PT-PT - Bidirectional asymmetric
		Video retrieval service	- Entertainment purposes - Remote education and training	- Demand/reserved - Point-to-point/multipoint - Bidrectional asymmetric[6]
Retrieval services (continued)	Text, data, etc. (continued)	High resolution image retrieval service	- Entertainment purposes - Remote education and training Professional image communications Medical image communications	- Demand/reserved - Point-to-point/multipoint - Bidirectional asymmetric[6]
		Document retrieval service	"Mixed documents" retrieval from information centres, archives etc.[4,5]	- Demand - Point-to-point/multipoint[6] - Bidirectional asymmetric
		Data retrieval service	- Telesoftware	
Distribution services without user individual presentation control	Video	Existing quality TV distribution service (PAL, SECAM, NTSC)	TV programme distribution	- Demand (selection)/permanent - Broadcast - Bidrectional asymmetric/unidirectional
		Extended quality TV distribution service - Enchanced definition TV distribution service - High quality TV ...	TV programme distribution	- Demand (selection)/permanent - Broadcast - Bidirectional asymmetric/unidirectional
		High definition TV distribution service	TV programme distribution	- Demand (selection)/permanent - Broadcast - Bidirectional asymmetric/unidirectional

Box 2.13 (continued)

TABLE 1 (continued 4)

Service classes	Type of information	Examples of Broadband services	Applications	Some possible Attribute Values[7,8]
		Pay-TV (pay-per-view, pay-per-channel)	TV programme distribution	- Demand (selection)/ permanent - Broadcast/multipoint - Bidirectional asymmetric/unidirectional
Distribution services without user individual presentation control (continued)	Test, graphics, still images	Document distribution service	- Electronic newspaper - Electronic publishing	- Demand (selection)/ permanent - Broadcast/multipoint - Bidirectional asymmetric/unidirectional[6]
	Data	High speed unrestricted digital information distribution service	- Distribution of unrestricted Data	- Permanent - Broadcast - Unidirectional
	Moving pictures and sound	Video information distribution service	- distribution of video/audio signals	- Permanent - Broadcast - Unidirectional
Distribution services with user individual presentation control	Text, graphics, sound, still images	Full channel broadcast videography	- Remote education and training - Advertising - News retrieval - Telesoftware	- Permanent - Broadcast - Unidirectional

Notes to Table 1

Note 1 - In this table only those broadband services are considered, which may require higher transfer capacity than that of the H1 capacity. Services for sound retrieval, sound main applications and visual services with reduced or highly reduced resolutions are not listed.

Note 2 - This terminology indicates that a re-definition regarding existing terms has taken place. The new terms may or may not exist for a transition period.

Note 3 - The realization of the different applications may require the definition of different quality classes.

Note 4 - "Mixed document" means that a document may contain text, graphic, still and moving picture information as well as voice annotation.

Note 5 - Special high layer functions are necessary if post-processing after retrieval is required.

Note 6 - Further study is required to indicate whether the point-to-multipoint connection represents in this case a main application.

Note 7 - At present packet mode is dedicated to non-realtime applications. Depending on the final definition of the packet transfer mode further applications may appear. The application of this attribute value requires further study.

Box 2.13 (continued)

Note 8 – For the moment this column merely highlights some possible attribute values to give a general indication of the characteristics of these services. The full specification of these services will require a listing of all values which will be defined for broadband services in CCITT Recommendation I.2xx.

given the task of creating standards for new data communication networks. The prefix "new" has since been dropped [17]. The 1989 edition of this family of Recommendations, the X-Series, encompasses 2230 tightly printed pages. Its best known member is Rec. X.25, which deals with interfaces between data terminals and *packet switching networks*. When X.25 was rushed through for approval by the Sixth P.A. in October 1976, some packet switching systems had been introduced in several countries. However, significant changes lay ahead for this new service and its technology. Adoption in 1976 of X.25 as an international standard was *a priori* in that its backers meant to force an evolving, new service into standard channels before too many different versions would be in place [18]. In fact, X.25 underwent substantial change and expansion in the three successive study periods of 1976 through 1988. In the CCITT *Blue Book* of 1989, X.25 occupies about two hundred pages, compared to thirty-five in the first publication of 1976. Box 2.14 highlights the evolution of data network standards.

2.6 STANDARDIZATION IS INNOVATION'S KEY TO THE MARKET

The development of new information network services is clearly caught in a paradox. On one hand, technology-driven innovations need much interaction with targeted users before products can be standardized. On the other hand, few potential users are prepared to invest in experimental systems that may prove incompatible with network standards a few years hence. Straddling this paradox are daring entrepreneurs who engineer first applications to characteristics suitable for a few, large-scale users. Initial offerings thus are not hampered by lack of industry standards. Neither is profitability a criterion for these entrepreneurs, who attempt to build a stake in capital growth of the new company. Occasionally, even a staid telecommunication service provider allows a special team to promote a new, unprofitable service with standards set by the service offerer alone.

The technical, economic, and political complexities of this given paradox are amplified by the differences between the two industries jointly involved in new services. The telecommunication industry's service providers have enormous capital investments in network transmission and switching plant all the way up to subscribers' premises. Under franchise they are obligated to provide service to all comers. Technical and operational decisions are made by career employees bound to their respective organizations' plans and amortization needs. International compatibility is assured under an intergovernmental treaty organization, ITU, where unanimous adoption of standards has guaranteed, noncoercive implementation worldwide.

Box 2.14 (a)
Data Transmission Milestones

DATA TRANSMISSION - MILESTONES

1960	First meeting of CCITT Working Party "Question 43" of Study Group XV. Over 100 attend. Stage is set for close collaboration with the computer industry.
Dec. 1960	CCITT Plenary Assembly (P.A.) adopts documentary texts and two draft Recommendations (Recs.) on Data Transmission. The study program is assigned to a new Special Study Group A. Standards coordination policy with ISO and IEC is explored by the Plenary Assembly.
1964	CCITT Third P.A. approves family of seven, letter "V" Series Data Recommendations. Also published are close to 100 supplements, which report on competing proposals and plans from leading countries.
1968	Fourth P.A. recognizes study of Data Networks , i.e., designed and optimized for data, not voice. It is given to a Special Joint Working Party, NRD (Nouveaux Réseaux de Données). Quickly, NRD explodes into one of the largest groups ever to meet.
1972	Fifth P.A. adopts NRD's first set of Definitions and "X" Series RECs for Public Data Networks. NRD becomes S.G. VII Public Data Networks, under congenial chairmanship of Vern C. McDonald (Canada). From here on Volume VIII of CCITT Books covers both V and X Series Recommendations.
1984	Eighth P.A. - End of a "founders' era." Canada's McDonald, first chairman of S.G. VII, retires. He is replaced by Wedlake of U.K. - AT&T's "Mr Data Modem" Vaughan relinquishes long-time chairmanship of S.G. XVII. Successor is Kern (Fed. Rep. of Germany).
1988	Ninth P.A. adopts Rec. No. A.22 on expanded collaboration with ISO/IEC, as reproduced on page 3 of this box.

Box 2.14 (b)

Parallel ISO Activities

Parallel ISO Activities

1960   ISO sets up a Technical Committee TC97 to cover standards for Computers and
        Information Processing. Its Subcommittee SC6 is to deal with data transmission.

1964   Demarcation lines for respective province of ISO and CCITT are drawn up. As
        adopted by CITT in REC.A.20, collaboration in Data Transmission is spelled out.
        This document acknowledges the interface between the Computer Industry and
        Telecommunicators.

1968   REC.A.20 successively reworded to keep it alive as guiding policy for
to   standardization in this complex field.
present

1979   ISO's Committee 97 adopts a Seven Layer model for Open Systems
        Interconnection (OSI). This model stratifies standard entry and exit
        interconnections of telecommunication networks and user terminal equipment.

N.B.   Note fundamental difference in modus operanti, ISO vs. ITU. ISO is not an
        intergovernmental treaty organization; ISO adopts standards by majority vote,
        after a prescribed time of consideration. Also, ISO's committees are located in
        many countries; a given country acts as secretariat for a given committee. But
        CCITT is headquartered at Geneva, where its small yet qualified staff acts as
        neutral secretariat.

Box 2.14 (c)

CCITT Draft Rec. A.22 (IXth Plenary Assembly, Geneva, 1988)

COLLABORATION WITH OTHER INTERNATIONAL ORGANIZATIONS

ON INFORMATION TECHNOLOGY

THE CCITT,

considering

(a)   that the purposes of the International Telecommunication Union and the
recognition of CCITT relations with other organizations were given in 1964 and later, in
CCITT Recommendation A.20 which concerns data transmission; and

Box 2.14 (continued)

(b)   that the principles of responsibility in regard to CCITT-defined Telematic services were given in 1980 and later, in Recommendation A.21 which mentions some subjects of mutual interest; and

(c)   that CCITT Resolution No. 7 in 1984 further recognized common interests with ISO and IEC concerning Information Technology and cooperation with them by appropriate means;

recognizes the following principles

1.   that in accordance with CCITT Recommendations A.20 and A.21 and Resolution No. 7, every effort should be made in establishing respective study programmes to identify overlapping studies with a view to avoiding duplication of work;

2.   that where subjects are identified in which coordination seems desirable, text should be drawn up mutually and kept aligned;

3.   that in carrying on the respective programmes of Information Technology studies, collaborative meetings at appropriate levels should be scheduled, where necessary. In drafting aligned text, it is necessary to take into account the respective timing for approvals and publication, particularly with the ISO/IEC Joint Technical Committee 1 (JTC1) on Information Technology;

4.   that commonality of text with ISO/IEC and cross-references is considered desirable in certain areas of mutual interest, such as:

-    Message Handling Systems,

-    Directory Systems,

-    Open Systems Interconnection (OSI) architecture - service definitions and protocol specifications,

-    certain areas of Interworking,

-    certain aspects of Telematic Services,

-    Document Architecture,

-    certain aspects of ISDN.

There is no such guarantee of implementation in the computer and affiliated terminal equipment industry. It operates in an open market with many dispersed competitors, although a certain manufacturer (e.g., IBM) may have dominating influence in that market for specific products. Obsolescence has been extremely rapid in these fields. The short product-life horizon makes imperative that standards, where and when they control market acceptance, be set in step with large-scale product introduction. While each manufacturer has a substantial investment in product development and tooling up for manufacture, including associated software where required, these outlays are expected to be recovered through sales within a few years. Industry standardization is negotiated through membership in national associations that are nongovernmental in some countries, semi-independent under a government charter in most others. Unanimity is not sought in the committees of these organizations, rather a compromise acceptable to the voting majority. The same approach carries over to international standardization. Cognizant organizations are the ISO (International Organization for Standardization) and IEC (International Electrotechnical Commission) [15]. In contrast with ITU, these two organizations do not have headquarters capable of organizing study group meetings and coordinating each group's transactions down to final publication of meticulously edited, approved texts. Instead, each individual committee created by ISO or IEC is placed under the responsibility of the national member that has accepted the secretariat for the particular subject study. Holding meetings, circulating drafts, and overseeing observance of rules are all tasks carried out by the respective national secretary and his or her assistants. Adoption of proposed standards is forced through a firm timetable, culminating in a "six-months rule" for final approval. A majority of those voting is sufficient to approve a new standard. A member of the outvoted minority may refuse to implement this standard in its national territory. However, some countries also participate in regional committees and institutes for "normalization" (in most languages but English, the *norm* is a standard codified for obligatory application). For Western European countries, an ISO standard may be converted to a norm of the CEN (Comité Européen de Normalisation), or its companion, CENELEC (Comité Européen de Normalisation Electrotechnique) [16]. Through such action, the particular ISO standard would become "*de facto*" binding for the industry, even of the country whose ISO member had voted against it.

Europe's CENELEC (founded in 1958) and CEN (1961) cover the same fields as IEC and ISO. In both older, worldwide organizations, European interests are represented by strong national member bodies. What, then, is the rationale for establishing separate committees for adoption of regional standards? The answer to this question opens additional perspectives on the sprawling activities that create ever more rigorous standards.

The goal of ISO and IEC standards is to assure interconnectability of specific equipment. A given standard usually has two additional goals: assured performance limits, and an incentive for reduced product variety in the marketplace. Within these three objectives, ISO and IEC stop short of dictating detailed design characteristics that would assure predictable interchangeability of equipment made by various manufacturers in different countries. The market effect of ISO and IEC standards is thus similar to that of most CCITT Recommendations.

In practice, such a standard specifies terminal characteristics for a given "black box," competing versions of which may differ substantially in other respects, as suits the policies of different countries. That lack of product interchangeability across national borders has been a serious obstacle to the European Community's plan for economic integration. CEN and CENELEC were created to overcome the obstacle. As a result, forthcoming products of the computer and associated terminal equipment industries are expected to meet uniform standards, regardless of European country of origin. A product cleared as meeting the specifications in one country automatically obtains market entry acceptance in all other countries of the EC.

Achieving this objective with respect to the computer industries has put a critical searchlight on the telecommunication Administrations. For ten or more years, CEPT has been pressured to produce definitive standards that would open all European countries to each other's equipment suppliers. Still, the Administrations resisted, protecting their respective national industries. Finally, in the 1986–1987 period, the EC's demand for action was met. A new European Institute for Telecommunication Standards has been founded. It is to become the ITU–CEPT counterpart link to the relations between ISO–CEN and IEC–CENELEC, respectively.

In summary, when all of these organizations are fully operational and coordinated, information network-plus-terminal procurement in any EC country will be according to uniform regional standards. Having been detailed by Europeans for the good of the EC, these standards are likely to pose barriers to non-European suppliers. Thus, the controlling power of standards will have traveled full circle, admitting insiders only to the sponsoring market. Control by one company or one administration indeed has been replaced by a multinational committee, but geopolitical expansion makes the power of these standards only more formidable. Most significantly, the power has resulted from external political pressure on the information service industries that have previously standardized by self-regulation. Most non-European countries continue to rely on internal forces for agreements, in particular through the ITU. Yet other international organizations, notably user associations and the INTELSAT (International Telecommunication Satellite Organization) consortium, express demands for worldwide equivalents of the European "norm" type of standard. In the United States, the clamor for maximum competitive access to all information market segments also points toward uniform, interchangeable product standards, as in EC.

The problems described in this section are taken up for closer examination in subsequent chapters. In particular, telecommunication reforms introduced in several countries are the subject of Chapter Four. Then, in Chapter Five, the effect of these reforms on standardizing activities and the standing of standards in the market is the main topic.

REFERENCES

1.   See Marc U. Porat, "Communication Policy in an Information Society," in *Communications for Tomorrow: Policy Perspectives for the 1980s,* Glen O. Robison, ed., New York: Praeger, 1978.
2.   See, for example, COMPUTOPOLIS plan for a "computerized city," as described in Chapter IV of *The Plan for an Information Society: A National Goal for the Year* 2000, Final Report of Japan Computer Usage Development Institute's Computerization Committee, Tokyo, May 1972. Republished in English by Diebold Europe's *Data Exchange,* July–August 1973. See also, pub-

lications of the HI-OVIS project, i.e., Higashi-Ikoma Optical Visual Information System; experimental in 1973; operational 1979. Several bibliographical references are given in NTIA Report 80-50, titled *Videotex Systems and Services,* by L.R. Bloom, A.G. Hanson, R.F. Linfield, and D.R. Wortendyke. Washington, DC, US Department of Commerce, October 1980.

3. Koji Kobayashi, *Computers and Communications: A Vision of C&C,* Cambridge, MA: MIT Press, 1986. (Translation of Japanese original published 1985.)

4. Valéry Giscard D'Estaing, "Informatique et Société," *Revue des Deux Mondes,* November 1979, pp. 257–267.

5. Marie Marchand, *The Minitel Saga: A French Success Story,* Paris: Larousse, 1988.

6. The predecessor organizations of CCITT, CCIF (International Telephone Consultative Committee) and CCIT (International Telegraph Consultative Committee), were focused on intra-European standards. They were founded in 1924 and 1925, respectively.

7. Reference is to the AT&T divestiture of its operating companies, under the *Modification of Final Judgment,* approved in the US District Court of the District of Columbia (Washington, DC), in August 1982; see Chapter Four for detailed excerpts.

8. Pertinent CCITT Recommendations are found in *Blue Book* (1988), Vol. V, i.e., Recs. P.11 and P.16; Vol. III, Recs. in the G.100, G.200, and G.800 subseries; also in the H and J series.

9. This text appears as a "Preliminary Note" at the front of each of the fourteen fascicles, i.e., separately bound volumes of Vol. VI of the *Blue Book.*

10. CEPT is the Conférence Européene des Postes et Télécommunications, founded in 1959 for the purpose of "harmonizing" the postal and telecommunication services in Europe. CEPT's membership includes many more countries than the European Economic Commission, so that it effectively coordinates all of Europe, excepting only the USSR and most of its allies. See Chapter Five for description.

11. See detail presented in Box 2.6.

12. Recommendations for signalling systems are found in CCITT *Blue Book,* Vol. VI, distributed over fourteen fascicles.

13. Recommendations for data communication networks are found in *Blue Book,* Vol. VIII, fascicles viii.2–viii.8.

14. As reported in *TE&M,* Vol. 92, No. 2, January 15, 1989, p. 9.

15. GTE Corporation, *1988 Annual Report to Shareholders,* Stamford, CT: March 1989, p. 18.

16. Bell Communications Research, *Catalog of Technical Information, 1988.,* Morristown, NJ: Bellcore, 1988.

17. At this writing, Study Group VII's title is "Data Communication Networks."

18. See Marvin A. Sirbu and Laurence E. Zwimpfer, "Standards Setting for Computer Communication: The Case of X.25," in *IEEE Communications Magazine,* Vol. 23, No. 3 (March 1985), pp. 35–45. Mr. Zwimpfer's more detailed analysis of this case, directed by Professor Sirbu, was published internally by MIT Center for Policy Analysis, as CPA81-13, January 1981.

19. A description of ISO and IEC with focus on telecommunication is included in Chapter Three. See also articles by Edward Lohse on ISO, and Sava Sherr on IEC in *IEEE Communications Magazine,* Vol. 23, No. 1 (January 1985); pp. 18–24 and 25–30, respectively.

20. CEN, founded 1961, is, in effect, a European regional coordinator with respect to ISO. CENELEC resulted from a merger of two predecessor organizations, CENELCOM and CENEL, effective January 1, 1973. Its secretariat is at Brussels, Belgium.

Chapter Three

Stratification and Arbitration of Standards*

3.1 DEFINITIONS

"Standards" is a broad term for a pyramid of requirements. The pyramidic structure will be discussed in Section 3.3, "Levels of Standardization." We should distinguish among the following.

(a) *True standards* (in French and German usage: *Normes, Normen*). Requirements imposed on an item (material or service) for its acceptance by end users, purchasers, or a regulatory authority. *Criterion*: Stated precision of the requirement to be met, including allowable tolerances within which an item conforms to the standard. Adoption by an authority capable of imposing penalties for noncomformance. Effective only within national borders because no international enforcing authority exists. However, national government agencies may be empowered and obligated to enforce a *norm*, as seems the case with European ETSI standards (see Chapter Four). *Example*: US MIL (i.e., military standards). Note that some originally internal standards of the AT&T's Bell Telephone System prior to divestiture (1984) also acquired the force of true standards. They remain effective not only in the Bell Operating Companies' service territories, but also in interconnected services and equipment supplied by others. The central staff of Bellcore dispenses these standards for a fee [1].

(b) *Regulations* (Regs.). International requirements, adopted under a treaty, that acquire the force of true standards in these two areas:

(1) sharing of the radio frequency (RF) spectrum [2]; and
(2) harmonized operation of public telecommunication services throughout the international network [3].

*The material in Sections 3.1 through 3.4 is a substantially revised version of a previously unpublished report by the author, prepared in 1977 for the US Department of Commerce. Principal investigator was Professor D. A. Dunn of Stanford University. The report's title was "International Standards as Nontariff Trade Barriers in Telecommunication."

A national government's participation in these Regulations is voluntary. However, once adopted, they become binding. This elevation to true standards, constraining and enforceable as under (a) above, is assured by giving the Regulations treaty status. Each participating country pledges formal ratification at home by its legislature. Thus, the ITU Regulations, and only these ITU technical outputs, become a matter of foreign policy. Regulations thereby become world standards legislated to the telecommunication industry by the executive arm of the government. In the United States, this involves the President, the Department of State, and the Senate's consent.

(c) *Recommendations* (Recs.). Requirements agreed in CCITT or CCIR committees, the observance of which is voluntary within each participating country. Origin of these requirements is the need for compatibility of telecommunication services transacted across national borders.

When telecommunication authorities of a given country adopt these Recommendations for use as binding standards within their own jurisdictions, they do so contrary to the professed spirit of the CCITT committees. In fact, some originators of a Recommendation's technical content often reserve their own administration's freedom of use and interpretation (British Telecom, in particular). Many Recommendations are deliberately broad, whereas others (e.g., those for data modens) specify fairly detailed equipment characteristics. Thus, some Recommendations are much more constraining than others. This is so because of divergent interests within the study groups and pressures from some developing countries for Recommendations that may serve as true standards.

We may subdivide the Recommendations into the following categories:

(1) *Performance Recommendations.* These remain somewhat general and are not so written as to pose as true standards. All take into account some statistical distribution of equipment arrangements or service events. A typical example is the noise power engineering of microwave radio systems; a perplexing problem whose straightforward solution has haunted CCIR Study Group 9 for many years [4].

(2) *Wire and cable system frequency plans.* These Recommendations are a step closer to true standards than performance Recommendations. A given equipment is either transmitting and receiving within an adopted plan or it is not. However, any such plan embodied in a Recommendation retains voluntary standing.

In wire and cable transmission, numerous CCITT Recommendations of the G-Serie include specific frequency plans. Older plans originated with the multinational European network situation. Countries adopting the same plan can interconnect at group and higher frequencies, thus eliminating the need for voice-channel demodulation at the border, which would be costly and transmission-degrading. Most North American plans for similar transmission systems differ from CCITT plans.

(3) *System and equipment specifications.* CCITT has standardized† many carrier systems that provide multichannel transmission over open wire, symmetrical pair cable, and coaxial cable. The majority of these systems have characteristics different from similar systems used in the United States. Moreover, CCITT standardized symmetrical pair cables, specially developed for multiplex carrier transmission, have not been used in the United States. In coaxial cables, too, applications outside AT&T have been minimal in the United States. Therefore, United States manufacturers are not in production for these heavy route systems. The background for this divergent trend in multichannel systems is discussed in Section 3.2.

3.2 ORIGIN AND ECONOMIC SIGNIFICANCE OF CCITT AND CCIR RECOMMENDATIONS

3.2.1 The CCITT Background

The weight of the ITU influence that can result in a competitive disadvantage of nonconforming telecommunication equipment in the world market seems to rest with the CCITT and CCIR Recommendations. These are not meant to be rigorous standards, but rather international compatibility agreements. Compatibility in international connections need not require compatible equipment throughout the national network. The latter step is a separate decision.

Administrations of importing countries seek to protect themselves against the hazards of using their own, limited, engineering judgment and of dependency on certain foreign suppliers by citing rigid specifications in the purchase, installation, and operation of telecommunication equipment.

In the absence of an international equivalent for military-like specifications, CCITT and CCIR Recommendations fill this need. Indeed, many developing coun-

---

†*Note on Terminology.* This writer has not discovered a perfect solution to the terminology problem associated with the words "*standard,*" *to standardize,* and *standardization.* The reader is reminded of the fact that CCITT and CCIR Recommendations are, legalistically speaking, just that: Recommendations, not true standards, as defined in Section 3.1. However, the word family of *standard* enjoys widespread and rather indiscriminate use, so much so that it shows up in documents prepared at CCI study group meetings. Moreover, precisely such a *de facto* transition from Recommendation to standard adopted by some countries has given some CCI Recommendations the powerful status as a potential trade barrier. Therefore, the terminology CCITT has standardized . . ." is used here purposefully. These particular Recommendations are standards cited in international trade.

tries limit their participation in CCITT and CCIR affairs to the articulation of demands for technical assistance in the form of complete specification books for systems and equipment. The CCITT and CCIR study groups are unlikely ever to fulfill this wish, but there is a definite trend toward more documentary information.

At one time, the CCITT (more precisely, its predecessors, CCIF and CCIT) was colloquially known as a European Club. Since about 1960, this has changed dramatically. Key study groups have or have had American, Canadian, and Japanese chairmen and vice-chairmen. People from these non-European countries, plus Australians and New Zealanders, also participate very actively in many groups. The US representation, on its part, has grown to include a wide spectrum of interests. For example, the data modem activities in CCITT Study Group (SG) XVII were guided for years by an American chairman who, at home, had been responsible for AT&T's interests in this field. During the same period (1972–1984), a Canadian was chairman of SG VII on data communication networks. Although both SG VII and XVII now have European chairmen, North American participation remains as strong as ever. The intra-US coordination committee was chaired by Mr. T. de Haas, recently replaced by Mr. Utlaut, members of the Commerce Department's telecommunication organization in Boulder, Colorado. The committee develops a US position on the current CCITT study group questions in data transmission; its membership assures a fair hearing for divergent views. US delegations to CCITT (SG XVII and VII) meetings have reported successful adoption of the US position on a fair percentage of items under study.

As a result of worldwide involvement, the US and Canadian telephone company practices have found more recognition in recent CCITT work. As a general rule, we can state that newer CCITT Recommendations are intended to be applicable worldwide in one or two ways: either there is only one right way stated (e.g., for echo suppressors [5]) or there is a choice. The latter situation is the case for most types of multiplex transmission systems including, in particular, regionally preferred signalling systems. This situation permits a specifying purchaser to choose from among CCITT Recommendations; if the purchaser did not choose the version prevalent in the US, he or she has nevertheless chosen from within the CCITT Recommendation's family.

The trend of most recent years favors single, worldwide standards, developed before divergent systems have found market acceptance. This significant trend has been discussed in Chapter Two.

The European Club had been revived in 1959, under the name of CEPT (European Conference on Posts and Telecommunication Administrations). Viewed from outside Europe, CEPT signifies a step toward regional cartelization, contrasting with the open character of the CCIs. The standardizing organization within CEPT has expanded in diversification and intensity of studies in response to pressures from the central bureaucracy of the European Community. Emergence of a supranational European bloc with unified telecommunication standards is CEPT's avowed objective.

This highly important development is one of two central issues taken up in Chapter Four.

In Chapter Two we had mentioned the now classic example of politically effective CEPT action with regard to adoption of standards for a wholly new transmission technology. As early as 1972, European countries as a bloc rallied around a candidate standard for PCM systems that was designed deliberately so as to be incompatible with an American system already in service [6]. Although the United Kingdom and Japan favored a world standard based on the US model, practically all other countries supported the European choice, albeit passively. Only a few developing countries take an active voice in CCITT study group affairs (e.g., Argentina, Brazil, India). For powerful historical reasons, these countries lean toward European practices. Thus, whenever competing proposals from Europe and the US vie for worldwide acceptance, the Europeans will have more support.

The reasons for this solid entrenchment of European practices around the world are themselves proof of solid market positions that were acquired without recourse to ITU standardization. Firms such as Siemens and L.M. Ericsson have invested heavily and methodically in many foreign countries; they have not just exported equipment but trained whole generations of technical people. They have also initiated some local assembly and manufacture of switching equipment, the principal product in demand. Perhaps, most important, in some countries their top representatives have "gone native," the very thing abhorred by American management. In this way, these companies are identified with the national temperament of the importing country.

Use of CCITT Recommendations for commercial leverage occurred later, with the advent of large scale transmission system investments. Local switching plant may be different in each city (and, in some countries, it almost is), but transmission systems are tools of interconnection and thus must be mutually compatible to some extent. After World War II, the art of transmission systems changed so rapidly that a company's entrenched position in switching equipment did not necessarily enable it to satisfy as well the transmission requirements of its loyal foreign customer. Therefore, since the late 1950s, most European suppliers saw the merits of collaborating across competitive rivalries. The goal is to educate all potential customers to a set of CCITT recommended transmission system characteristics that all suppliers profess to meet, regardless of whether each of them is ready to deliver the equipment at the time. To choose these characteristics in such a way that they would also satisfy the border-crossing interconnection requirements in Europe made elementary economic sense.

Now, consider the peculiar situation and needs of the European telecommunication entities after World War II. The old wire and cable plant was either destroyed or outmoded and in bad repair. Populated areas are closely spaced together and can be connected by relatively short, economical cable links. Thus, the basic transmission plant of Western Europe developed on a backbone of new cable routes, using either a specially designed symmetrical pair or coaxial cable for multichannel systems. The European coaxial systems benefited from hindsight at the Bell System's "L" coaxial system, and, in fact, AT&T's chosen building block of a 60–108 kHz base group became a key "European" CCITT Recommendation. Nonetheless, European development in paired cable systems went far beyond any US use of this medium. The situation in the United States did not require such solutions; there was a multimillion pair mile plant of open-wire and voice-frequency type of cables in good condition. Also, the occurrence of many long gaps between population centers favors the alternative use of radio, which is more flexible, requiring no installations between radio stations. Therefore, the different development of transmission systems in the United States cannot be blamed on the existence of the Bell System, but rather on different physical and economic conditions [7].

Indeed, the US manufacturing industry outside Western Electric never developed a product line of coaxial carrier systems. The cost of installation, the first cost of basic equipment, and the acquisiton of rights of way in suitably level terrain, all demand a certainty of high-density, long-distance traffic. Only the Bell System had this certainty, whereas several thousand independent telephone companies served divided and fragmented territories, predominantly in nonmetropolitan areas. The spectacular development of suburban areas, coupled with consolidation of small independents into large organizations, was still to come. Yet even the few large, multistate, independent telephone companies found little use for coaxial systems.

As a result of the conditions indicated above, the core of CCITT Recommendations, created during the CCIF period prior to 1960, described systems and characteristics developed in Europe. Noncompatibility with US practices was mutually acknowledged and accepted for the respective reasons. Nevertheless, a few US manufacturers, serving the fast-growing independent telephone operations, were able to survive in the relatively small volume of world exports to be had in transmission systems. This was possible for several reasons:

(1) The CCITT books had not yet achieved worldwide acceptance, partly because they were available in French only;

(2) Many developing countries in need of equipment had low-density, widely spaced traffic centers, similar to those in the US independent telephone service area;

(3) Some US-made light-to-medium capacity open-wire and radio-channelized systems were technologically advanced and economically attractive;

(4) The European and Japanese manufacturers were straining at domestic needs, building up capacity and offering exasperatingly long delivery intervals; and

(5) These countries were not yet rich enough to offer long-term, low-interest-rate financing.

In a little more than ten years, these gaps have been completely closed. The CCITT books are now published in English and Spanish, in addition to French; even Arabic and Chinese editions are published, with some delay. Recommended systems and performance characteristics in the books presumably have worldwide support, including that of the US industry. Several of the paired cable carrier systems developed in Europe have become historical relics, but so, too, have open-wire carrier systems in all except a few of the least developed areas. In coaxial, microwave, and PCM-exploited paired cable systems, the technology as well as the application objectives are essentially the same the world over.

Nevertheless, if the CCITT books describe more than one recommended type of system in a given application category, the reason is not lack of opportunity for better agreement. In addition to the reasons already cited, we may ponder the sustained different styles in vehicular transportation, where Mercedes and Volvo defy the dominance of "standard" US and Japanese automobile designs, not to mention Citroen and Renault, both as typically French as Ford and Buick are American.

3.2.2 Radio Communication

Origin and economic significance of ITU standards in the field of radio differ somewhat from considerations and historical background given for the CCITT's field of competence.

Transborder telegraph service was perceived as a collaborative enterprise from the outset, but radio had a turbulent and hostile start in international collaboration. Earliest demonstrations of working radio transmission, outside laboratories, were pioneered by inventor-entrepreneur Guglielmo Marconi.

Let us focus on Marconi's story. In 1901, he demonstrated transatlantic radio transmission, a starting point for radiotelegraphy over long distances. He founded companies to exploit his innovations. There was an immediate market for communication with ships at sea, an obvious application for *wireless* connections between points on land and moving, distant stations. Marconi had dual national loyalty—to his native Italy and to England through his mother. His companies in these two countries wanted a worldwide monopoly; naturally, other countries balked. In 1903, the first radiotelegraph conference was called by Germany, but Italy and the United Kingdom blocked agreement. Pressure developed on the Marconi interests to collaborate with other nations. Some competitive systems made their appearance, threatening Marconi's monopoly. His companies retaliated by refusing to accept messages that originated from ships outside the Marconi monopoly (i.e., those that communicated by use of another manufacturer's equipment). By persuasion and compromise, the first formal international agreement in radiotelegraphy was worked out at the second Berlin conference, in 1906. The basic principle adopted states that telegraphic communication between coastal stations and ships at sea should be possible, regardless of the radio system used. This seemingly simple principle is the grandfather of all subsequent worldwide agreements on the uses of radio frequencies. The conference of 1906 put on record the first *Radio Regulations*. They set a pattern of standards that are accepted as obligatory by the signatory governments.

Present-day Radio Regulations form the source book of worldwide and regional frequency allocations for dozens of separately defined radio services. In that respect, the Radio Regulations are much more definitive, binding, and all-inclusive than the contents of any other ITU book. There is simply no escape from the purview of these regulations, which cover amateur radio as well as broadcasting and the fixed service that transmits myriad messages of telephone, telex, data, and visual terminal end-users. Even the passive "listening" for cosmic radiation or postulated extraterrestrial civilizations is included in the Radio Regulations. As radio waves do not by themselves respect national borders, and because reception can be made practically useless by interference from unwanted transmissions or noise, national governments have no alternative but to collaborate in the exploitation of this peculiar resource. Therefore, large political and economic values are built into international allocations. That there are always more applicant users of radio frequency assignments than can be accommodated without harming each other's transmissions or receptions has become axiomatic. Actual assignments are the responsibility of national governments, whose agencies distribute to the various services in accordance with the constraints of the Radio Regulations.

In the United States, radio station licensing by the FCC bestows a coveted frequency assignment that may be contested by competitors. When an established radio or television broadcasting station changes ownership, a new owner is expected to pay a very large sum for the privilege of a place in the crowded airwaves. With respect to similar assignments for telephone and other public telecommunication service providers, the high ecnonomic value is less flagrantly displayed in the marketplace, but it exists there just the same.

Behind an assignment from an international allocation is a set of technical standards. They are developed and approved in the CCIR. A substantial number of these standards are integrated with the Radio Regulations, thus becoming as binding as the allocations. However, many system standards are adopted as Recommendations, similar to those of the CCITT. Also, the CCIR has recourse to guidelines that stop short of formal Recommendation status in documents known as *Reports*. The reader should understand that CCIR deals with much scientific exploration and analysis, as in studies of radio propagation and its optimal uses or radio astronomy.

Traditionally, the United States has had a high profile in this work. Not by coincidence has the office of CCIR Director been occupied by an American since 1966 [8]. These individuals have come to the post from a career in government service as experienced specialists.

The United States has powerful representation in CCIR Study Groups. In fact, on many occasions of study group meetings, the US delegation may number from fifteen to thirty percent of total participation. The United States contributes a disproportionally high percentage of documentation. In the United States, the US CCIR National Committee subjects all contributions to a rigorous, wide-range industry comment and approval routine. In short, we can say that the CCIR is as American as it may be European or Asian in its perception and actual work.

The importance of radio frequencies for applications other than common carrier type of telecommunication accounts for a long-standing, productive participation in ITU Radio Conferences and CCIR on the part of several US government agencies. Yet these same agencies help perpetuate terminologies and frequency band designations that have no standing in the Radio Regulations or any other international standards book. A notorious example is the persistent use of the letter-labelled bands (e.g., C and Ku) in technical and commercial publications. These US designations do not coincide with frequency bands that are precisely allocated to specific services. A C or Ku band may earmark a particular hardware technology to an amateur or designer of radio equipment, but the continued use of such nonstandard designations helps maintain barriers between American engineers and suppliers, on one hand, and their counterparts elsewhere. This is a serious obstacle in a world governed by standards.

3.3 LEVELS OF STANDARDIZATION

3.3.1 Standards Adopted at Intergovernmental Level

Levels of standards may be represented by a hierarchical structure, as in Figure 3.1. At the top of this pyramid are standards adopted at the intergovernmental treaty level. Because of their regulatory force, these standards are often designated as Regulations. At this level, standards are adopted with the intent of making them international law. Their ratification by a member state is equivalent to incorporating them into the law of the land. As with any other law in the country, this standard stands above the citizens. Its observance is backed by the powers of the state to prescribe, prosecute, and punish. In establishing and enforcing standards by law, the authorities of the state preempt voluntary adherence. Thereby also preempted are flexibility of application to specific cases and judgment with regard to discretionary tolerances.

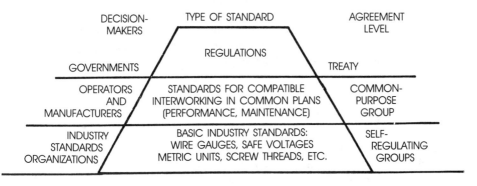

Figure 3.1 The Pyramid Structure of International Technical Standards.

Elementary wisdom would suggest that such a formal standardization should be reserved to fields and cases that justify the state's authoritative involvement. Allocation of scarce resources is a field in which some legalistic standardization is a *sine- qua-non*. This is illustrated by the case of the Radio Regulations, an elaborate body of technical specifications that accompany the allocation of uses of the radio frequency spectrum. As an example, the allocation of the same spectrum space for shared use by terrestrial line-of-sight microwave and satellite communication systems is made feasible only by detailed engineering instructions controlling the choice of locations for the stations operating in the respective services. These engineering instructions form part of the intergovernmental treaty known as Radio Regulations, described in the preceding section.

The ITU promulgates one other set of regulations, known for many years as *Telegraph and Telephone Regulations* (T&T). Unlike Radio Regulations, the T&T Regulations do not allocate a scarce resource. They deal with operational and accounting rules that must be observed by national service providers among each other, and with respect to the general public.

Until 1973, when a World Administrative T&T Conference (WATTC) adopted a major simplification, these regulations included a substantial part of detailed agreements, particularly in regard to telegraphy. Agreement was reached to relegate much of this detail to the CCITT Recommendations, so that the pair of Telegraph and Telephone Regulations henceforth reads like a contract among managers, not a book of standards. The managerial commitments were worded carefully to enable the United States to sign this category of Recommendations for the first time since their inception [9].

A new milestone was reached in late 1988 at the Melbourne WATTC. The *Final Acts* of this conference emerged with the title of *Telecommunication Regulations,* in recognition of the "menu" of services now offered and yet to be offered. Although the precise wording of the relatively few Articles was the subject of lengthy debates because of deep-seated policy disagreements, a working compromise was attained [20].

In their present form, the Telecommunication Regulations are a concise intergovernmental policy instrument, well above the standards of Recommendations. Nevertheless, observance of applicable CCITT Recommendations is written into Article 1.

3.3.2 Study Group Level

The next lower level of the pyramid includes technical and operational standards for compatible interworking. These standards are the outcomes of agreements in the study groups of the CCI technical committees. Study groups are international common-purpose groups, in that they are held together only by a common functional interest. Operation of telephone and telegraph message traffic across national borders is such a common interest. Service-oriented agreements among telecommunication operators that do not require formal adoption at treaty level may seem to be free from governmental controls. However, exclusion from intergovernmental cognizance does not shield this standardization work from individual governmental intervention in the proceedings. In other words, what is not an affair of state by international agreement may yet be an affair of state at national option.

In the United States, a government agency opts for control over these standards if it is charged with regulation or surveillance of a commercial activity such that, in effect, the agency allocates the right to use a resource. Government's allocation, according to prescribed standards, safeguards competition against the potentially sole survival of a giant monopoly. Under this regulatory system, certain allocations and their associated standards can become rather inflexible, as each competitor bases its economic decisions on the opportunities allotted to it. An example of this may be found in the tradition of US participation in the International Telegraph Consultative Committee (CCIT) portion of the ITU family. The FCC has long played a unique role as regulator for several record carrier companies that offer telegraph and telex services linking the United States and overseas points. The FCC is, in fact, cast as a cartel manager for this business. The agency has not only allocated certain services to certain points, but for years has spoken in the CCIT (later absorbed into the CCITT) on behalf of these carriers in matters of technical and operational standards [11]. This spokesmanship might have appeared incongruous to outsiders, considering that the FCC had neither operating nor engineering design responsibilities in this business. This particular situation has been modified, though not eliminated, since about 1965. The State Department directs a US National CCITT Study Group Coordination Committee, which develops unified national positions prior to international conferences.

Another problem arises when a government or dominant industry standard serves as the preferred universal standard for the telecommunication industry suppliers. This problem must be considered, particularly in view of the increasing possibility of large government expenditures on technological systems developed and produced by private industry. A leading industry might be so heavily engaged in supplying to its government or a single, large nongovernment user that the industry could not contemplate supplying other users with similar products built to different standards. Such an industry would enter the international common-purpose group with a prior bias in favor of the standards to which their production is geared.

In telecommunication, the past, long dominance of AT&T in the United States has occasioned some decisive inflexibility when standardization of a new technology was at issue. The case of pulse code modulation (PCM) digital systems has been cited before. As highlighted in Box 2.6, Chapter Two, AT&T's choice of system characteristics had been made final in the early 1960s. The T-1 carrier system and its Canadian as well as US non-AT&T counterparts quickly became the most widely installed multiplex systems throughout North America. It was established as a *de facto* standard by the time CCITT put PCM systems for study, at the 1964 Plenary Assembly, under chairmanship of Mr. Boyd of AT&T Bell Laboratories.

Thus, industry's investment in this particular standard was so heavy in North America that only modest changes could be considered. Between 1969 and 1972, CCITT's newly created Study Group Sp-D, later renamed SG XVIII, confronted opportunities for compromise between the North American existing standard and a European counterproposal yet to be agreed. However, the gap could not be bridged. As a result, CCITT Recommendations have offered a choice of two similar but incompatible standards ever since.

The choice of two standards not only divides the world market for such equipment, it obstructs end-to-end compatibility of international circuits. In a smooth-functioning worldwide network, compatibility through to users' terminals is preferable to translation from one regional or national standard to another at international switching points (also called *gateways* in US practice).

The *international network* is not a homogeneous, single entity. It is an administrative, operational, and technical superstructure that ties together the participating national networks. With almost complete, all-embracing automation, this complex structure of networks relies on compatible standards. This means that specified types of electronic signals, when transmitted, are correctly acknowledged and interpreted at a distant receiving station. These requirements of compatibility are in addition to standards of transmission quality, freedom from noise and interruption, and around-the-clock availability. At the terminals, users are and ought to be unaware of the service provider's standards. Therefore, international telecommunication standards have the additional task of facilitating users'(nationals of different jurisdictions) interfacing with dispersed terminals of the international network.

From the viewpoint of each nation-state's agencies, the standards that enable worldwide users to interchange messages represent potential interference with the state's control over property rights and service regulations in its territory. Of all ITU member countries, the US delegations have most consistently and tenaciously resisted encroachment of CCITT Recommendations on prerogatives of national government or the free marketplace, respectively.

The history of CCITT Recommendations for the telephone and telegraph service tells the story of a gradual penetration of worldwide compatibility standardization into the sacred territories of national telecommunication operations run or licensed by the state. The CCIF, predecessor of the CCITT in the field of telephony, was founded to provide compatibility for the long-distance lines in Europe and the Mediterranean area. As long as the service employed manual operators, they acted as buffers between the international lines and the domestic network. Required compatibility from there to the local terminals could be limited to some reference standards for voice signal intelligibility and loudness, guaranteeing a useful call setup after interconnection of the domestic transfer points.

During the years since then, the specific demands for compatibility have increased for three reasons. First, interconnectability on a worldwide basis has become technically feasible and commercially demanded. Second, systems used for long-distance transmission have become more complex, providing larger numbers of channels over different types of cable and radio facilities. Third, the increased traffic has given impetus to automation, initially at the level of operators providing national-international transfer, and finally at the subscriber terminal level. For many years the CCITT (and two CCIR) study groups were well occupied with work on the details necessary for compatible systems that would carry the traffic over the international lines connecting the national-international transfer points. The domestic side of these transfer points and the whole domestic network, including the subscriber terminals, were exempted from the purview of CCI Recommendations. Thus, the interference with state prerogatives was limited to the international service from the gateway points. Each state legalized the international connection arrangements and regulated the tariffs; the necessary technical and administrative standards could be settled in the study groups, with nominal approval by the states.

Progressive automation coupled with growing volume and diversity of traffic has brought about a need for specified compatibility of the national system and the local systems within it. No longer can the manual long-distance operators stay on the line to ensure that the called subscriber has answered, a connection of satisfactory quality has been established between calling and called parties, and the connection is duly ended with an appropriate service signal function at both ends, including the record of chargeable service time. All these functions must be performed by electronic machinery. While some functions can be handled at the gateway points or a few major distribution centers served by it, the total performance of these functions depends on close coordination with the signals handled by the subscriber's telephone set and the local office serving his line. Moreover, the assurance of adequate talking quality of a random selected connection assumes that all possible national and local lines will meet a certain minimum transmission standard. This standard has to be derived from a model for international connections. CCITT has incorporated into its Recommendations several models, allowing for the different situations in small or large countries and for very complex or more average tandem circuit buildups of international connections (see Section 2.4).

As a counter-example (i.e., lack of compatibility), we mention the status of coin-operated public telephones. These are likely to be the last holdouts of national, in some countries even local, individuality in a worldwide telecommunication environment. The reason for this is the location and functional application of these service terminals. Not by chance are they called "public" telephones. These are the access points provided for the most diverse imaginable cross section of users. In home and office, a very restricted sampling of possible users will interface with the terminals. To most users, the telephone becomes part of the furniture, which one respects as a property item and learns to use with reasonable care. No such relationship need exist between a random user and a public phone. The apparatus must be designed to withstand deliberate or aimless physical abuse, imaginative misuses by adults or children, tricks by people trying to avoid paying for the service, and thieves' attacks on the coin storage. However, the machine should be easy to use, requiring only a minimum of detailed instructions to be read before use. These requirements together are rather difficult to meet. If all cannot be met with equal firmness, which requirements take priority over others? The answer to this question can vary from one society to another because the value systems and cultural habits vary.

In some societies, the respect for public installed property is greater than in others; in another society the probability of cheating may loom large *et cetera*. Consequently, the service organizations in various countries, collaborating with the manufacturers, have developed different types of public telephones with diverse service features. In some European countries (e.g., the United Kingdom), even a local call can only be completed if the caller presses a button after the called party has answered. By this action the inserted coin is actually collected. Such a protective provision where a unit of small change is at stake will be objectionable to the general public in the United States, where, by contrast, an automatic coin return is expected if the call cannot be completed. Corresponding to these individual features, the electronic signals used between public telephones and the telephone office will also vary. This is not a fertile field for compatibility standardization, and there has not been much public pressure in this direction.

3.3.3 The Self-Regulating Group Level

Industry product standards are set at the self-regulating level. Several international organizations are active in this field. Two have particular importance with respect to telecommunication: the ISO (International Organization for Standardization), and the IEC (International Electrotechnical Commission). Both operate through committees, each of which is given a specific product line or category. A detailed description is given in Section 3.4 to follow.

The ISO has taken major responsibility in the data processing field and interacts with the CCITT by preparing contributions to the cognizant study groups, Data Transmission and Public Data Networks. This interaction with both ISO and IEC is itself "standardized" by the vehicle of CCITT Plenary Assembly-level Recommendations A.20 and A.22, cited before.

Coordination between IEC and CCITT on other subjects is recognized by several CCITT Recommendations and one Resolution on cable standards. In 1960, IEC's then new technical committee, TC 46, was expected to stay out of the territory of cables used in "public telecommunication networks." Its subcommittee, 46C, had a charter to standardize "low frequency cables and wires" for indoor use. However,

46C's chairmanship decided to embark on standardization of local (telecommunication) network cable for *outdoor use*. This decision troubled CCITT's central staff and several study group chairmen. Without close coordination, an IEC telecommunication cable standard might conflict with CCITT's Recommendations for transmission over such facilities. This concern led to Resolution No. 8, which was hence used as a memorandum of demarcation lines of IEC's and CCITT's respective competence in this particular field. Resolution No. 8 has been updated to the present, its significance having been enhanced by the ubiquitous use of optical fiber cable in telecommunication plant. See Box 3.1.

The most fundamental standards traditionally agreed at the self-regulating level are those of units and quantities. In recent years, graphic symbols have joined this group. Both CCITT and CCIR have had ongoing preoccupation with questions of terminology and standard units. In CCITT, standard units were accepted in the 1960s, but work on terminology fared poorly for some years, partly because the corresponding Study Group VII (as then numbered, since reassigned) did not have a forceful chairman. However, obstruction from chairmen of telegraph and telephone technical study groups delayed efforts at unified terms and definitions. Autonomy in the assigned specialization was, and has continued to be, a hallmark of CCITT study group work. Each chairman feared that accepted standard terms would hamper his study group's readiness for agreement, often depending on the choice of a few words. By contrast, the radio people seemed much more prepared to have the central secretariat propose terms and definitions as the need arose.

Thus, CCIR initiative for a joint group on vocabulary, including units and symbols, came to engulf the CCITT in the late 1970s, well after the ISO and IEC had each begun work on entire families of electrical and electronic terms, definitions, and units. Agreement to collaborate across study groups as well as with ISO and IEC, by way of Joint Study Group *CMV*, has helped CCITT's internal requirements of newly defined terms in the burgeoning fields of data communication and telematic services, in particular. The Plenary Assembly conferences, held once every four years, also review the pertinent CCITT Recommendations assembled in the B-Series. Recommendation B.3 endorses the use of basic and derivative metric units, known collectively as International System of Units (SI). Thus, cable dimensions given in inches and length in miles, as is still standard in the United States, have no place in CCITT Recommendations.

Ad hoc conversion of specified values from or to metric numbers is, of course, possible. However, in telecommunication transmission and performance specifications, accurate values of tolerances can be of decisive importance. Therefore, service providers and users everywhere except the United States expect system and service descriptions as well as testing and maintenance to be based on internationally standard units. US suppliers at variance with SI and related standards must be prepared to suffer the consequences, a lack of acceptance of their product in overseas markets.

Box 3.1

CCITT Resolution No. 8 with Annex A and Appendix I on Cooperation between CCITT and IEC

RESOLUTION No. 8

Cooperation with the IEC on the standardization of cables,
wires, optical fibres and waveguides

The CCITT,

considering

(a) that the International Electrotechnical Commission has set up a Technical Committee (TC 46) to prepare international standards on cables, wires, optical fibres[1], waveguides and accessories intended for use in telecommunication equipment and in devices employing similar techniques;

(b) that the cables with metallic conductors and optical fibres[1] and waveguides intended for use in public telecommunication networks are not included in the scope of this Committee, with the exception of polyolefin insulated LF cables for outdoor use covered by the present scope of IEC TC 46 (see Appendix I);

(c) that other points of the scope of this Committee have not been narrowly defined and that its work in this respect should be coordinated with that of the CCITT;

(d) that telecommunication Administrations reserve the right to establish some of the specifications for wires, optical fibres and cables for use in public telecommunication networks whenever they consider it advisable;

instructs

the Director of the CCITT to take any useful measures to ensure efficient liaison between the CCITT and IEC TC 46 in accordance with the principles given in Annex A below;

recommends

to member Administrations of the CCITT whose countries participate in the work of the IEC to take an active part — each within the National Committee of the IEC — in work connected with the activities of IEC TC 46, so that the views of telecommunication Administrations may be duly taken into account.

ANNEX A

Principles of cooperation between the CCITT and IEC Technical Committee 46

A.1 The aim of the standardization envisaged by the IEC is to cut down the number of types of cables to be made, so that the price may be lowered and so that the cables made by different manufacturers will be interchangeable. This policy is analogous to that followed by the CCITT as regards those types of cables for which it alone is competent. The IEC can study the standardization of internal cabling for use for various purposes in electronics, including telecommunications, polyolefin insulated low-frequency cables for outdoor use covered by the revised scope of IEC TC 46 and cables containing optical fibres not intended for use in public telecommunication networks. Although Standards for cables, wires or optical fibres [with the exception mentioned in (b) of Resolution No. 8] for use in public telecommunication installations are not in the scope of IEC TC 46,

---

[1] *Note by the CCITT Secretariat:* The Technical Committee currently responsible for matters relating to optical fibres is IEC Technical Committee 86.

Box 3.1 (continued)

IEC will endeavour to develop standards which are also in accordance with CCITT Recommendations concerning public telecommunication installations and which in any case are not at variance with them. In particular it is important that the characteristics of the cables are compatible with CCITT Recommendations on transmission, screening and protection drawn up by relevant Study Groups.

A.2 It therefore seems very desirable for the draft standards studied by TC 46 to be forwarded to the CCITT for examination. To simplify cooperation, the result of this examination should preferably be expressed in one of the following forms:

a) the CCITT has no comment to make on this draft, or

b) draft standard ... should be brought into line with CCITT Recommendation ..., or

c) the CCITT is at present studying the point dealt with in draft standard ..., which it considers as being within its terms or reference, or

d) the CCITT is of the opinion that this draft is not of interest for the CCITT.

As a general rule, this examination should be carried out by the appropriate CCITT Study Group but since IEC procedure involves time-limits that may not be exceeded (and which are sometimes rather short), the Plenary Assembly leaves it to the Director to take any appropriate practical measures.

A.3 The Director of the CCITT will continue to supply the IEC with any useful documentation regarding CCITT work and to send observers to the meetings of TC 46 and its subcommittees studying the problems which are of interest to the CCITT.

APPENDIX I

(to Resolution No. 8)

Technical Committee No. 46: cables, wires and waveguides
for telecommunication equipment

Scope

To prepare international standards regarding cables having metallic conductors and/or optical fibres wires, waveguides, optical fibres and accessories for use with electrical and guided optical telecommunication equipment and with devices employing similar techniques. Where appropriate, the work of TC 46 and the ITU shall be coordinated. TC 46 shall also coordinate the fibre optics activities within the IEC.

Cables and waveguides intended for use in public telecommunication networks are not included in the Scope of the Committee, with the exception of polyolefin insulated low-frequency cables for outdoor use.

Discrete or integrated photo-emitting and/or photo-sensitive solid state devices that may be used in fibre optic systems or sub-systems, but which are specified as COMPONENTS for purposes of trade and commerce, as well as fibre optics face-plates for cathode-ray tubes, are also excluded from the Scope of TC 46.

3.4 STANDARDS IN NATIONAL TELECOMMUNICATIONS

3.4.1 Fields of Application

We distinguish two fields of operations to which telecommunication standards can be applied:

- Service offerings;
- Material suppliers' operations.

Each of these fields can be divided into several subfields, in which standards may originate from different motivations. These subfields are outlined below.

Service Offerings

1. The performance of a service function, offered by the provider to the general public.
2. The performance of a service function, offered by the provider to individual users on a contractual basis.
3. The performance of a service function by one provider to another, within the flow of service performed by the latter for the user.
4. The performance of a service function by one provider to another, outside the flow of service offered to the user (e.g., telephone company role line attachment service offered to cable television (CATV) operators).

Material Suppliers' Operations

1. Supply of materials to a service provider.
2. Supply of materials to a service user by sale or lease.
3. Supply of materials to another supplier that sells to a service provider.

3.4.2 Interaction of Service Offering and Supply of Materials

As illustrated in Figure 3.2, a complete telecommunication service function involves several interactions of users, providers, and suppliers. In the most simple case, this model may be reduced to a fixed interraction between the user and a provider on one hand, and between the provider and a supplier on the other. In more typical cases, a publicly authorized provider offers services to many users. Network access to other users is an integral part of such services. The typical relationship involves at least one provider with a variety of users, some of which require compatibility with users in a geographical or administrative area covered by another provider. As

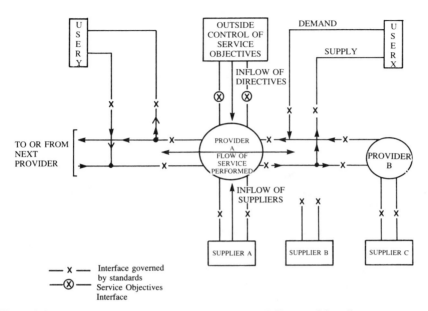

Figure 3.2 Model of a Service Provider's Relationship with Users and Suppliers.

regards the provider-supplier interaction, some providers may have a tightly controlled, exclusive relationship with a sole supplier. Thus, the provider's readiness
for a variety of interactions is not as typical at the "supply" port as it is at the user's
ports.

3.4.3 Logic of a National Standards Hierarchy

Keeping in mind the general model of Figure 3.2, a logical hierarchy of standards
may be devised. Perception of a need for standards starts logically at the points of
interaction between service provider and service user. Recognizing this logical origin
of a standard is important because it may not coincide with the historical origin.
Every service operation will eventually be governed by standards that are cited in
the provider-user relationship. This logic is not changed by the fact that, in a given
case, user-oriented standards historically may have come *after* standards have been
developed within the provider-supplier sphere of operations. This logic seeks to put
the user's expression of preference above an equipment supplier's image of it. In
practice, user preferences are stimulated by trial offerings of new services based on
new equipment.

In the market testing phase of new services, equipment-related standards may
be developed before those related to the service users. This is particularly true for
new services offered to the general public because, by definition, the general public

encompasses a much wider range of possible preferences than any preselected class of users. By contrast, in the case of a single user contracting for a specific service from one provider, the one-to-one relationship allows service standards to be recognized early and to be integrated with the contract. However, such standards negotiated between one provider and one user may not be suitable for offerings to the general public, or even to a single class of users. Thus, in the first fifteen years or so of rapid growth in computer-communication services, leading providers of interconnected services separately developed standards for individually negotiated applications. Examples are private network designs and installations for airlines, major industrial organizations, and US government agencies. When considering standards for general-purpose service offerings to the general public, the task is much more complex. Instead of the definitive case of one user, a range of offerings must meet threefold requirements, as follows.

The general purpose standards must be:

- technically and economically attractive to the service providers;
- technically and economically attractive to the suppliers of equipment; and
- economically and functionally attractive to a sufficient number of users. By functionally attractive, we mean the ability of the service to offer value to the user, at the place, time, quantity, and quality appropriate to his or her needs.

Determination of the general public market that would satisfy these three sets of requirements can be a controversial and time-consuming task. The first European study of the data transmission market may be cited as a case in point [12].

A market initiative is often based on new equipment design that may stimulate new service offerings. At this introductory stage, the equipment will be designed to certain standards, assumed by the manufacturer as appropriate for a contemplated service. However, the service provider that acquires this equipment may or may not have collaborated in the assumed standards. Interaction with users enables the provider to draft standards for the service. If the service provider has collaborated with the equipment manufacturer, the provider is likely to see the user standards as an adaptation of the equipment-related standards. If, however, the service provider has no collaborative ties to a manufacturer, the user standards are likely to be independently conceived. Under this latter condition, user standards may function as a challenge to manufacturers, exerting pressure on them to change equipment standards that they may have already assumed to be satisfactory.

3.4.4 Provider-Supplier Relationship: A National Variable

Focus on the relationship of service provider and supplier of manufactured equipment helps clarify peculiar conditions in specific telecommunication markets.

Until 1984, in the United States, AT&T had a completely integrated business.

Equipment standards flowed through the branches of the same organization, from research and development in Bell Telephone Laboratories (BTL) to manufacture by Western Electric (WE), becoming service standards in the hands of the Bell Operating Companies (BOC). In a given case, it may have been difficult, perhaps pointless, to determine whether the required service standard was first perceived by a BOC, BTL, or the AT&T central headquarters staff at New York. What matters is the fact that AT&T controlled standards setting in all directions of the diagram in Figure 3.2, *supra*. Further, by virtue of AT&T's dominant national position, it was the *de facto* trust administrator for the entire telecommunication industry. Under the *Consent Decree* of 1956, AT&T was also *de jure* obligated to share its standards at reasonable licensing terms. Moreover, a coordinating committee with the US independents (several thousand telephone companies, individually owned) met regularly. It included major non-AT&T manufacturers, so that provision of compatible products could be planned by others than WE.

The leading European and Japanese telecommunication administrations never were in the enviable position of predivestiture AT&T. They were, and most still are, government departments or government-controlled corporations, responsible to the general public via the respective country's legislative process. Recent reforms toward some degree of privatization have stopped short of severing the umbilical cord to government's oversight, generally at the ministerial level (see Chapter Four). These administrations are expected to develop service standards on their own initiatives. Manufacturers are separate, privately owned and operated businesses. Depending on the government for their orders, they must nevertheless take initiative on design and standards of equipment. This is so because the manufacturers alone have the responsibility for staying abreast of new developments and reporting satisfactory results to the stockholders. A strong competitive position in the export market is an additional incentive for in-house research and development.

The resulting relationship of service provider and manufacturer takes on a strong national flavor. Variables are such fundamentals as the country's size, its political system and current legislative trend, and the socioeconomic importance attached to telecommunication service at the national level, and the significance of the administration's orders compared to the total business volume of the national supplier or suppliers. Thus, mutual accommodation of user and equipment standards is a national variable.

In France, the administration has traditionally taken strong initiatives in both standards applied to the service and to equipment that it buys. While France Telecom (formerly PT&T) and industry collaborate, there seems to be no question about who is boss in writing the standards. We can ascertain characteristic French administration standards in telephone service, as well as in long lines systems and central office equipment, which are obligatory to the French manufacturing industry. Prospective sales of similar equipment to other administrations often require the manufacturers to accept different standards. By contrast, the Federal Republic of Germany's administration engages in more of a "give-and-take" collaboration with German manufacturers. In this case, the administration stimulates industry standards, which it evaluates and possibly modifies. The climate of this interaction is that of an equal partnership in a common purpose. The goal is to offer service standards that the administration can publicly promulgate as just and reasonable, after ascertaining that the industry can meet these by matching equipment standards. The industry's position on the export market is also a factor in the German administration's attitude regarding standards. The German collaborative scheme therefore seems to approximate the now legendary AT&T unity of purpose. However, a fundamental difference is that in Germany the two partners, government and industry, must avoid appearances of collusion and the accommodation process consumes more time than necessary under a unified organization's goals.

We suggest that the service-provider–materials-supplier relationship is a national variable. Therefore, a broad generalization regarding the effects of standards in the equipment trade would ignore the sometimes decisive criteria for a given country. Precisely this variation from country to country has been a thorn in the side of the EC's central bureaucracy. The diversity has led to initiatives for unified European standards, justified by the EC objective of a "Europe without Frontiers." Achieving this goal by 1992 is a formidable challenge. Our Chapter Four focuses on these European plans for "harmonized" telecommunications." One policy cornerstone may be stated here: the EC has obtained agreement by member governments and leading manufacturers to submit to a single, centralized organization's standards.

Let us consider now the United States. The virtual center for standardization, AT&T until 1984, has been made impotent by legal action. The national market has been fragmented simultaneously in two dimensions: network operations, on one hand, and the service provider-supplier relationship, on the other.

With respect to the national network, there is none left that deserves this title. Long-distance and "local area" services (substantial territories within 50 states) have been redefined as separate lines of business. A provider is allowed to operate in one or the other, but not both; yet, there are individually rationalized exceptions. Furthermore, the legal and regulatory climate with regard to more advanced services beyond plain old telephone service (POTS) is in a state of flux. The EC's appraisal of this situation, though of late 1987 vintage and thus not fully up-to-date, makes enlightening reading. We excerpt it in the material of Chapter Four (Section 4.2.1).

In this fragmented US market, the competing companies, old and new, would be left without a central standards-coordinating agency as AT&T Bell Laboratories had constituted in the past. Yet the very complex, multiple-network structure more than ever requires equipment compatibility—if any customer's calls are to be routed and completed through this maze. The need was recognized in a timely manner, and new standards organizations were set up. The primary ones are called out in the next section (Section 3.5). Their effectiveness is reviewed in Chapters Four and Five.

With this perception of the fluid market situation in the United States, we may reconfirm our earlier statement that the service-provider–materials-supplier relationship is a national variable. Again, in the present-day United States, for example, service providers are beleaguered by competing suppliers from everywhere in the world. By what criteria are they to choose when the objective is standards compatibility, not only attractive price? Reliance on CCITT Recommendations is not sufficient to certify a product to each significant detail. The BOC's centrally contracted staff at Bellcore (see [1] *supra*) attempts to fill the void by issuing specifications for US companies. However, these publications are worded carefully to reflect "Bellcore's View" and therefore lack the voice of binding authority. In clear contrast, Europe's scheme seeks normative specifications, *norms*. While the administrations and manufacturers of member countries have their say in the drafting and final approval of these norms; once promulgated, they must be recognized by all. The future will reveal how European specifications will guide the relationship between an individual country's buying organization and competing suppliers from several other countries.

3.5 TWO INTERNATIONAL BODIES WITH COGNIZANCE AND CLOUT

3.5.1 Introductory Remarks

Two large, diversified, and globally dispersed organizations together standardize everything in information processing, including computer-communications, that is not claimed by ITU. They are the IEC and the ISO. The latter changed to the present full title from the original International Standards Organization, but retained its well established three-letter acronym.

The administrative and operating structures, as well as rules of procedure, of IEC and ISO are reasonably similar, but quite different from ITU's. One fundamental reason is ITU's standing as an intergovernmental treaty organization, whereas ISO and IEC are nongovernmental—at least, at the level of international agreements. Referring to our pyramid, introduced in Section 3.3, both IEC and ISO are intended to function at the industry self-regulating level. Moreover, their focus is on numerous, unrelated products in general use, whereas ITU's mandates center on interrelated services offered to the public, usually through elaborate networks with attendant long-term investments and several layers of operating management. For the ITU, telecommunication's need for end-to-end compatibility sets up unanimous agreement in standards as a necessary objective. By contrast, majority vote seems the only realistic methodology when standardizing manufactured products offered in the open, competitive market.

From conceptual and juridical differences flow different policies and operating methods. Both IEC and ISO delegate the chairmanship and secretariat of each separately defined specialization under standards preparation to the national member committee volunteering for the task. ITU's CCITT and CCIR study groups and working parties are also headed by chairmen and vice-chairmen volunteered by member countries. However, in accepting these positions, chairmen of CCITT and CCIR must coordinate closely with the central secretariats at Geneva. All official documentation is prepared, translated as required, and distributed under ITU central headquarters' direct responsibility. The respective central secretariats of ISO and IEC are small by comparison; their principal function is coordinating the dispersed committees and properly recording as well as validating their final outputs.

The three organizations have had encounters with overlap and duplication of effort, particularly in the interface regions, where the products of the computer industry meet telecommunication lines and terminal apparatus. Since about 1960, all three have worked out coordination policies and procedures, aided in some cases by the same person playing a dual role in the work of ISO and CCITT. We have already cited relevant CCITT Resolutions and Series A Recommendations. Additional examples of current coordination subjects are given in this chapter's concluding section (Section 3.5.4).

3.5.2 The International Electrotechnical Commission (IEC)

The IEC was initiated in 1904–1906 to facilitate the coordination and unification of various national electrotechnical standards. IEC predates ISO, to which it is historically related, by forty years. Although affiliated, the IEC and ISO operate as autonomous bodies.

The IEC's roots are operational and technical, as are those of the CCITT. Besides component measurements, the IEC is concerned with information processing systems and the safety of data processing and office machine services, including the electrical connector itself. These interests continue to broaden.

Each of the forty-four member countries of the IEC has a national committee, which represents the full spectrum of IEC interests within the country. The American National Standards Institute (ANSI) has oversight for the US National Committee (USNC). Although official delegates to IEC meetings are approved by the USNC, other non-ANSI individuals may serve as expert members in working groups.

The IEC Plenary Assembly occurs each year and the General Secretariat (Geneva) provides central management in the interim between meetings. The IEC work is divided into the following six divisions or groups:

1. Basic standards;
2. Materials;
3. Electrical equipment and installations;
4. Industrial equipment;
5. Power generation, transmission, and distribution; and
6. Electronic components, devices, instruments, and systems.

Although all six groups have some interest in information systems and tele-communication, this interest is particularly centered in Division 6. To support the work of the six groups, IEC has eighty-two technical committees (TCs) and six subcommittees of the International Special Committee on Radio Interference (CISPR). The TCs deal with fundamentals of electrical parameters, measurements, components, rules of practice, *et cetera*.

The technical committees and their subcommittees related to telecommunication are listed in Box 3.2. The IEC TC 46 is of particular current interest because it deals with cables, wires, and waveguides. Its detailed definitions and standards for optical fiber cable brought about an intense coordination activity with CCITT that has spread over many years since the mid-1970s. Another long-term involvement with CCITT and CCIR is on terminology. IEC's commitment to preparation of a new International Electrotechnical Vocabulary (IEV), *the task* of TC 1, triggered a formal agreement with both CCITT and CCIR, regarding those terms and definitions that are of primary concern to these ITU technical committees. In view of the fundamental importance of defined terms in any published standard, we report on the functioning of this little known joint IEC-ITU activity in Section 3.5.4.

3.5.3 The International Organization for Standardization (ISO)

The ISO traces its beginnings to World War II. The United States and its allies needed interface characteristics among several aspects of information systems as well as in certain other technical domains, and these characteristics were not covered by existing IEC standards. As a result, an *ad hoc* standardization effort was begun, and this was upgraded in 1946 into the ISO. It is a nontreaty agency of the United Nations.

Scope of Studies (ISO)

The scope of studies in ISO is very broad and includes such fields as agriculture, nuclear systems, fabrics, documents used in commerce, library science, computer systems, and computer communication. The latter two are of interest to the tele-communication industry. The ISO encompasses both fundamental and highly complicated topics in its collective programs, all of which are user-oriented.

Organizational Structure (ISO)

The ISO at present has seventy-two "member bodies" or member countries; the United States, through ANSI, is one of them. There are also about eighteen developing countries that have an associated relationship in ISO. Upon request, a developing

Box 3.2
IEC Technical Committees and Subcommittees Related to Telecommunication

IEC TECHNICAL COMMITTEES AND SUBCOMMITTEES RELATED TO TELECOMMUNICATIONS	
TC/SC NO.	**COMMITTEE TITLE**
TC-1	Terminology
TC-12 SC-12A SC-12C SC-12D SC-12E SC-12F SC-12G SC-12H	Radio Communications Radio Receiving Equipment Radio Transmitting Equipment Aerials (Antennas) Microwave Systems Equipment Used in Mobile Services Cabled Distribution Systems Written Message and Graphic Systems Primarily Intended for Use on Television Terminals
TC-13	Electrical Measuring Equipment
TC-18 SC-18A	Electrical Installations in Ships Cables and Cable Installations
TC-46 SC-46A SC-46B SC-46C SC-46D	Cables, Wires and Waveguides for Telecommunications Equipment Radio Frequency Cables Waveguides and Their Accessories Low Frequency Cables and Wires Connectors for Radio Frequency Cables
TC-47	Semiconductor Devices and Integrated Circuits
TC-48 SC-48B	Electromechanical Components for Electronic Equipment Connectors
TC-57	Telecontrol, Teleprotection and Associated Telecommunications for Electrical Power Systems
TC-60 SC-60C	Recording Systems of Audio-visual and Electronic Technology (for Information and Communication)
TC-65 SC-65A SC-65C	Industrial-Process Measurement and Control Systems Considerations Digital Data Communications for Industrial-Process Measurement and Control Systems
TC-66	Electronic Measuring Equipment
TC-74	Safety of Data Processing Equipment and Office Machines
TC-76	Laser Equipment
TC-77	Electromagnetic Compatibility between Electrical Equipment Including Networks
CISPR	International Special Committee on Radio Interference
ACET	Advisory Committee on Electronics and Telecommunications

country's member body receives full documentation of an ISO technical committee's activities. Not all of these developing countries are obliged to pay membership dues, nor are they obliged to participate in ISO activities. The associated developing countries do not enjoy voting privileges on administrative or standards-related matters.

Each member country has a designated national agency to represent that country in the ISO. These national agencies are of two types. In the first case, the national agency (e.g., ANSI) is a private, voluntary member supported by participating companies. Some participants *may be* government representatives. In the second case, the member body *is* a government agency, and may have some private sector participation.

The ISO members meet in plenary session about every three years, usually in a different host country. Interim management is provided by the Central Secretariat, located in Geneva. In addition, each ISO technical committee, as well as each subcommittee (SC) and working group (WG), has its own secretariat, located in the country of the member body that has accepted responsibility for the particular committee. The ISO thus is a generally decentralized type of standardizing body, where the Central Secretariat coordinates the work of the various technical secretariats located throughout the world.

The majority of the work in ISO is handled in the TCs and their subunits. The TC is primarily a management, policy-making, and review body; it is assisted by a secretariat advisory group (SAG). Although each TC conducts its business under the broad direction of ISO, it also has its own, more specific rules appropriate to its particular work. These rules affect the degree of substructure, the time between meetings, and the number of active projects.

The TCs of most active interest currently include TC 46 (Automation and Library Science), TC 68 (Banking), TC 154 (Documents Used in Commerce and Industry), and TC 97 (Information Systems). TC 97 is discussed below, both for the relevancy of its studies and for its structure, which is illustrative of the ISO's technical committee organization.

Technical Committee 97 (ISO)

TC 97 was born at a Paris roundtable in 1960 and eventually absorbed TC 95 (Office Machines). The scope of TC 97 is the standardization (including terminology) of information processing systems from the perspective of free-standing computer systems, office machinery, and data communication implementation.

The structure of the SCs and WGs of TC 97 is shown in Box 3.3. These SCs are responsible for the technical accuracy of the information industry standards created by TC 97. For the telephone industry, the two most relevant US SCs of TC 97 are SC 6 (Data Communication) and SC 16 (Open Systems Interconnection, OSI). SC 18, dealing with text preparation, will also be relevant.

Box 3.3

Titles and Secretariats for ISO TC 97 Subcommittees

SC	WG	TITLE	SECRETARIAT OR CONVENOR
	WG 1	Data Encryption	UK
SC1	WG 1	Maintenance	France
	WG 2	Editing	France
	WG 3	Methodology	France
SC2	WG 1	Code Extension Techniques	UK
	WG 4	Coded Character Set for Text Communication	Netherlands
	WG 5	Coding for MICR and OCR	Germany
	WG 6	Additional Control Functions	USA
		Registration Authority	France
		Registration Advisory Group	France
	WG 7	Revision of ISO 646	Canada
		Registration Advisory Group	Switzerland
SC 5	WG 1	Prog. Languages for the Control of Industrial Processes (PLIP)	Germany
	WG 2	Graphics	Netherlands
	WG 3	Data Base Management Systems (DBMS)	USA
	WG 4	PASCAL	UK
	WG 5	DBMS Coordination	France
	WG 6	APL	France
	EG	COBOL	USA
	EG	FORTRAN	USA
	EG	ALGOL	Netherlands
	EG	PL/1	USA
	EG	Computer Language for Processing of Text (CLPT)	USA
	EG	BASIC	ECMA
	EG	Ada	USA
	EG	DBMS/DDL	USA
SC 6	WG 1	Data Communications Control Procedures	USA
	WG 2	Public Data Networks	UK
	WG 3	Physical Interface Characteristics	Germany
SC 7	WG 1	Symbols, Charts and Diagrams	UK
	WG 2	Items for Documentation	UK
	WG 3	Program Design	Canada
	WG 4	Decision Tables	France
SC 9	WG 1	Input Language	UK
	WG 2	CLDATA	France
	WG 3	Technological Description	UK
	WG 4	Language Subdivision	USA
SC 13	WG 1	Process Interfaces for Computer Systems	Germany
	WG 2	Interface Standards Administration	UK
	WG 3	Lower Level Interface Functional Requirements & L-L Interfaces	Germany
SC 14	WG 1	Standard'n Guidelines for the Representation of Data Elements	UK
	WG 2	Check Character Algorithms	UK
SC 15	WG 1	Flexible Disks	UK
	WG 3	Interchangeable IRV-Coded Data Files	USA
SC 16	WG 1	OSI Reference Model	France
	WG 4	OSI Application and Systems Management	Japan
	WG 5	OSI Application and Presentation Layers	UK
	WG 6	OSI Session and Transport Layers	USA
SC 17	WG 1	Physical Characteristics and Test Methods for ID Cards	Germany
	WG 3	Passport Cards	Sweden
	WG 4	Integrated Circuit Cards	France
	WG 5	Registration Advisory Group	USA
	WG 6	Magnetic Stripes on Savings Books	USA
	WG 7	Data Content, Track 1 and 2	Sweden
SC 18	WG 1	User Requirements	Italy
	WG 2	Symbols and Terminology	Japan
	WG 3	Text Structure	UK
	WG 4	Procedures for Text Interchange	France
	WG 5	Text Preparation and Presentation	Canada
SC 19	WG 1	Monochrome Test Chart for Document Copying Machines	UK
	WG 2	Duplicating and Document Copying Machines	UK
	WG 3	Keyboards for Office Machines and Data Processing Equipment	Italy
	WG 4	Mail Processing Machines	Germany

LEGEND:
EG = Expert Group   SC = Subcommittee
TC = Technical Committee
WG = Working Group

The SC members are of two types—voting, P (primary), members and non-voting, O (observing), members. Approximately ten to twenty member bodies have active voting participants in any particular SC. About 25% additional members send observer delegations to the SC (or lower level) meetings. These O members may also make comments on ballots, and their contributions are valued.

The SCs are divided, as needed, into working groups, expert groups (EG), *ad hoc* groups, and rapporteur groups. The latter groups generally work on short-term assignments. In most cases, the specific writing of standards is assigned to the WG. For the TC, SC, or WG meetings, each member sends a delegation and a head of delegation, with appropriate instructions from the member body, including the degree of freedom permitted to the delegation. The positions and contributions are cleared through the member body, flowing up (as is the case of the United States, for example) from the individual contributor to the senior representative.

Most decisions are made through written ballot voting. This process takes between four and five months. In its ongoing process of updating, ISO requires a five-year review of all ISO standards. The TC 97 plenary meeting occurs about every two years. The subunits meet at the discretion of the chairman or secretariat, as the case may be.

Few industry standards have the far-reaching importance of ISO's OSI reference model and its derivatives. All CCITT study groups dealing with ISDN and the associated plethora of new or expanded services are guided by OSI. We are reproducing (Box 3.4) one application of OSI, as published in Annex III to CCITT Rec. T-101, "International Interworking for Videotex Services." This particular text explains the use of the general OSI seven-layer model with respect to the North American Presentation Level Protocol Syntax (NAPLPS). In this context, the words "layer" and "level" are used interchangeably.

3.5.4 Joint Coordination Becomes Effective

By the late 1980s, coordinating procedures among ISO, IEC, and CCITT had become so effective that they rarely needed to be cited before representatives of the respective organizations would act together. This section highlights only a few milestones, marking the remarkable progress on the path of intercommittee collaboration.

In the mid-1960s, the IEC set about to revise and expand its International Electrotechnical Vocabulary (IEV). This is a classic bilingual reference, first published in 1938, when it listed and defined about 2000 terms. For a completely new edition, the IEC, through the Secretariat of its TC No. 1 (Terminology), obtained agreement with ISO to include terms relating to the data processing field. As far back as 1964, CCITT adopted Rec. A.12, "Collaboration with the International Electrotechnical Commission on the Subject of Definitions for Telecommunications." We quote from Rec. A.12, text prior to the 1988 Plenary Assembly:

It is understood that for this purpose there shall be established:

—a joint coordination group composed of members of the IEC and of the ITU;

—a number of groups of technical experts to be set up by the joint coordination group to prepare the drafts of various sections of the *Telecommunications Vocabulary*.

It is furthermore understood that the joint-coordination group will be composed of twelve members and that the ITU (itself represented by equal numbers of members of the CCIR and CCITT) will be represented on equal footing with the IEC in the joint coordination group

—the chairman will be chosen from among members of the ITU (CCITT and CCIR);

—the Secretary will be chosen from among members of the IEC, which will also provide the secretariat.

Box 3.4
OSI and its Seven Layers:
(a) Reference Model

Open System Interconnection (OSI) Reference Model

The following extracts from the text of the OSI Reference Model standard describe the concept of open systems interconnection:

"Open Systems Interconnection (OSI) refers to standardised procedures for the exchange of information among terminal devices, computers, people, networks, processes etc., that are 'open' to one another for this purpose by virtue of their mutual use of these procedures.

" 'Openness' does not imply any particular systems implementation, technology or interconnection means, but rather refers to the mutual recognition and support of the standardised information exchange procedures." (para. 2.1)

"In the concept of OSI, a system is a set of one or more computers, the associated software, peripherals, terminals, human operator, physical processes, information transfer means, etc., that forms an autonomous whole capable of performing information processing.

"OSI is concerned with the exchange of information between systems (and not the internal functioning of each individual system).

"The transfer of information between systems is performed by physical media for systems interconnection. . . The physical media initially considered in developing OSI standards is of the telecommunication type (other media will be considered later)." (para. 2.2)

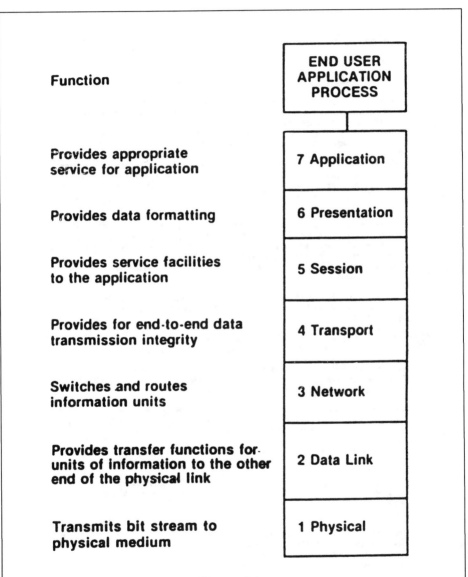

Figure A1

The Seven Functionally Separate Layers of the OSI Model

Box 3.4

(c) NAPLPS Standard [Appendix A to CCITT Rec. T.101 (Videotex); Data Syntax III]

Appendix A

Layered Architecture Model

The Basic Reference Model for Open Systems Interconnection is described in ISO DIS 7498-1983. A similar concept is also defined in CCITT (Draft) Recommendation X.200. The layered system architecture is an assembly of interrelated protocols required to define an entire communication system. The layered system architecture allows an "open systems interconnection" (ie, data exchange) between participating systems. Each layer covers an independent aspect of a communications system in such a way that other protocols may be substituted at various layers in order to operate over different media. Figure A1 illustrates the model. The coding scheme described in this Data Syntax addresses itself to the user data conveyed by the presentation layer of the Basic Reference Model, and is independent of the protocols used to transfer data between systems.

Both videotex and teletext services make use of the same presentation layer protocol data syntax and semantics but may have different protocols at other layers. The protocols for other layers for teletext are defined in CCIR Report 957, Characteristics of Teletext Systems, Document 11/5001-E, October 1981; Broadcast Specification BS-14, Department of Communications, Canada, Telecommunications Regulatory Service, June 1981; and the North American Basic Teletext Specification (NABTS).

The seven layers may be viewed in two major groupings. Layers 1 to 4 treat the transference of data while layers 5 to 7 treat how the data is processed and used.

(1) The physical layer provides mechanical, electrical and procedural functions in order to establish, maintain, and release physical connections.

(2) The data link layer provides a data transmission link across one or several physical connections. Error correction, sequencing, and flow control are performed in order to maintain data integrity.

(3) The network layer provides routing, switching, and network access considerations in order to make invisible to the transport layer how underlying transmission resources are utilized.

(4) The transport layer provides an end-to-end transparent virtual data circuit over one or several tandem network transmission facilities.

(5) The session layer provides the means to establish a session connection and to support the orderly exchange of data and other related control functions for a particular communication service.

(6) The presentation layer provides the means to represent information in a data coding format in a way that preserves its meaning. The detailed coding formats for the scheme described in this document provide the basis of a presentation layer protocol data syntax for videotex, teletext, and related applications.

(7) The application layer is the highest layer in the reference model and the protocols of this layer provide the actual service sought by the end user. As an example, the information retrieval service commands of a videotex application form part of the application layer.

The CCITT had, at the time, a Study Group VII assigned to Definitions and Symbols. The CCIR had its own counterpart study group that had become quite active and respected because of the weight attached to terms and definitions in the often binding agreements of radio communication. By contrast, the CCITT tradition encouraged complete independence of study groups when terminology was involved. Frequently, a particular term or its *ad hoc* definition would allow a new Recommendation to sail through approval; after all, these Recommendation were always intended for voluntary observance.

The failure of CCITT to participate in joint work with IEC during the first half of the 1970s is thus attributable to the reluctance—in some instances, outspoken obstruction—on the part of study group chairmen. Each feared interference with the group's autonomous prerogatives when drafting Recommendations, much in the same way that business organizations' line departments resent coordination with advisory staff. Still, with the chairmen's consent, the CCITT Plenary Assembly of 1972 had broadened older Rec. A.10, so as to make intergroup collaboration on definitions more of a reality. The push was provided by the CCIR, which proposed a Joint CCIR-CCITT Vocabulary Committee, called *CMV* after the French initials. Also, the new CMV could now be recognized as official mouthpiece of ITU as a whole with regard to IEC's work on the IEV. In other words, the six ITU members on the Joint Coordination Group (JCG) envisaged in Rec. A.12, would be designated by CMV.

Yet it was not until early 1978 that CMV began to make joint CCI terminology decisions in earnest. As often happens in similar international collaboration, time has to do its work in softening opposition; also, an energetic and persuasive person has to assume chairmanship. Both conditions were met in 1978. Since 1976, several CCITT study group chairmen had chosen so-called "special rapporteurs," assigned to preparing for group approval lists of terms and definitions peculiar to the work of the respective group. The most pressing need for terminology standardization was experienced by the people drafting Recommendations for data networks in new SG VII. It was given this number after CCITT abolished its separate vocabulary study group that had been denoted by the same numeral, curiously enough. Additional demand for an agreed vocabulary, standardized in a Recommendation of its own, arose in other new fields: digital systems and optical fiber cable systems, in particular. Thus, from 1976 onward, several study groups, grappling with rapidly evolving innovations, formulated vocabularies that overlapped, at least in part, with the province of data processing or that of cables, fields in the purview of IEC or ISO. Eventually, by the time of the Seventh Plenary Assembly of 1980, all CCITT study groups were brought into the vocabulary coordination scheme overseen by the CMV. Already, since 1978, the JCG with IEC had really come to life, processing hundreds of terms (and their definitions), with the initiative of those CCITT study group terminology rapporteurs who spoke for the fast developing technologies and services.

Some ten years later, entire chapters of the IEV have come out of a fully co-ordinated cycle of redrafting and face-to-face sessions of a dedicated dozen people constituting the JCG. The CCITT has had occasion to strengthen further the study groups' commitments to this work, ensuring CMV almost routine participation. The chairman of CMV, Mr. Thué of France, a radio specialist designated by the CCIR, has persevered over several CCITT Plenary Assemblies. This steady tenure contrib-uted to the spirit of cooperation on terminology that had been resisted by many chairmen in earlier years.

In CCITT's *Blue Book* of 1988–1989, numerous Recommendations allude to specific coordination with ISO or IEC, as the case may be. Terminology and other conventions of a given text are cross-referenced. The newly expanding Series X.400 (Message Handling Systems) was prepared in such a coordinated format. The CCITT-ISO-IEC collaboration in data networks and telematic services systems or terminals has come as far as parallel adoption of essentially identical Recommendations (CCITT) and Standards (ISO, IEC). A list prepared by the Vice-Chairman of Data Networks Group VII, Mr. Bertine of AT&T Bell Laboratories, identifies more than forty such parallel Recommendations in the Blue Book issue. The road ahead for beneficial coordination is ever clearer, since ISO and IEC formed a *Joint Technical Committee One* (JTC 1) in November of 1987. The scope of JTC 1 is given as "Standardization in the field of information technology." At the Ninth Plenary Assembly (Melbourne, 1988), CCITT endorsed its collaboration with JTC 1 by way of an additional Series A Recommendation, A.22, cited *supra*.

The computer-communication "marriage," at last, appears ready to be con-summated, through the good offices of determined standards-makers who straddle both camps.

REFERENCES

1. *Catalog of Technical Information,* Morristown, NJ: Bellcore, 1988.
2. *Radio Regulations,* Geneva: ITU, 1988.
3. *International Telecommunication Regulations,* Geneva: ITU, 1989.
4. See CCIR Recommendation 393, "Allowable Noise Power in the Hypothetical Reference Circuit for Radio Relay Systems for Telephony Using FDM," editions of 1956, 1959, 1963, 1966, 1974, 1978, 1982, and 1986. See also, companion Rec. 395 "Noise in the Radio Portion of Circuits to be established over Real Radio Relay Links for FDM Telephony."
5. CCITT Recs. G.161 and G.164 for Echo Suppressors; Rec. G.165 for Echo Cancellers. Note that required compatibility among these services is written into the recommendations. Rec. G.161 has remained unchanged since 1976; the other two were first adopted in 1980.
6. This has been described as a case of failure to obtain worldwide agreement in the article by Gerd D. Wallenstein, "The Internationalization of Telecommunications Systems Development," *Telecom. J.,* Vol. 41, No. 1, 1974 (ITU, Geneva).
7. Gerd D. Wallenstein, "A Review of Telephone Development in Western Europe and in Under-developed Areas," *Trans. AIEE,* pp. 15–21, 1959 (L).

8. Jack Herbstreit, NBS, Boulder, CO, to June 1974; Richard C. Kirby, Office of Telecommunications, Boulder, CO, elected 1974.

9. "Report of the Chairman of the United States Delegation to the Meeting of the World Administrative Telegraph and Telephone Conference of the International Telecommunication Union," Department of State, Office of Telecommunications, TD Serial No. 37, Washington, DC, May 24, 1973.

10. See *Telecommunications Reports*, Vol. 54, No. 48 (December 5, 1988), pp. 36–37; Vol. 54, No. 49 (December 12, 1988); pp. 41–42; and Vol. 55, No. 1 (January 16, 1989), pp. 13–16.

11. Meetings of the CCITT study groups concerned with telegraph, telex, and facsimile standards were attended by US delegations, usually headed by a knowledgeable member of the FCC. By contrast, US participation in the telephone transmission and signalling study groups was left to the service providers (AT&T, COMSAT, GTE) free from government agencies' protocol. See Chapter Five for policy changes of the late 1980s.

12. *Eurodata 1972–1985*. A market study on data communication in Europe, by P.A. International Management Consultants, March 1973, New York: Quantum Science Corporation, 1973.

Chapter Four

Perestroika West: An Era of Telecommunication Reform

перестро́йка *ж.* 1. (*зда́ния*) ré|búild-
ing [-'bɪl-], ré|constrúction; 2. (*идео-
логи́ческая*) ré|òrientátion; 3. (*реор-
ганиза́ция*) ré|òrganizátion [-naɪ-]; ~
рабо́ты ré|òrganìzátion of work, ré|-
formátion of procédure [...-'siːdʒə]; co- (*)

4.1 PREVIEW OF THIS CHAPTER'S CONTENT

Assembled here are the most important documents of current telecommunication reforms, adopted in much of the western world. "West" is to be understood here as
a geopolitical, not geographic, affiliation. Thus, our country focus includes Japan
along with the United States and Western Europe.

As is the case with most historically significant events, these reforms, too, have
cast their shadows before. Some knowledge of the preparatory steps that led to new
regulatory and market policies would enhance an engaged person's perspective. With
this aim, we have included excerpts of, or clear references to, documents of key
decisions that paved the way. In all cases, the "reformers" (i.e., government agency
officials, judges, or members of specially appointed commissions) speak directly
through their published output. In this writer's view, there has been too much piecemeal citation, selective commentary, and interpretation of these famous cases. Too
few of the many people affected by telecommunication reform have learned about
it "from the horse's mouth." The present chapter attempts to remedy this shortcom-
ing.

European reform, slated to be in place by 1992, is documented first. The EC
proposals were made final, well after the AT&T break-up and related reforms took

(*)Source: *Russian-English Dictionary*, New York: E.P. Dutton, 1966 (7th Ed.).

effect in the United States. The reader may note the emphasis on a unified European market, based on common standards. Competition is promoted as a vehicle toward a stronger Europe.

The following section brings the full text of the *Modified Final Judgment* (MFJ) of 1982, ending the legal case of US *versus* AT&T and its group of companies. The acronym *MFJ* has been among the most frequently printed words in trade publications, continuously since about 1984. Yet its substance is less well known and will offer the reader valuable insights into ensuing events. The MFJ is, at present, the end of a line that had its formal start in 1956. Our documentation traces the line from that date onward.

Section 4.4 is devoted to user group organizations. A new phenomenon since the late 1970s, these groups have expressed demands for accelerated and more effective standardization. Their presence thus constitutes strong support of standards as a power in their own right.

National reforms adopted in three countries are documented in Sections 4.5, 4.6, and 4.7. The documentation varies in depth, depending mainly on the material available to us. Germany's restructuring of telecommunication is most thoroughly presented, starting with the *Report* of a high-level commission, released in 1975. The other two countries are the United Kingdom and Japan.

4.2 THE GREEN PAPER'S UNIFIED EUROPE

Documentation:

4.2.1 COM (88) 48, Brussels, 9 February 1988, "Implementing the Green Paper . . ."

4.2.2 COM (87), 290, Brussels, 30 June 1987, "*Summary Report*" of Green Paper on the Development of the Common Market for Telecommunications Services and Equipment. (Not reproduced here are the pages titled "Presentation of the Green Paper," which precede the Summary Report. Also omitted is the Green Paper's full-length text (213 pp.).)

Bibliographic Reference:

The EC has published, in paperback book form, an analytical description, with supporting material as used by the European Commission's staff. The book is well edited and profusely illustrated. *Telecommunications in Europe* by Herbert Ungerer, with collaboration of Nicholas P. Costello. Brussels: The European Perspectives Series, 1988 (260 pp.). Published in the EC's nine languages: Danish, Dutch, English, French, German, Greek, Italian, Portuguese, Spanish.

4.2.1 Implementing the Green Paper

TOWARDS A COMPETITIVE COMMUNITY-WIDE TELECOMMUNICATIONS MARKET IN 1992: IMPLEMENTING THE GREEN PAPER ON THE DEVELOPMENT OF THE COMMON MARKET FOR TELECOMMUNICATIONS SERVICES AND EQUIPMENT. Commission of the European Communities, COM (88) 48 Final, Brussels, 9 February 1988.

SUMMARY

On 30th June 1987, the Commission submitted its Green Paper on the future development of telecommunications sector, the major driving force for the entry of the Community's economy into the information age [*Towards a Dynamic Economy—Green Paper on the Development of the Common Market for Telecommunications Services and Equipment"*, *(COM (87) 290)*].

As set out in the Green Paper, the *current wave of technical innovation resulting from the convergence of telecommunications and computer technology* has led to reviews in all Member States, and at world-level, of the future organisation of the telecommunications sector and its necessary regulatory adjustment. The strengthening of European telecommunications has become one of the major conditions for *achieving the Community-wide market for goods and services in 1992.*

The Green Paper was intended to initiate debate and attract comment from a broad spectrum of opinion: "the Council; the European Parliament and the Economic and Social Committee; the Telecommunications Administrations and Recognized Private Operating Agencies, referred to as "Telecommunications Administrations"; the European telecommunications, data processing, and services industry; the users who must be the main beneficiaries of the new opportunities; and the trade unions and other organisations which represent the social interest in this field.

In the meantime, the *Commission has received a wide range of comments.* The broad consensus apparent from these comments now seems to give a strong basis on which to define further a determined campaign to develop the Community's telecommunications market, with the overall objective of fully achieving a Community-wide open competitive market by 1992.

On this basis, the *in order to facilitate the consideration of the Green Paper* and future Community policy in the sector by the Council, the European Parliament and the Economic and Social Committee, this Communication sets out a *programme of action,* both as regards measures to be undertaken by the Commission under Community competition rules and its general mandate, and as regards future proposals to Council, in order to achieve progressive opening of the telecommunications market in the Community to competition. It reviews the proposals advanced in the *Green Paper in the light of the comments received up to now, establishes priorities and proposes strict deadlines for implementation.*

(I) INTRODUCTION

The Commission published on 30th June 1987 a Green Paper on the future development of the telecommunications sector [*"Towards a Dynamic Economy—Green Paper on the Development of the Common Market for Telecommunications Services and Equipment,"* (COM (87) 290), hereinafter referred to as the *Green Paper*].

The Commission has set out its basic motivations in the opening statement to the Green Paper. It emphasized that "the strengthening of European telecommunications has become one of the major conditions for promoting a harmonious development of economic activities and a competitive market throughout the Community and for achieving the completion of the Community-wide market for goods and services by 1992."

The Commission further stated: "Information, exchange of knowledge, and communications are of vital importance in economic activity and in the balance of power in the world today. Telecommunications is the most critical area for influencing the 'nervous system' of modern society. To flourish, it has to have optimum environmental conditions."

In this respect, the convergence of telecommunications, computing and applications of electronics in general has now made possible the introduction of a wide variety of new services. The traditional form of organisation of the sector does not allow the full development of the potential of these new services. In order to create an open and dynamic market in this area, it therefore seems necessary to introduce regulatory changes to improve the sector's environment.

These changes should allow the full development of the supply of services and equipment, thus making it possible for industry to take full advantage of this potential. In particular national frontiers should not be allowed to hamper the development of a consistent communications system within the European Community."

Telecommunications must now be seen as the major component of a conglomerate global sector comprising the management and transport of information which already represents more than ECU 500 billion worldwide. The world market for telecommunications equipment has reached ECU 90 billion by 1986, of which ECU 17.5 billion was accounted for by the Community. In 1985 world revenue from telecommunications services was almost ECU 300 billion, of which the Community represented ECU 62.5 billion.*

It is estimated that by *the end of the century, up to 7% of the gross domestic product of the Community will result from telecommunications* and adjacent activities, as against 2% today. Via information technology, more than 60% of Community employment will depend, to an important degree, on telecommunications by the year 2000.

The situation in the Community is in flux. All Member States are envisaging or discussing necessary adjustments of regulatory conditions to the new requirements. Managing together this challenge will be *essential for the Community to achieve the Internal Market; improve the competitiveness of the European economy; and strengthen Community cohesion.*

As set out in detail in the Green Paper, the necessary definition of common regulatory goals can build on the achievements of Community telecommunications policy to date, on the programme set out by Council on 17th December 1984, and on previous positions taken by the European Parliament and the Economic and Social Committee. The adjustment of the Community's telecommunications market involves a complex process and should be undertaken on a broad basis.

The Green Paper emphasized that "regulatory changes in telecommunications must take account of the views of all parties concerned, in particular private and business users, Telecommunications Administrations, the Administrations' work force, competing enterprises, and the telecommunications and data-processing industry."

---

*ECU = European Currency Unit; see Glossary.

With this in mind, the Commission has undertaken, *since June 1987, an extensive consultative process on the Green Paper*. A broad range of reactions has been received from the wide spectrum of interests concerned. In parallel, substantial discussion has been carried on with the Senior Officials Group on Telecommunications (SOG-T), the [Directors-General] of the Telecommunications Administrations and the European Committee of the Postal, Telegraph and Telephone Trade Unions.

At this stage, the Commission considers it appropriate to draw preliminary conclusions on the results of this process of broad consultation. This is the purpose of this Communication.

The Communication is intended to facilitate the further consideration of the Green Paper in Council, the European Parliament, and the Economic and Social Committee, by reviewing the proposals advanced in the Green Paper in the light of the reactions received up to now, establishing priorities and proposing strict deadlines for implementation.

The overriding objective, supported by all comments, must be to "develop the conditions for the market to provide European users with a *greater variety* of telecommunications services, of *better quality* and at *lower cost,* affording Europe the full internal and external benefits of a strong telecommunications sector" and "the development in the Community of a strong telecommunications infrastructure and efficient services" in order to achieve this goal.

It involves obtaining the full benefits of the opportunities deriving from the Treaty in this sector: the *full implementation of the free movement of goods and the freedom to provide services;* the establishment of a competitive environment; and the strengthening of Community cohesion.

(II) THE GREEN PAPER APPROACH

The *consultative process* undertaken and the reactions received *must be seen against the positions* set out in the Green Paper.

The objectives set out in the Green Paper correspond to three major concerns which must be dealt with at the European level:

—*Technological change is penetrating irreversibly* the European and world market and requires adjustment of market conditions. Over recent years, the speed of technological diversification (signal digitisation, optical cables, cellular telephony, satellites, etc.) has dramatically accelerated.

Digitisation—the transmission of information in the form of bits in computer language, and the best indicator of the convergence of telecommunications and computer technology—will be an economic fact in the Community by the end of this decade. By 1990, on average in the Community, approximately 70% of long distance transmission will be digitised, 50% of long-distance switching and 30% of local switching.

A major consequence in regulatory terms flowing from technological and market development will derive from the simple fact that those connected to the network will be able to carry out many more activities via this network. This poses the *fundamental problem of how in the future current constraints on these new possibilities will be handled*;

—The current change of technological and market conditions is *leading all Member States to undertake or envisage changes in regulatory conditions*. As set out in the Green Paper, the Community must make sure that "the necessary European scale and dimension are introduced into the current phase of transformation; no new barriers are created within the Community during the adjustment of regulatory conditions; existing barriers are removed in the course of this adjustment";

—*The Treaty obligation of achieving the completion of the Community Market by 1992* sets a strict deadline for full application of the Treaty to this sector. As a result of on-going changes, telecommunications will come to play a central role in the Community's technology and service markets. Even today, services account for nearly two thirds of Community output and employment.

The future importance of telecommunications for overall economic development and growth makes a Community-wide market in this sector indispensable for reaching the 1992 goal for the Community market as a whole. This implies full and speedy application of the opportunities and obligations deriving from the Treaty to the sector: the free movement of goods; the freedom to provide services; competition rules; the common commercial policy.

In the *Green Paper,* the Commission:

—*pleads strongly for recognising*—and using the potential of—the new technological and market trends;

—*acknowledges fully the traditional public service tasks* of the Telecommunications Administrations. It accepts safeguards in order to maintain their capability to develop networks and services and envisages their full participation in the newly emerging markets in both the services and terminal equipment fields;

—emphasises, however, that *any service monopoly which is maintained implies constraints* on the activities of those connected to this network or using network facilities. The justification of continued exclusive provision where it still exists must therefore be weighed carefully against the restrictions which this may impose on those connected to the network concerning present and future application for their own use, shared use or provision to third parties.

As a consequence, the Green Paper clearly considers that, with a view to 1992 and the full development of new economic activities with their potential for employment, a *more liberal and flexible competitive environment for the telecommunications services and equipment market is indispensable* for the overall development of the Community's technology and service markets. At the same time, it recognises the continuing central role of the Telecommunications Administrations in ensuring the long-term convergence and integrity of the network infrastructure and the supply of a broad range of services in the Community.

With the Green Paper, the Commission has tried to achieve a careful balance:

"The Green Paper acknowledges the differences in current situations and the variety of trends. It proposes essentially a hard core of proposals designed to ensure Community consistency in telecommunications. The proposed process is iterative; it accepts the existence of a movement, not all aspects of which can be defined today.

The fundamental purpose of the measures is therefore to set off a dynamic process that will give the political, economic and social actors involved a better understanding of their own interests and to optimise their activities in the construction of the Community."

(III) STATE OF DISCUSSIONS

The Green Paper translates the foregoing considerations into ten detailed "Proposed Positions" and a number of "Proposed Actions Lines" to support the transformation process. The comments received have concentrated on these Positions and Action Lines. They are therefore recalled in [Box 4.1] *and* [Box 4.2] *for easy reference.* More detailed explanation is given in the Green Paper.

As set out in the introduction to the Green Paper, the Green Paper was intended "to launch a debate and to attract comment from a broad spectrum of opinion." The Commission announced that it would draw preliminary conclusions at the end of 1987, in order to focus debate and to facilitate consideration in the Council, the European Parliament and the Economic and Social Committee.[1]

Since June 1987, the Green Paper has stimulated a very broad response by the users, telecommunications and data-processing industry and other parties concerned. More than 45 organisations representing different interests in the field, both at Community and national level, have forwarded formal comments. The full text of the comments is *available on request.*

As already mentioned, in parallel, intensive discussion was carried on with the Senior Official Groups on Telecommunications (SOG-T), the Director Generals of the Telecommunications Administrations, and the Trade Unions in the field.

While for details reference should be made to the full text of the comments, *summarising* the following can be said:

—the consultation process has been a major success in itself. This is the very first time in the Community that an in-depth broadly based discussion between all actors involved in the future of the sector has taken place;

—the process has proved that, while respecting different national situations and perceptions, a broad consensus in this field can be developed in the Community;

—during the process of discussions and consultation, a clear will to arrive at common regulatory aims for the sector has emerged on the part of all major actors.

Regarding the reactions to the main proposals set out in [Boxes 4.1, 4.2], the situation seems to be that (while there are different qualifications with regard to the exact wording) *there is*:

—a broad consensus regarding the full liberalisation of the terminal equipment market, with a reasonable period for transition;

---

[1]The Economic and Social Committee has given, at its meeting of 18th November 1987 an initial opinion on the Green Paper (OJ No C 356, 31.12.1987). It announced that it reserves the right to re-examine specific problems when the Commission presents its proposals for attaining the objectives of the Green Paper.

Box 4.1

Proposed Positions

(*Note*: For easy reference, the following are reproduced in their original form from the *Green Paper*, COM (87) 290.)

PROPOSED POSITIONS

A) *Acceptance of continued exclusive provision or special rights for the Telecommunications Administrations regarding provision and operation of the network infrastructure. Where a Member State chooses a more liberal regime, either for the whole or parts of the network, the short and long term integrity of the general network infrastructure should be safeguarded.*

Closely monitored competitive offering of two-way satellite communications systems will need further analysis. It should be allowed on a case-to-case basis, where this is necessary to develop European-wide services and where impact on the financial viability of the main provider(s) is not substantial.

Common understanding and definition regarding infrastructure provision should be worked out under E) below.

B) *Acceptance of continued exclusive provision or special rights for the Telecommunications Administrations regarding provision of a limited number of basic services, where exclusive provision is considered essential at this stage for safeguarding public service goals.*

Exclusive provision must be **narrowly** *construed and be subject to review within given time intervals, taking account of technological development and particularly the evolution towards a digital infrastructure. 'Reserved services' may not be defined so as to extend a Telecommunications Administration service monopoly in a way inconsistent with the Treaty. Currently, given general understanding in the Community, voice telephone service seems to be the only obvious candidate.*

C) *Free (unrestricted) provision of all other services ('competitive services', including in particular 'value-added services') within Member States and between Member States (in competition with the Telecommunications Administrations) for own use, shared use, or provision to third parties, subject to the conditions for use of the network infrastructure to be defined under E).*

'Competitive services' would comprise all services except basic services explicitly reserved for the Telecommunications Administrations (see B).

Box 4.1 (continued)

D) *Strict requirements regarding standards for the network infrastructure and services provided by the Telecommunications Administrations or service providers of comparable importance, in order to maintain or create Community-wide inter-operability. These requirements must build in particular on Directives 83/189/EEC and 86/361/EEC, Decision 87/95/ EEC and Recommendation 86/659/EEC.*

Member States and the Community should ensure and promote provision by the Telecommunications Administrations of efficient European-wide and worldwide communications, in particular regarding those services (be they reserved or competitive) recommended for Community-wide provision, such as according to Recommendation 86/659/EEC.

E) *Clear definition by Community Directive of general requirements imposed by Telecommunications Administrations on providers of competitive services for use of the network, including definitions regarding network infrastructure provision.*

This must include clear interconnect and access obligations by Telecommuni cations Administrations for trans-frontier service providers in order to prevent Treaty infringements.

Consensus must be achieved on standards, frequencies, and tariff principles, in order to agree on the general conditions imposed for service provision on the competitive sector. Details of this Directive on Open Network Provision (O N P) should be prepared in consultation with the Member States, the Telecommunications Administrations and the other parties concerned, in the framework of the Senior Officials Group on Telecommunications (SOG-T).

F) *Free (unrestricted) provision of terminal equipment within Member States and between Member States (in competition with Telecommunications Administrations), subject to type approval as compatible with Treaty obligations and existing Directives. Provision of the first (conventional) telephone set could be excluded from unrestricted provision on a temporary basis.*

Receive Only Earth Stations (ROES) for satellite down-links should be assimilated with terminal equipment and be subject to type approval only;

G) *Separation of regulatory and operational activities of Telecommuni-cations Administrations. Regulatory activities concern in particular licensing, control of type approval and interface specifications, allo-cations of frequencies, and general surveillance of network usage conditions;*

H) *Strict continuous review of operational (commercial) activities of Telecommunications Administrations according to Articles 85, 86 and 90, EEC Treaty. This applies in particular to practices of cross-subsidisation of activities in the competitive services sector and of activities in manufacturing;*

Box 4.1 (continued)

I) Strict continuous review of all private providers in the newly opened sectors according to Articles 85 and 86, in order to avoid the abuse of dominant positions;

J) Full application of the Community's common commercial policy to telecommunications. Notification by Telecommunications Administrations under Regulation 17/62 of all arrangements between them or with Third Countries which may affect competition within the Community. Provision of information to the extent required for the Community, in order to build up a consistent Community position for GATT negotiations and relations with Third Countries. (*)

(*) GATT = General Agreement on Tariffs and Trade

Box 4.2
Proposed Action Lines
(*Note*: For easy reference, the following are reproduced in their original form from the *Green Paper*, COM (87) 290.)

1 ACCELERATION OF EXISTING ACTION LINES

- ENSURING THE LONG-TERM CONVERGENCE AND INTEGRITY OF THE NETWORK INFRASTRUCTURE IN THE COMMUNITY

- RAPID ACHIEVEMENT OF FULL MUTUAL RECOGNITION OF TYPE APPROVAL FOR TERMINAL EQUIPMENT

- RAPID PROGRESS TOWARDS OPENING UP ACCESS TO PUBLIC TELECOMMUNICATIONS PROCUREMENT CONTRACTS

2 INITIATION OF NEW ACTION LINES

I SUBSTANTIAL REINFORCEMENT OF THE DEVELOPMENT OF STANDARDS AND SPECIFICATIONS IN THE COMMUNITY / CREATION OF A EUROPEAN TELECOMMUNICATIONS STANDARDS INSTITUTE

II COMMON DEFINITION OF AN AGREED SET OF CONDITIONS FOR OPEN NETWORK PROVISION ("O N P") TO SERVICE PROVIDERS AND USERS

III COMMON DEVELOPMENT OF EUROPE-WIDE SERVICES

Box **4.2** (continued)

IV COMMON DEFINITION OF A COHERENT EUROPEAN POSITION
REGARDING THE FUTURE DEVELOPMENT OF SATELLITE
COMMUNICATIONS IN THE COMMUNITY

V COMMON DEFINITION OF A COHERENT CONCEPT ON
TELECOMMUNICATIONS SERVICES AND EQUIPMENT WITH REGARD TO
THE COMMUNITY'S RELATIONS WITH THIRD COUNTRIES

VI COMMON ANALYSIS OF SOCIAL IMPACT AND CONDITIONS FOR A
SMOOTH TRANSITION

—a broad consensus on the liberalisation of value-added services, the high-value end of
the overall spectrum of telecommunications services which is proposed in Fig. I to be
open to competitive provision;

—full endorsement in principle of the separation of regulatory and operational responsibilities of the Telecommunications Administrations;

—general recognition of the fact that tariffs should follow overall cost trends;

—strong support, in principle, regarding standards, in order to maintain or create Community-wide and worldwide interoperability, while safeguarding the capability for innovation. Strong support for a clear definition of general requirements imposed by Telecommunications Administrations on providers of competitive services and other users
for use of the network (ONP—Open Network Provision);

—broad acceptance of the fact that Telecommunications Administrations should be able
to participate in the newly open competitive sectors, on an equal footing;

general acceptance of the need to apply the general rules of competition law to the
operational (commercial) activities of both the Telecommunications Administrations and
other private providers, in a symmetric way;

Support for the line taken in the Green Paper, that, while this implies on the one hand
clear requirements for transparency of operations, in particular with regard to cross-
subsidisation and procurement of equipment, it should imply on the other hand relaxing
of organisational and financial constraints imposed on Telecommunications Administrations which may inhibit their ability to compete;

—general support for existing Community programmes, actions and proposals aimed at
strengthening the long-term convergence and integrity of the network infrastructure in
the Community. This concerns in particular the development of Integrated Broadband
Communications (IBC) (the RACE programme);† the Integrated Services Digital Network (ISDN); and the introduction of Digital Mobile Communications.

---

†RACE = A program of the European Communities; see Glossary.

A second category of positions has also met with general support, while at the same time receiving criticism from both possible perspectives: of going too far in the opinion of some *and* of not going far enough in the opinion of others.

This concerns in particular:

—the acceptance of the continuation of exclusive provision for network infrastructure. This has met acceptance in most comments while receiving some criticism from both sides.

—the degree of competition in services other than value-added services. There is broad general support for accepting exclusive provision of voice telephony, as long as it is defined as switched voice telephony intended for the general public and as long as this is subject to review.

A number of comments hold that either special authorisation schemes or exclusive provision for other services, in particular telex and switched data communications intended for general public use, are required. Special authorisation schemes have been suggested as a possible option for movement towards market opening in this area.

Generally, comments hold that a broad provision of efficient Europe-wide and world-wide communications to the public must be ensured.

Regarding competition in satellite communications, a consensus still does not seem possible. On this issue, there seems only to be a general readiness to open competition for Receive-Only Equipment as long as not connected to the public network.

Regarding other major issues, further discussion and definition is needed. This concerns in particular:

—the development of a coherent European position on satellite communications in order to create or deepen consensus in this key technology;

—the rapid promotion of Europe-wide services and development of concrete concepts for a market led approach and of tariff principles for these services;

—the development of a common position on the Community's relations with third countries and on international problems, in particular with regard to multilateral issues.

Special concern has been expressed with regard to future discussions of international regulation in the 1988 ITU World Administrative Telegraph and Telephone Conference (WATT-C), concerning especially the future openness of the international environment.

Broad support was given for thorough concertation in preparation of the new GATT Round. Comments have called for ensuring foreign market opening in services and equipment for Community providers, as a corollary to Community market liberalisation;

—a further strengthening of the use of advanced telecommunications for developing the less favoured regions, on the basis of the STAR programme, and the consideration of the special problems of the peripheral regions of the Community; [‡]

‡STAR = A program of the EC; see Glossary.

—the further promotion of the social dialogue and the discussion of effective means to match the requirements for training/re-training in the sector.

Discussion should be broadened to include more clearly general social consensus in this area, in particular the protection of privacy and of personal data, and general long-term social implications of different options in the development of telecommunications in the Community.

(IV) PROGRAMME FOR ACTION:
ACHIEVING PROGRESSIVELY A COMPETITIVE COMMUNITY-WIDE MARKET BY 1992

The reactions received to date, and the broad consensus apparent from these comments seem to give now a strong basis on which to define in more detail, a determined policy to develop the Community's telecommunications market, with the overall objective of fully achieving a *Community-wide open competitive market by 1992.*
    As set out in the Green Paper,

"given their importance and wide ramifications, regulatory changes in telecommunications can only be introduced progressively. Time must be allowed for present structures, which have grown up historically over a long period, to adjust to the new environment."

It seems therefore appropriate to define the *future approach according to three areas*:

—areas where the development of concrete policy actions seems possible now;

—areas where comprehensive policy consensus still has to be worked out;

—areas where existing policies must be confirmed/strengthened.

(IV-1) Areas where the development of concrete policy actions is possible now.

For a number of areas the development of consensus seems sufficiently advanced on the one hand, the need for clarification and the obligation to act speedily are evident on the other.

    Given the overriding aim of achieving the Internal Market before the 31st December 1992, the obligation fully to apply the Treaty to the sector and the broad consultation process, a strong basis now exists for the *opening of the Community's telecommunications market, according to defined deadlines and according to the following principal measures*:

(i) *Rapid full opening of the terminal equipment market to competition.*

Community-wide opening should be fully achieved for terminal equipment *by 31st December 1990 at the latest.* This should allow a sufficient transition period for all equipment including the first (conventional) telephone set.
Opening must ensure free (unrestricted) provision of terminal equipment within Member States and between Member States (in competition with the Telecommunications Administrations), subject to type approval as compatible with Treaty obligations and existing Directives.
Fair type approval procedures must involve, amongst others, full publishing of the type approval procedures in force, and appropriate cost and time required for the

completion of the procedures. A network termination point appropriate for suitable connection of terminal equipment must be made available to the subscriber on request. The Commission will, before end-March 1988, issue a Directive under Article 90 (3) regarding the liberalisation of the terminal equipment market.

In parallel, the Commission will rapidly propose a Directive on full mutual recognition of type approval before end-1988, building on Directive 86/361/EEC on the progressive introduction of the NETs (see v.4).(**)

(ii) *Progressive opening of the telecommunications services market to competition from 1989 onwards.*

Continued exclusive provision or special rights for the Telecommunications Administrations regarding provision and operation of the network infrastructure, and at this stage of voice telephone service, is accepted.

All other services should be opened *by 31st December 1989.*

However, special consideration will need to be given to the telex service and packet and circuit switched data services intended for general public use. Provision will be made for a period of transition to be defined, sufficient to allow the elaboration of schemes to ensure future service provision for the general public for this type of service.

Opening must ensure free (unrestricted) provision of services within Member States and between Member States (in competition with Telecommunications Administrations), for own use, shared use, or provision to third parties, subject to fair conditions of access, and the lifting of restrictions on use and interconnection where they exist. Implementation of these principles will involve the closer definition of the limitations of the Telecommunications Administrations service monopoly, in order to prevent wide differences in the scope of the monopoly from Member State to Member State and definition of principles guiding access to and use of the network (see Open Network Provision—ONP, v.2 below).

By 1st January 1992, any remaining exclusive provision of services will have to be reviewed "taking account of technological development and particularly the evolution towards a digital infrastructure." The development of trade must not be affected to such an extent as would be contrary to the interests of the Community.

(iii) *Full opening of receive-only satellite antennae,* as long as they are not connected to the public network, *by 31st December 1989.*

It is believed that liberalisation for this specific segment of equipment can be advanced rapidly as no major technical obstacles exist.

(iv) *Progressive implementation of the general principle that telecommunications tariffs should follow overall cost trends.*

If reasonable overall cost-related tariffs are not achieved *by 1st January 1992,* the whole approach with regard to the future evolution of the telecommunications sector will have to be re-evaluated.

**NET = European Telecommunication Standard

(v) *Setting in motion of a number of accompanying measures,* necessary to allow the competitive environment to function and to ensure market participation by all on fair terms.

This concerns, at this stage:

v.1. *Clear separation of regulatory and operational activities,*
in order to prevent possible abuses of a dominant position in type approval, licensing, etc. by the Telecommunications Administrations acting both as regulator and as competing operator;

v.2. *Definition of details for Open Network Provision* (ONP).

The clear *Community-wide definition* of general requirements imposed by Telecommunications Administrations on providers of competitive services for use of the network has been recognised generally as central to the future functioning of a competitive market.
In the meantime, the SOG-T's subgroup GAP (Group for Analysis and Forecasting) has started to define the general approach to the concept. (***)
In order to allow timely input to the Community-wide definition of fair access and usage conditions, it is suggested to concentrate on those issues most critical to providers of competitive services and a competitive market environment and to work according to a stringent time schedule:
—analysis of conditions of open provisions of leased lines to be completed *by mid-1988*;
—analysis of conditions of open provision of the general public data networks to be completed *by end-1988*;
—analysis of conditions of open provision of the future Integrated Services Digital Network (ISDN) to be completed *by mid-1989*.

In a subsequent study period, the conditions of access to frequencies may be a suitable subject.
Analysis should cover technical interfaces, tariff principles, and conditions of use. It should include the clear definition of network termination points where appropriate.
Allowing for comment by all concerned—including users, industry, and potential service providers—will be essential to reach a general consensus.

v.3. *Establishment of a European Telecommunications Standards Institute,*

in order to accelerate substantially work in this area.
In September 1987, the CEPT took a basic decision to establish such an institute *by April 1988*. Details are currently being worked out. (*)

***SOG-T = Senior Officials Group—Telecommunications.

*CEPT = European Conference of Postal and Telecommunications Administrations; see Section 5.3.

In the Green Paper, the Commission has emphasised that "this action should build on and complement the Community's current policy on telecommunications and information technology standards," within the framework of the Community's general promotion of open international standardisation.

The comments received have shown a broad conviction that a substantial reinforcement of resources applied to standardisation is a necessary requirement for a truly open competitive market.

The planned Institute will best serve this objective if it is open both to those involved in telecommunications and to those involved in information technology and allows for full active participation of industry and users.

The Commission expects that, as a result of the efforts currently being devoted to the establishment of the Institute, such a body will be in a position efficiently to draft the specifications with the status of standards, with the participation of all interested parties, in full alignment with the Community principles applicable to technical harmonisation and with adequate links with existing European standardisation bodies.

v.4. *Rapid introduction of full mutual recognition of type approval to terminal equipment.*

Full mutual recognition of type approval is a necessary corollary for the effective Community-wide opening of the terminal equipment market. The Green Paper's proposal concerning rapid extension of the current Directive 86/361/EEC to include full mutual recognition of type approval has found universal backing. The Commission therefore intends to submit a draft Directive on full mutual recognition of type approval *before end-1988.*

v.5. *Creating transparency in the financial relations between Member States' governments and the Telecommunications Administrations, and a fiscal environment within which Telecommunications Administrations will be able to participate* in the competitive market on fair terms.

As set out in the Green Paper, "participation in a competitive market will offer new opportunities to the Telecommunications Administrations, if at the same time organisational and financial constraints imposed on them are relaxed."

Participation in the competitive markets on fair terms requires a stable financial environment for Telecommunications Administrations.

The Commission intends fully to apply *Directive 80/723/EEC* (extended to Telecommunications by Directive 85/413/EEC) *which requires transparency in the financial relations* between Member States' governments and their public undertakings, to the sector.

The abolition of fiscal frontiers and the objective to arrive at a state of equal competitive conditions in the sector, requires adapting the fiscal conditions of the Telecommunications Administrations to the new competitive environment.

In a number of Member States, public telecommunications are currently still exempted from *Value-Added Tax.* The Commission presented on 17th June 1987, an amended proposal for *an 18th VAT Directive which makes provision for obligatory taxation* of these supplies with effect *from 1st January 1990.*

v.6. *Ensuring fair conditions of competition.*

Ensuring an open competitive market makes continuous review of the telecommunications sector necessary.

The Commission intends to issue guidelines regarding the application of competition rules to the telecommunications sector and on the way that the review should be carried out.

v.7. *Ensuring the independence of procurement decisions and the opening of public procurement.*

In the Green Paper, the Commission announced that the results of the voluntary and partial opening of procurement of the Telecommunications Administrations achieved by Recommendation 84/550/EEC are currently under review. The Commission has also announced that it will undertake a determined campaign to introduce open purchasing procedures in those sectors, which are still excluded from the existing Directives.

The essential objective will be to *ensure non-discriminatory open procurement in the telecommunications sector,* subject to commercial criteria and free from undue influences, *allowing fair open tendering.*

The Commission is currently considering a number of options, in order to attain this objective in the most efficient way. A detailed analysis is required to take into account the specifics of the sector. Comments have pointed in particular to the influence of the competitive environment within which Telecommunications Administrations operate, on procurement behaviour.

While the Community-wide opening of the *terminal equipment* market to competition should rapidly ensure open purchasing procedures in the best commercial conditions, under the pressure of a competitive market place, special measures will be needed to ensure fair Community-wide purchasing practices in the field of *network equipment* or in those sectors of the terminal market where Telecommunications Administrations continue, for the time being, to exercise exclusive or special rights.

Measures should concern both ensuring open tendering for network equipment suppliers throughout the Community through appropriate tendering procedures as well as the establishment of a monitoring system.

The Commission will propose appropriate measures *in March 1988.*

Procedure envisaged

As set out, the Commission will, *before end-March of 1988,* issue a Directive under Article 90 (3) regarding the liberalisation of the terminal equipment market.

The progressive opening of telecommunications services from 1989 onwards and the problem of separation of operational and regulatory functions will be dealt with by a Commission Directive to be presented *before mid-1988* and to be adopted *before end-1988.*

As set out, the Commission will further submit *before end-1988* a proposal to Council concerning a Directive on the full mutual recognition of type approval of terminal equipment. Regarding the Community-wide opening of public procurement, it will propose appropriate measures *in March 1988.*

Regarding Value-Added Tax, the Council is currently considering the Commission's amended proposal for an 18th VAT Directive which makes provision for obligatory taxation of telecommunications.

Moreover, it will submit Directive(s) on Open Network Provision (ONP), as definition work proceeds according to the schedule set out.

(IV-2) Areas where a comprehensive policy consensus still has to be worked out.

During the consultations a number of areas have been identified, where discussion has still not sufficiently progressed but where there is general agreement that they form topics of key importance. For these areas, the Commission proposes that *further discussions should lead to defined common policies before the end of 1988.*
This concerns in particular:

(i) *A coherent European Position regarding the future regulation and development of satellite communications in the Community.*

The discussions have singled out the importance of reaching common positions on:

• future regulation of two-way satellite communications;
• development of the earth station market in Europe, in particular with regard to common standards;
• the future development of space segments in particular the relationships between EUTELSAT, national, and private systems, and the full use of the technological potential of the European Space Agency;
• the development of international satellite communications, in particular with regard to INTELSAT and INMARSAT.

(ii) *A pro-active concept for the promotion of Europe-wide services, by a market-led approach, and definition of common tariff principles.*
Consultations have given full support for discussing major issues raised in this regard in the Green Paper:

• *defining a pro-active approach to develop Europe-wide compatibility and inter-operability of telecommunications services,* required for both business activities and the needs of the general public.
In addition to efficient telephony and telex, new services such as packet switched and circuit switched data services, videotex, services provided under ISDN as defined in Recommendation 86/659/EEC, and future digital mobile communications, as defined in Recommendation 87/371/EEC and Directive 87/372/EEC should be available universally at the European level.
This could involve joint Community-wide service provision and network planning, as far as compatible with Community competition rules.
The Memorandum signed by Telecommunications Administrations for the joint implementation of digital mobile communications in Europe may serve as an example;
• *development of common tariff principles, as far as compatible with a market led approach,* with a view to seeking convergence on tariff structures.
Regarding intra-Community and international tariffs, higher transparency and convergence should be sought in order to avoid excessive divergences of tariffs and possible distortion of competition.

Provision of switched and leased lines services at reasonable rates must be an essential feature of Open Network Provision;

- *full use of programmes at Community level* for stimulating private and public initiatives for developing Europe-wide value-added and information services. This concerns in particular the TEDIS programme concerning electronic data interchange and the programme for the establishment of a Community-wide information market (see IV.3.ii).

In addition, new initiatives should be considered, to put new advanced services rapidly at the disposal of the European user, as technological opportunities develop.

Toward this end, the Commission will shortly submit a Communication on the Community-wide introduction of *advanced broadband services for business use,* using fully the technologies being developed in the RACE programme.

The initiative will be based on the analysis of SOG-T/GAP, regarding the co-ordinated introduction of broadband services in the European Community.

(iii) *Defining a European position on the major international questions in telecommunications.*

Strong backing has been found in the discussions regarding the common definition of a coherent concept of telecommunications services and equipment with regard to the Community's relations with third countries.

As set out in the Green Paper, this concerns in particular:

- multilateral issues:
  the preparation of the new GATT round and future relations with international organisations such as the International Telecommunications Union.
  While further discussion will be needed, comments have emphasised the importance of the forthcoming World Administrative Telegraph & Telephone Conference (WATT-C), December 1988, which will review the international regulation of telecommunications. The working out of a *common position on the WATT-C,* in agreement with the regulatory consensus developed in the Community, should be a high priority objective for discussions in this area during 1988.
  Future international regulations should be flexible enough fully to allow the implementation of the internal market in the Community in this area and to arrive, in the framework of the *new GATT Round,* at the definition of a fair open trading environment for both telecommunications equipment and services.
  The Commission will need to build up the necessary international relationships, in order to dispose of the necessary position and information to undertake policy formulation.
- bilateral issues:
  in particular the evolving relationship in this field with:
  - the EFTA countries,
  - the United States and Japan,
  - and with the Third World.

(iv) *Developing the social dialogue and taking full account of social concerns.*

The requirement for common analysis of social impact and conditions for a smooth transition has been singled out in the discussions as *the single most important issue.*

It has been generally agreed that, in the long term, this is a crucial factor for the future evolution of the telecommunications and information technology sector, both at the national and Community level.

Positions must be worked out in particular regarding:

- best ways to intensify the social dialogue, on the basis of joint analysis and informed debate;
- a clear view on *future skill requirements and their impact on training/re-training,* in order to manage the shift in job qualifications required by the change of technology and to expand employment in the new service provision.

Analysis should result in concrete proposals on how best use can be made of the instruments available at the national and Community levels to facilitate change;

- extending the debate on the requirements for acceptability of new services and activities, both in the business and the private sector.

Special attention will have to be paid to develop a *common position regarding the protection of individuals with regard to personal data.* The issue is addressed in the framework of the Community's policy for the development of an information services market.

Currently, the Commission has engaged in an intensive dialogue with the trade unions in the field. A first common study concerning the analysis of the state of employment, requirements for future skills and requirements for training/re-training has been initiated.

(IV-3) Areas where existing policies must be confirmed/strengthened.

(i) *Ensuring the long-term convergence and the integrity of the network infrastructure in the Community.*

The ensuring of the long term convergence and integrity of the network infrastructure in the Community, the major goal of Community telecommunications policy since 1984 has found universal confirmation. The Community's RACE programme is essential in this context, as it is intended to lay the foundations for Europe's telecommunications infrastructure of the nineties.

The major policy goal in the sector must be the *rapid implementation of the RACE programme* which has recently been adopted. Further central goals must be the full application of Recommendation 86/659/EEC on the co-ordinated introduction of the *Integrated Services Digital Network (ISDN)* and the full application of Recommendation 87/371/EEC on the co-ordinated introduction of Public Pan-European Cellular *Digital Mobile Communications* in the Community, based on Directive 87/372/EEC on frequency bands to be reserved for this service.

Further, rapid progress on the *implementation of infrastructure projects of common interest,* according to the work programme agreed by the Council of Ministers at its meeting of 17th December 1984 should be made. This should concern in particular the progressive Community-wide introduction of broadband communications for business use (see IV.2.ii).

(ii) *Promoting a strong European presence in both the services and industrial field.*

As set out in the Green Paper, "intensified co-operation within the Community must ensure that European industry will fully benefit from the opening of the markets."
More than 100 companies have submitted proposals for the *RACE Main Programme*. The programme is turning out to be a major factor in the formation of the Community's future industry and research structure in the sector. The rapid full launching of the programme will bring this effect to full fruition.
On the services side, Community programmes exist or are being introduced around which substantial initiatives can develop. This concerns in particular the *TEDIS initiative*, adopted by Council on 5th October 1987, which will offer major stimuli to European cooperations in the crucial field of electronic data interchange.
In neighbouring fields, the *Community's INSIS and CADDIA programmes* are now starting to exert their full influence as a spearhead of development in Community-wide cooperation in data communication, electronic mail, electronic message systems, and the operational interconnection of large sophisticated data bases.
In a broader context, *the ESPRIT programme* in the field of Information Technology on the one hand, the programme for the *Development of an Information Services Market* on the other, create the favourable environment which Europe needs for a strong entry into the information age [*"The Establishment of a Policy and a Plan of Priority Actions for the Development of an Information Services Market,"* COM(87)360, submitted to Council on 24th July 1987*].†

(iii) *Ensuring full participation, on equal terms, of the less-favoured regions of the Community in the new Community-wide markets.*

Throughout the discussions, strong emphasis has been given to the important role which telecommunications infrastructure, services and markets will play in the future for *strengthening Community cohesion*. Concern has been voiced to ensure the full participation of the Community's less favoured regions in the new growth potential and to take account of their special problems.
As set out in the Green Paper, the Community's telecommunications policy has, in particular through the launching of the *STAR programme,†* aimed at regional development and funded by the European Regional Development Fund, demonstrated that it will take full account of this fundamental concern. The development of a Community-wide competitive market for telecommunications services and equipment will represent for the regions a special potential for future growth on the one hand, a major challenge on the other.
In depth discussion will be necessary, in particular concerning:
• how to ensure that regions are fully integrated into the new markets, on an equal footing;

---

†TEDIS, CADDIA, ESPRIT/STAR see Glossary for the derivation of these acroynms that designate European programs.

• how to ensure that the growth potential is put to best use, in order to reduce the gap in economic development which currently separates these regions from the more prosperous parts of the Community.

The implementation of the Community-wide market for telecommunications equipment and services *will give the peripheral regions a new opportunity to better integrate into a future, information-based, Community-wide economy*. It is believed that the experience gained in the STAR approach will serve as a very useful starting point for future discussion.

(V) CONCLUSIONS

The *wide consultative process on the Green paper during the last six months* has allowed, according to the Commission's opinion, to identify a *broad consensus on major regulatory orientations* in the sector, to define clear priorities and to develop a progressive approach which should lead to full market opening by 1992.

The *proposals concentrate on priority issues* which must be resolved at Community level for all Member States. They leave out, according to the line taken in the Green Paper, "questions which are important but fall to the national level, such as which status for Telecommunications Administrations is best suited to facing the developing competitive market, and related questions of finance, organisation and employment relations." Community policy in the area can and should support and complement the current transition.

The proposals, at this stage, concentrate on the use of the main network infrastructure. As pointed out in the Green Paper, for a number of infrastructure/services adjacent to the main network infrastructure, special consideration is needed. "This concerns in particular satellite communications, mobile radio communications and cable-TV networks." Out of these, satellite communications have been singled out as an area on which a common position must be most urgently reached.

The Commission considers that, at this stage, the implementation of the objectives and proposals set out can be pursued within the given institutional framework, by applying the Treaty's competition rules and by submitting proposals to Council as appropriate, as well as by providing the Community framework as a focus for policy formulation.

Comments have drawn attention to the requirement for a broad involvement of users, industry and trade unions in the policy formulation process. The Commission will propose appropriate mechanisms to achieve this end.

The future development of a *Community-wide open competitive market in telecommunications services and equipment* will be one of the major conditions for implementing the Community-wide market for goods and services *in 1992* as a whole. Rapid progress towards a Community-wide market will also be the necessary pre-condition for reaching fair and balanced agreements for the Community with Third Countries in this field.

The Commission will work vigorously towards these ends. It transmits this Communication to Council, the European Parliament, and the Economic and Social Committee *to facilitate the consideration of the Green Paper and future Community policy in the telecommunications sector*. [Commission of the European Communities, February 1988.]

4.2.2 Summary Report of the Green Paper

TOWARDS A DYNAMIC EUROPEAN ECONOMY: GREEN PAPER ON THE DEVEL-

OPMENT OF THE COMMON MARKET FOR TELECOMMUNICATIONS SERVICES AND
EQUIPMENT.
Commission of the European Communities, COM(87) 290 Final, Brussels, 30 June 1987.

(I) INTRODUCTION

The strengthening of European telecommunications has become one of the major conditions
for *promoting a harmonious development of economic activities and a competitive market
throughout the Community* and for achieving the completion of the Community-wide market
for goods and services by 1992.

The current wave of technical innovation resulting from the convergence of telecommunications and computer technology has now led to reviews in all Member States, and
elsewhere, of the future organisation of the telecommunications sector and its necessary regulatory adjustment. The Commission considers it timely to aim at achieving maximum syn-
ergy between current developments and debates in the Member States, drawing fully on the
potential offered by them to meet the objectives of the Treaty.

This report is intended to launch a debate and to attract comment from a broad spectrum
of opinion: the Council; the European Parliament and the Economic and Social Committee;
the Telecommunications Administrations and Recognized Private Operating Agencies, hereinafter referred to as the "Telecommunications Administrations"; the European telecommunications, data processing and services industry; the users who must be the main beneficiaries
of the new opportunities; and the trade unions and other organisations who represent the social
interests in this area.

Ensuring that the varying national situations are fully taken into account in a European
approach requires a wide-ranging debate over the whole of the Community.

The paper advances proposals for common positions and lines of action, in order to
ease the current transition.

The overriding aim is to develop the conditions for the market to provide European
users with a *greater variety* of telecommunications services, of *better quality* and at *lower
costs,* affording Europe the full internal and external benefits of a strong telecommunications
sector.

(II) ACHIEVEMENTS OF COMMUNITY TELECOMMUNICATIONS POLICY TO DATE

A technically advanced, Europe-wide and low-cost telecommunications network will provide
an essential infrastructure for improving the competitiveness of the European economy, achieving
the Internal Market and strengthening Community cohesion—which constitute priority Community goals reaffirmed in the Single European Act. Telecommunications have a great influence not only on services in general, such as financial services, transport and tourism, but
also on trade in goods and on European industrial co-operation.

The emerging new telecommunications services—and notably so-called value-added
and information services—will *have a major impact on the future tradeability of services in
general and on the location of economic activities.*

By the end of the century up to seven per cent of the Gross Domestic Product of the
Community will result from telecommunications, as against over two per cent today. The
combined world equipment and services market for telecommunications and information technology already represents more than ECU 500 billion. It is estimated that, via information
technology, more than 60% of Community employment may depend on telecommunications
by the end of the century.

Since 1984, the Community has made substantial progress in this field, by implementing a policy aimed at:

—promoting the creation of an advanced European telecommunications infrastructure;

—contributing to the creation of a Community-wide market for services and equipment;

—contributing to the competitiveness of European industry and service providers.

In following these objectives, the Commission has, within the last two years, made proposals and achieved *rapid agreement by Council* along five main lines:

—co-ordination regarding future development of telecommunications in the Community and common infrastructure projects. This concerns in particular the principal future stages of network development—the Integrated Services Digital Network (ISDN), digital mobile communications, and the introduction of future broadband communications;

—creation of a Community-wide market for terminals and equipment. This concerns in particular the promotion of Europe-wide open standards, in order to give equal opportunity to all market participants;

—the launch of a programme of pre-competitive and "prenormative" R&D covering the technologies required for integrated broadband communications (the RACE programme);

—promoting the introduction and development of advanced services and networks in the less-favoured peripheral regions of the Community;

—building up common European positions with regard to international discussions in this area.

During 1986 alone, Council achieved agreement, on proposal by the Commission, on six major measures which will become fully effective during 1987. [Box 4.3] gives an overview of decisions taken and of proposals currently before Council.

In parallel, the Commission has taken up a number of cases, related to the opening of telecommunications markets, under the Treaty's competition rules.

Box 4.3

COUNCIL DECISIONS TAKEN IN THE FIELD OF TELECOMMUNICATIONS

SINCE 1984

COUNCIL RECOMMENDATION OF 12 NOVEMBER 1984 concerning the
implementation of a common approach in the field of
telecommunications (84/549/EEC)

Box 4.3 (continued)

COUNCIL RECOMMENDATION OF 12 NOVEMBER 1984 concerning the first
phase of opening up access to public telecommunications contracts
(84/550/EEC)

COUNCIL DECISION OF 25 JULY 1985 on a definition phase for an R&D
programme in advanced communications technologies for Europe (RACE)
(85/372/EEC)

COUNCIL RESOLUTION OF 9 JUNE 1986 on the use of videoconference and
videophone techniques for intergovernmental applications (86/C
160/01)

COUNCIL DIRECTIVE OF 24 JULY 1986 on the initial stage of the
mutual recognition of type approval for telecommunications terminal
equipment (86/361/EEC)

COUNCIL REGULATION OF 27 OCTOBER 1986 instituting a Community
programme for the development of certain less-favoured regions of
the Community by improving access to advanced telecommunications
services (STAR programme) (86/3300/EEC)

COUNCIL DIRECTIVE OF 3 NOVEMBER 1986 on the adoption of common
technical specifications of the MAC/packet family of standards for
direct satellite television broadcasting (86/529/EEC)

COUNCIL DECISION OF 22 DECEMBER 1986 on standardisation in the
field of information technology and telecommunications (87/95/EEC)

COUNCIL RECOMMENDATION OF 22 DECEMBER 1986 on the co-ordinated
introduction of the Integrated Services Digital Network (ISDN) in
the European Community (86/659/EEC)

PROPOSALS CURRENTLY BEFORE COUNCIL

PROPOSAL FOR A COUNCIL REGULATION OF 29 OCTOBER 1986 on a Community
action in the field of telecommunications technologies (RACE)

PROPOSAL FOR A COUNCIL REGULATION OF 1 DECEMBER 1986 introducing
the preparatory phase of a Community programme on trade electronic
data interchange systems (TEDIS)

Box 4.3 (continued)

PROPOSAL FOR A COUNCIL RECOMMENDATION OF 9 FEBRUARY 1987 on the co-ordinated introduction of public pan-European digital mobile communications in the European Community and PROPOSAL FOR A COUNCIL DIRECTIVE on the frequency bands to be made available for the co-ordinated introduction of public pan-European digital mobile communications in the European Community (*).

(*) approved by Council on 11th June 1987

(III) CURRENT ADJUSTMENT OF INSTITUTIONAL AND REGULATORY CONDITIONS

To complement the progress achieved to date, it now seems timely to initiate a common thinking process regarding the *fundamental adjustment of the institutional and regulatory conditions* which the telecommunications sector now faces. This world-wide transformation is due to the profound technical change which is currently taking place: the progressive merger of telecommunications and computing technology, and the growing integration of spoken, written and audio-visual communication.

Telecommunications has taken 140 years to develop from a single service to a dozen services in the early eighties. The new technological capabilities will now lead to considerable *growth and multiplication of services and applications* within a single decade. [See Figure 4.1.]

Mastering this transformation requires certain readjustments in the organisation of the sector in all Member States. The form of these adjustments must take into account the particular position of European countries and the requirements of the establishment of a unified market.

As set out in this Green Paper, the Community must make sure that:

—the necessary European scale and dimension are introduced into the current phase of transformation;

—no new barriers are created within the Community during the adjustment of regulatory conditions;

—existing barriers are removed in the course of this adjustment.

The search for common positions in the complex field of future regulation of the tele-

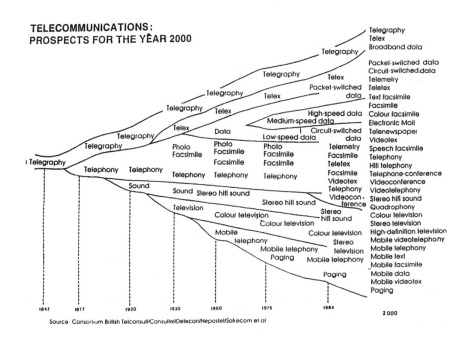

Figure 4.1 Telecommunications: Prospects for the Year 2000.

communications sector must take into account a number of major requirements, if it is to contribute to strengthening the European economy:

—firstly, differing regulatory traditions in the sector. Careful analysis of current reviews and debates in the Member States must identify those areas on which common positions can be reached. It is on those areas that efforts towards developing consensus should be concentrated, in order to increase convergence over time in the Community;

—secondly, opportunities and obligations deriving from the Treaty, in particular regarding: the free movement of goods; the freedom to provide services; competition rules; the common commercial policy;

—thirdly, the external relations of the Community, in particular regarding its major trading partners—the EFTA countries, the United States and Japan, the Third World. The opportunities and obligations deriving for the Community from the GATT agreement and the new GATT round must be taken into account. The impact on the Community's industrial and trading position must be kept clearly in mind;

—fourthly, the evolution of social perceptions in the Member States regarding the new technologies. This concerns the social consequences of the new technologies and associated regulatory policies, the conditions for the integration of these technologies into both private and work life, and measures to facilitate the transition by generating new employment opportunities and protecting legitimate interests.

The convergence of telecommunications, data processing and audio-visual technologies is outdating traditional boundary lines between the telecommunications network and the terminals sector, and between services traditionally provided under monopoly and those provided in a competitive environment. Satellites are now able to provide services within and between countries, at a world level.

There are now many service functions and features that can be performed either by the public network or by a private network or the terminal equipment attached to the network. All countries are confronted by two options:

—either to try to maintain the current regulatory framework, which would imply imposing additional and permanent restrictions and regulations on the use of data processing equipment connected to the network;

—or to define the telecommunications regulatory framework more narrowly and to give more room for competition.

The worldwide trend points towards the latter.

(IV) CONVERGENT TRENDS IN THE CURRENT DEBATE IN THE COMMUNITY ON STRUCTURAL ADJUSTMENT IN TELECOMMUNICATIONS

In the Community, the situation is in flux. The United Kingdom has substantially modified the organisation of its telecommunications sector and issued recently a new general license for value-added and data services. France has seen substantial changes of legislation in the telecommunications/audio-visual field and will introduce major new proposals for its future telecommunications policy in 1987. Reviews or changes are underway in Germany, the Netherlands, Belgium, Italy, Spain, Portugal, and other Member States. For its part, the European Conference of Postal and Telecommunications Administrations (CEPT) is reviewing its organisation, in response to, and in close interaction with, the development of Community telecommunications policy, and in close co-operation with the Commission.

Analysis of the regulatory situation and of current trends of adjustment in the Member States shows that there are convergent trends in current thinking. There is therefore the *genuine possibility of finding agreement for broad common regulatory aims* for the telecommunications sector in the Community.

There seems to be agreement on the following *basic orientations*:

—New services and terminal equipment require market conditions which favour innovation, experimentation, and a high degree of flexibility.

—the current and future integrity of the basic network infrastructure must be maintained or created. This implies in particular a continuing strong role for Telecommunications Administrations in the provision of network infrastructure, and strong emphasis on Europe-wide standards in this area. It also implies safeguarding the financial viability of Telecommunications Administrations in order to ensure the build-up of the new generations of telecommunications infrastructure and the necessary level of investment.

—securing a wide range of choice for the consumer requires that Telecommunications Administrations be able to provide, alongside other suppliers, those services which are opened to competition even if this may involve complex problems of regulation.

—employment growth requires a growth-oriented policy, particularly in the future conglomerate sector of telecommunications/information technologies within which jobs will shift from traditional activities to new opportunities. An intense dialogue with the social partners will be necessary, in order to ensure a smooth transition.

(V) POINTS TO BE CONSIDERED FOR A COMMON APPROACH

The following points to be considered for a solution are discussed in more detail in the Green Paper:

—Given their importance and wide ramifications, regulatory changes in telecommunications can only be introduced progressively. Time must be allowed for present structures, which have grown up historically over a long period, to adjust to the new environment. The major objective must be the completion of the Internal Market by 1992.

—Regulatory changes in telecommunications must take account of the views of all parties concerned, in particular private and business users, Telecommunications Administrations, the Administrations' work force, competing enterprises and the telecommunications and data-processing industry;

—There is consensus in the Community that competition in the telecommunications services and terminal equipment sectors must be substantially expanded, in order to react to technological, economic and world market trends;

—There is also consensus that the role of the Telecommunications Administrations in the provision of network infrastructure must be essentially safeguarded, in order to allow them to fulfill their public service mandate;

—A stable "natural" boundary line between a "reserved services" sector and a "competitive services" sector (including in particular "value-added services") is not possible. Due to technological development—the trend towards integration—any definition (and reservation) of a service can only be temporary and must be subject to review if it is not to impede the overall development of telecommunications services. There is however in practice consensus between the Member States that voice telephone service is a basic service. Currently, this service is reserved in all Member States for provision by the Telecommunications Administrations. At present, this service corresponds to 85%–90% of telecommunications revenues.

—As one counterpart of a more open market environment, the time it takes for the establishment and common application of international standards must be substantially reduced, in order to maintain future network integrity and to promote the availability and interoperability of efficient Europe-wide and worldwide services.

—Telecommunications Administrations generally are—and should be—allowed to participate in the newly emerging competitive services and terminal equipment market. This requires that in the future regulatory responsibility must be separated from operational responsibility. Regulation concerns in particular licensing, control of conformity testing and obligatory interface specifications, frequency administration, and general surveillance including tariff principles;

—Entry of the Telecommunications Administrations but also of the computer and data-processing multi-national companies into a competitive telecommunications sector implies the danger of abuse of a dominant position. Control measures with regard to both types of dominant market participants will have to be strengthened;

—Action at Community level must be taken towards narrowing the differences between Member States regarding the provision of network facilities to the newly emerging competitive services and terminal equipment sector. Otherwise a Community market for services will not develop rapidly. This has implications both for technical regulations and network termination points and for usage conditions and tariff principles;

—The long-term convergence of telecommunications with audio-visual technologies must be taken into account, in addition to the current convergence between the telecommunications and data-processing sectors. This affects in particular policies concerned with satellite communications and cable-TV networks.

Where cable-TV network infrastructure and satellite communications are also used for two-way communications, close surveillance with regard to their relationship and interfacing with the overall telecommunications network will be needed, in order to ensure the long-term overall integrity of the telecommunications infrastructure.

—Two-way satellite communications and the regulation of up-links will need case-by-case consideration. Closely monitored competition should be a possibility in those cases where unacceptable interference with other satellite or radio communications systems is not to be expected and where the revenue base and financial viability of the general network infrastructure provider is not put into question. In the case of very small satellite antennae (VSAT or "microterminals") suitable for data exchange only, this situation should normally be assumed automatically.

—Given the trend in satellite communications towards point to multi-point 'broadcasting' applications for closed user groups, the regulatory regime for receive only earth stations (ROES) for satellite communications should be assimilated to the regime for telecommunications terminals and TV receive-only satellite antennae and fully opened to competition.

—With the growing importance of services, the Community will face in its external relations a growing number of telecommunications-related issues. Consensus must be achieved in time for the preparation of the new GATT round which will include telecommunications services.

Consensus must be further developed at Community level regarding telecommunications issues and the Community's overall framework of external relations, in particular with the EFTA countries and CEPT, with the United States and Japan and with the international organisations in this field, such as the International Telecommunication Union (ITU). (*)

---

*EFTA = European Free Trade Association; see map in Chapter Six.

(VI) PROPOSED COMMUNITY POSITIONS

With these points in mind, in the Green Paper proposals for *positions are developed,* which are set out in [Box 4.1] (see the immediately preceding section, titled "Implementing the Green Paper").

The proposals concentrate on those issues which must be resolved at Community level for all Member States. They leave out questions which are important but fall to the national level, such as which status for Telecommunications Administrations is best suited to facing the developing competitive market environment, and related questions of finance, organisation, and employment relations.

The proposals foresee the continuation of those aspects of the current regimes where there is compatibility with the Treaty. Within the framework of the current adjustment and according to their economic appreciation and perception, Member States may, of course, choose their own position with regard to these aspects, such as a more liberal regime regarding the whole or parts of the network infrastructure. As regards *required change at the Community level,* [the *Proposals* in Box 4/1, *supra,*] insist on these essential modifications:

—*PHASED COMPLETE OPENING OF THE TERMINAL EQUIPMENT MARKET TO COMPETITION*

In the long run this must include all terminals including the subscriber's first telephone set, given the trend towards integration of functions and the Integrated Services Digital Network.

In the short term, transitional solutions will have to be found, taking into account that at the present stage the large majority of Member States wish to maintain their monopoly covering the first (conventional) telephone set.

—ACCEPTANCE BY THE TELECOMMUNICATIONS ADMINISTRATIONS OF CLEAR OBLIGATIONS TO INTERCONNECT WITH AND PROVIDE ACCESS TO TRANS-FRONTIER SERVICE PROVIDERS

Generally, the network must be opened, under fair competitive conditions, to service providers from other Member States. This is a pre-condition for implementation of the Internal Market for the Community's future service economy.

Insofar as Member States continue, for the time being, to reserve certain basic services for exclusive provision by their Telecommunications Administrations, reserved services must be construed narrowly and not interfere with service provision from other Member States, in accordance with Treaty rules.

—*CLEAR SEPARATION OF REGULATORY AND OPERATIONAL FUNCTIONS OF TELECOMMUNICATIONS ADMINISTRATIONS,*

in those Member States where this still has not been carried out. In a more competitive environment, the Telecommunications Administrations cannot continue to be both regulator and market participant, i.e. referee and player. Regulatory functions concern in particular licensing, control of type approval and binding specifications, frequency allocation, and surveillance of usage conditions.

The need for this separation is confirmed by the trends and debates in all Member States which are envisaging more competition for the sector.

The Telecommunications Administrations should be market participants in the competitive sectors, in an improved competitive environment, in order to ensure full service to the whole spectrum of users and industry.

Substantial differences will continue to exist between Member States but must be accommodated. This concerns the *different status of the network operators (public/private)* but also the policy regarding provision of leased lines and resale of capacity. All Member States agree currently on the necessity of securing the financial viability of their Administrations, either by excluding pure resale of voice (telephone) on leased lines or by tariff schemes which make resale of voice to third parties unattractive, such as usage-based tariffs. Both methods will have to be accommodated in the Community. However, both methods must be limited to a legitimate level of protection of financial viability and most not represent the abuse of a dominant position. Current charges for leased lines both at the national and Community level show in some cases wide and unexplained divergences.

The proposals aim at progressively introducing full Community-wide competition to the terminal equipment market, and as far as possible and justified at this stage to telecommunications services. In pursuing the implementation of these proposals, and the lifting of existing restrictions, the Commission will take full account of the fact that the competition rules of the Treaty apply to Telecommunications Administrations, in particular to the extent that they engage in commercial activities.

(VII) LINES OF ACTION TO HELP IMPLEMENTATION OF THESE POSITIONS

In order to create the environment for reaching the objectives set out, the Commission proposes a number of actions:

—to smooth the transition towards a more competitive Community-wide market;
—to promote a strong European presence in both the services and industrial field;
—to prepare the Community for its discussions of future trading relations in this field with its outside partners, in particular in the framework of GATT.

It is envisaged:

—to accelerate the implementation of existing action lines;
—to initiate a number of new action lines needed to complement and facilitate the transition.

(VII.1) ACCELERATION OF EXISTING ACTION LINES

As regards the acceleration of implementation of the action lines defined by Council in December 1984 for the Community's telecommunications policy, *the Commission foresees*:

—*ACCELERATED ADOPTION OF THE PROPOSALS FOR ENSURING THE LONG TERM CONVERGENCE AND INTEGRITY OF THE NETWORK INFRASTRUCTURE IN THE COMMUNITY*

A pan-European telecommunications infrastructure with full interoperability is the only basis on which a Community-wide open competitive terminal equipment and services market can thrive. Intensified industrial cooperation within the Community must ensure that European industry will fully benefit from the opening of this market.

This concerns in particular:
* rapid adoption of the RACE MAIN programme which is fundamental to longer term network development in the Community and for Community-wide standards for the future Integrated Broadband Communications, and promotion of related projects for the progressive Community-wide introduction of broadband communications;
* rapid adoption of the proposals for the introduction of digital mobile communications;
* full application of Recommendation 86/659/EEC on the co-ordinated introduction of the Integrated Services Digital Network (ISDN);
* rapid application of the STAR programme for advancing infrastructure in the regions, with the aim of increasing economic cohesion during the current transition.

—*RAPID EXTENSION OF DIRECTIVE 86/361/EEC TO INCLUDE FULL MUTUAL RECOGNITION OF TYPE APPROVAL FOR TERMINAL EQUIPMENT*

According to the current Directive 86/361/EEC on the mutual recognition of testing required for type approval, proposals for full mutual recognition of type approval must be submitted by July 1989 at the latest. The Commission proposes to accelerate this measure which is vital for the development of a competitive, Community-wide terminal market.

—*REPLACING RECOMMENDATION 84/550/EEC ON THE FIRST PHASE OF OPEN-ING UP ACCESS TO PUBLIC TELECOMMUNICATIONS CONTRACTS BY A DI-RECTIVE,*

on the opening of procurement contracts applying to public and private Telecommunications Administrations to which the Member States confer exclusive or special rights. The future participation of Telecommunications Administrations in the competitive markets requires more transparency in their purchasing behaviour.

(VII.2) INITIATION OF NEW ACTION LINES

As regards new action lines needed to facilitate the transition towards a more competitive, Community-wide environment, *the Commission believes that the following are necessary*:

I. *SUBSTANTIAL REINFORCEMENT OF THE DEVELOPMENT OF STANDARDS AND SPECIFICATIONS IN THE COMMUNITY—CREATION OF A EUROPEAN TELECOM-MUNICATIONS STANDARDS INSTITUTE,*

based on the current cooperation of the Telecommunications Administrations within CEPT and with CEN-CENELEC (**) A substantial reinforcement of resources applied to standardisation is a necessary requirement for a truly open competitive market.
Jointly financed, the institute, based on a small core team of permanent staff and independently managed according to best business practice, should draw flexibly on experts from both the Telecommunications Administrations and industry, in order substantially

---

**CEN. CENELEC = European Committee for Standardization, and for Electrotechnical Standardization, respectively. Regional counterparts to ISO and IEC; see Section 3.5.

to accelerate the elaboration of standards and technical specifications, indispensable for an open competitive market environment and the development of Europe-wide services. This action would build on and complement the Community's current policy on telecommunications and information technology standards.

II. *COMMON DEFINITION OF AN AGREED SET OF CONDITIONS FOR OPEN NETWORK PROVISION ("ONP") TO SERVICE PROVIDERS AND USERS*

Working out in common the principles of the provision of the network to competitive service providers is a necessary requirement for a Community-wide competitive market for terminal equipment and for competitive services, including in particular value-added services, if a long period of case-to-case decisions is to be avoided.

This concerns in particular the definition of clear Europe-wide network termination points, usage conditions and tariff principles and availability of frequencies where relevant.

The work should be carried out by the Commission in close collaboration with the Senior Officials Group on Telecommunications (SOG-T), based on hearings with all parties concerned. Subsequently, the Commission would submit a corresponding Directive on ONP to Council.

III. *COMMON DEVELOPMENT OF EUROPE-WIDE SERVICES*

Future intra-Community communications will depend on achieving three objectives:

—Europe-wide compatibility and inter-operability of those services provided by the Telecommunications Administrations. In addition to efficient telephony and telex, new services such as teletex, videotex, packet-switched and circuit-switched data services, mobile communications and the future ISDN, as defined in Recommendation 86/659/ EEC should be available universally at the European level. This could concern joint Community-wide service provision, network planning, and tariff principles;

—Rapid development of intra-Community provision of value-added services. It is proposed to set into motion at the Community level a number of measures aimed at promoting the emergence of European value-added services, building on current efforts such as the TEDIS initiative.

—Rapid development of the Community's policy on the information market, to promote Europe-wide information services, in particular fully mobilising the potential of private initiatives.

IV. *COMMON DEFINITION OF A COHERENT EUROPEAN POSITION REGARDING THE FUTURE DEVELOPMENT OF SATELLITE COMMUNICATIONS IN THE COMMUNITY*

The international satellite communications sector is currently going through rapid changes. In the light of the positions described in *Fig. 3,* based on prevailing technological trends, common positions will in particular be required regarding:

• development of the earth station market in Europe, in particular with regard to common standards;

• future development of satellite links (space segment), in particular the relationships between EUTELSAT, national, and private systems, and the full use of the technological potential of the European Space Agency;

• development of international satellite communications, in particular with regard to INTELSAT and INMARSAT.

V. *COMMON DEFINITION OF A COHERENT CONCEPT ON TELECOMMUNICATIONS SERVICES AND EQUIPMENT WITH REGARD TO THE COMMUNITY'S RELATIONS WITH THIRD COUNTRIES*

An intensification of co-ordination with regard to Third Countries and the position on the international regulatory environment is urgently needed.

This concerns in particular the preparation of the new GATT ROUND and future relations with international organisations such as the International Telecommunications Union.

It concerns further the evolving relationship in this field with the EFTA countries, with the United States and Japan and with the Third World.

VI. *COMMON ANALYSIS OF SOCIAL IMPACT AND CONDITIONS FOR A SMOOTH TRANSITION*

In the long term, the most important factor for the future evolution of the telecommunications and information technology sector and its regulatory environment, both at the national and the Community level, will be the degree of social consensus which can be achieved regarding the new technologies.

Common discussions and positions will be needed regarding the best ways to master the shift in job qualifications required by the change in technology and to expand employment in new service provision.

An essential condition for achieving a true Common Market in this area will therefore be the development of a Europe-wide consensus in the analysis of the social consequences of the new technologies and the associated regulatory evolution and policies. Analysis of the conditions for acceptability of new services and activities, and the impact on work life and employment will be a permanent task. [Commission of the European Communities, June 1987.]

This must include continuous in-depth research of evolving user requirements for the new services, taking fully into account broader trends in economic activity, in the transformation of life-styles and in the social concerns of the European citizen.

A vital contribution which can be made at Community level towards evolving this consensus should be the launching of joint analysis and study, in order to lay a better factual basis of knowledge, increase the perception of developments in the other Member States, prepare informed debate and facilitate discussions and negotiations between the social partners. [Commission of the European Communities, June 1987.]

4.3 THE GREENE COURT'S FRAGMENTED UNITED STATES

We summarize below the contents of this section.

4.3.1—The *Modification of Final Judgment* (MFJ), also referred to as "Modified Final Judgment," is reproduced without editing or omissions, as it became effective on September 13, 1982. Divestiture of the Bell System's Operating Companies and attendant reorganization of other parts of AT&T began on this date. The official entering into operational force was set for January 1, 1984. Several of Judge Greene's restrictions that remain under his oversight are open to review after seven years, i.e., as of September 1989.

4.3.2—Judge Greene's *Opinion*, preceded the MFJ by one month, and provides a reasoned catalog of the court's considerations; it is here represented by its introduction and a detailed contents, specially prepared for this book.

4.3.3—"Regulatory Developments in the U.S." Reproduced is Appendix to the EC Green Paper of 1987.

4.3.4—Twenty-five Years of FCC's Rule-Making to Open Up AT&T's Monopoly. A one-page summary is presented with key title references.

4.3.1 Modification of Final Judgment (MFJ)

First published in *Federal Register* on September 13, 1982, subsequently cited as 552 F. Supp. 131 (1982).

MODIFICATION OF FINAL JUDGMENT

Plaintiff, United States of America, having filed its complaint herein on January 14, 1949; the defendants having appeared and filed their answer to such complaint denying the substantive allegations thereof; the parties, by their attorneys, having severally consented to a Final Judgment which was entered by the Court on January 24, 1956, and the parties having subsequently agreed that modification of such Final Judgment is required by the technological, economic and regulatory changes which have occurred since the entry of such Final Judgment;

Upon joint motion of the parties and after hearing by the Court, it is hereby

ORDERED, ADJUDGED, AND DECREED that the Final Judgment entered on January 24, 1956, is hereby vacated in its entirety and replaced by the following items and provisions:

I

AT & T Reorganization

A. Not later than six months after the effective date of this Modification of Final Judgment, defendant AT & T shall submit to the Department of Justice for its approval, and thereafter implement, a plan of reorganization. Such plan shall provide for the completion, within 18 months after the effective date of this Modification of Final Judgment, of the following steps:

1. The transfer from AT & T and its affiliates to the BOCs, or to a new entity subsequently to be separated from AT & T and to be owned by the BOCs, of sufficient facilities, personnel, systems, and rights to technical information to permit the BOCs to perform, independently of AT & T, exchange telecommunications and exchange access functions, including the procurement for, and engineering, marketing and management of, those functions, and sufficient to enable the BOCs to meet the equal exchange access requirements of Appendix B;

2. The separation within the BOCs of all facilities, personnel and books of account between those relating to the exchange telecommunications or exchange access functions and those relating to other functions (including the provision of interexchange switching and transmission and the provision of customer premises equipment to the public); provided that there shall be no joint ownership of facilities, but appropriate provision may be made for sharing, through leasing or otherwise, of multifunction facilities so long as the separated portion of each BOC is ensured control over the exchange telecommunications and exchange access functions;

3. The termination of the License Contracts between AT & T and the BOCs and other subsidiaries and the Standard Supply Contract between Western Electric and the BOCs and other subsidiaries; and

4. The transfer of ownership of the separated portions of the BOCs providing local exchange and exchange access services from AT & T by means of a spin-off of stock of the separated BOCs to the shareholders of AT & T, or by other disposition; provided that nothing in this Modification of Final Judgment shall require or prohibit the consolidation of the ownership of the BOCs into any particular number of entities.

B. Notwithstanding separation of ownership, the BOCs may support and share the costs of a centralized organization for the provision of engineering, administrative and other services which can most efficiently be provided on a centralized basis. The BOCs shall provide, through a centralized organization, a single point of contact for coordination of BOCs to meet the requirements of national security and emergency preparedness.

C. Until September 1, 1987, AT & T, Western Electric, and the Bell Telephone Laboratories, shall, upon order of any BOC, provide on a priority basis all research, development, manufacturing, and other support services to enable the BOCs to fulfill the requirements of this Modification of Final Judgment. AT & T and its affiliates shall take no action that interferes with the BOCs' requirements of nondiscrimination established by section II.

D. After the reorganization specified in paragraph I(A)(4), AT & T shall not acquire the stock or assets of any BOC.

II
BOC Requirements

A. Subject to Appendix B, each BOC shall provide to all interexchange carriers and information service providers exchange access, information access, and exchange services for such access on an unbundled, tariffed basis, that is equal in type, quality, and price to that provided to AT & T and its affiliates.

B. No BOC shall discriminate between AT & T and its affiliates and their products and services and other persons and their products and services in the:

1. procurement of products and services;

2. establishment and dissemination of technical information and procurement and interconnection standards;

3. interconnection and use of the BOC's telecommunications service and facilities or in the charges for each element of service; and

4. provision of new services and the planning for and implementation of the construction or modification of facilities, used to provide exchange access and information access.

C. Within six months after the reorganization specified in paragraph I(A)(4), each BOC shall submit to the Department of Justice procedures for ensuring compliance with the requirements of paragraph B.

D. After completion of the reorganization specified in section I, no BOC shall, directly or through any affiliated enterprise:

1. provide interexchange telecommunications services or information services;

2. manufacture or provide telecommunications products or customer premises equipment (except for provision of customer premises equipment for emergency services); or

3. provide any other product or service, except exchange telecommunications and exchange access service, that is not a natural monopoly service actually regulated by tariff.

III

Applicability and Effect

The provisions of this Modification of Final Judgment, applicable to each defendant and each BOC, shall be binding upon said defendants and BOCs, their affiliates, successors and assigns, officers, agents, servants, employees, and attorneys, and upon those persons in active concert or participation with each defendant and BOC who receive actual notice of this Modification of Final Judgment by personal service or otherwise. Each defendant and each person bound by the prior sentence shall cooperate in ensuring that the provisions of this Modification of Final Judgment are carried out. Neither this Modification of Final Judgment nor any of its terms or provisions shall constitute any evidence against, an admission by, or an estoppel against any party or BOC. The effective date of this Modification of Final Judgment shall be the date upon which it is entered.

IV

Definitions

For the purposes of this Modification of Final Judgment:

A. "Affiliate" means any organization or entity, including defendant Western Electric Company, Incorporated, and Bell Telephone Laboratories, Incorporated, that is under direct or indirect common ownership with or control by AT & T or is owned or controlled by another affiliate. For the purposes of this paragraph, the terms "ownership" and "owned" mean a direct or indirect equity interest (or the equivalent thereof) of more than fifty (50) percent of an entity. "Subsidiary" means any organization or entity in which AT & T has stock ownership, whether or not controlled by AT & T.

B. "AT & T" shall mean defendant American Telephone and Telegraph Company and its affiliates.

C. "Bell Operating Companies" and "BOCs" mean the corporations listed in Appendix A attached to this Modification of Final Judgment and any entity directly or indirectly owned or controlled by a BOC or affiliated through substantial common ownership.

D. "Carrier" means any person deemed a carrier under the Communications Act of 1934 or amendments thereto, or, with respect to intrastate telecommunications, under the laws of any State.

E. "Customer premises equipment" means equipment employed on the premises of a person (other than a carrier) to originate, route, or terminate telecommunications, but does not include equipment used to multiplex, maintain, or terminate access lines.

F. "Exchange access" means the provision of exchange services for the purpose of originating or terminating interexchange telecommunications. Exchange access services include any activity or function performed by a BOC in connection with the origination or termination of interexchange telecommunications, including but not limited to, the provision of network control signalling, answer supervision, automatic calling number identification, carrier access codes, directory services, testing and maintenance of facilities and the provision of information necessary to bill customers. Such services shall be provided by facilities in an exchange area for the transmission, switching, or routing, within the exchange area, of interexchange traffic originating or terminating within the exchange area, and shall include switching traffic within the exchange area above the end office and delivery and receipt of such traffic at a point or points within an exchange area designated by an interexchange carrier for the connection of its facilities with those of the BOC. Such connections, at the option of the interexchange carrier, shall deliver traffic with signal quality and characteristics equal to that provided similar traffic of

AT & T, including equal probability of blocking, based on reasonable traffic estimates supplied by each interexchange carrier. Exchange services for exchange access shall not include the performance by any BOC of interexchange traffic routing for any interexchange carrier. In the reorganization specified in section I, trunks used to transmit AT & T's traffic between end offices and class 4 switches shall be exchange access facilities to be owned by the BOCs.

G. "Exchange area," or "exchange" means a geographic area established by a BOC in accordance with the following criteria:

1. any such area shall encompass one or more contiguous local exchange areas serving common social, economic, and other purposes, even where such configuration transcends municipal or other local governmental boundaries;

2. every point served by a BOC within a State shall be included within an exchange area;

3. no such area which includes part or all of one standard metropolitan statistical area (or a consolidated statistical area, in the case of densely populated States) shall include a substantial part of any other standard metropolitan statistical area (or a consolidated statistical area, in the case of densely populated States), unless the Court shall otherwise allow; and

4. except with approval of the Court, no exchange area located in one State shall include any point located within another State.

H. "Information" means knowledge or intelligence represented by any form of writing, signs, signals, pictures, sounds, or other symbols.

I. "Information access" means the provision of specialized exchange telecommunications services by a BOC in an exchange area in connection with the origination, termination, transmission, switching, forwarding or routing of telecommunications traffic to or from the facilities of a provider of information services. Such specialized exchange telecommunications services include, where necessary, the provision of network

control signalling, answer supervision, automatic calling number identification, carrier access codes, testing and maintenance of facilities, and the provision of information necessary to bill customers.

J. "Information service" means the offering of a capability for generating, acquiring, storing, transforming, processing, retrieving, utilizing, or making available information which may be conveyed via telecommunications, except that such service does not include any use of any such capability for the management, control, or operation of a telecommunications system or the management of a telecommunications service.

K. "Interexchange telecommunications" means telecommunications between a point or points located in one exchange telecommunications area and a point or points located in one or more other exchange areas or a point outside an exchange area.

L. "Technical information" means intellectual property of all types, including, without limitation, patents, copyrights, and trade secrets, relating to planning documents, designs, specifications, standards, and practices and procedures, including employee training.

N. "Telecommunications equipment" means equipment, other than customer premises equipment, used by a carrier to provide telecommunications services.

O. "Telecommunications" means the transmission, between or among points specified by the user, of information of the user's choosing, without change in the form or content of the information as sent and received, by means of electromagnetic transmission medium, including all instrumentalities, facilities, apparatus, and services (including the collection, storage, forwarding, switching, and delivery of such information) essential to such transmission.

P. "Telecommunications service" means the offering for hire of telecommunications facilities, or of telecommunications by means of such facilities.

Q. "Transmission facilities" means equipment (including without limitation wire, cable, microwave, satellite, and fibre-optics) that transmit information by electromagnetic means or which directly support such transmission, but does not include customer premises equipment.

V

Compliance Provisions

The defendants, each BOC, and affiliated entities are ordered and directed to advise their officers and other management personnel with significant responsibility for matters addressed in this Modification of Final Judgment of their obligations hereunder. Each BOC shall undertake the following with respect to each such officer or management employee:

1. The distribution to them of a written directive setting forth their employer's policy regarding compliance with the Sherman Act and with this Modification of Final Judgment, with such directive to include:

(a) an admonition that non-compliance with such policy and this Modification of Final Judgment will result in appropriate disciplinary action determined by their employer and which may include dismissal; and

(b) advice that the BOCs' legal advisors are available at all reasonable times to confer with such persons regarding any compliance questions or problems;

2. The imposition of a requirement that each of them sign and submit to their employer a certificate in substantially the following form:

The undersigned hereby (1) acknowledges receipt of a copy of the 1982 *United States v. Western Electric* Modification of Final Judgment and a written directive setting forth Company policy regarding compliance with the antitrust laws and with such Modification of Final Judgment, (2) represents that the undersigned has read such Modification of Final Judgment and directive and understands those provisions for which the undersigned has responsibility, (3) acknowledges that the undersigned has been advised and

understands that non-compliance with such policy and Modification of Final Judgment will result in appropriate disciplinary measures determined by the Company and which may include dismissal, and (4) acknowledges that the undersigned has been advised and understands that non-compliance with the Modification of Final Judgment may also result in conviction for contempt of court and imprisonment and/or fine.

VI

Visitorial Provisions

A. For the purpose of determining or securing compliance with this Modification of Final Judgment, and subject to any legally recognized privilege, from time to time:

1. Upon written request of the Attorney General or of the Assistant Attorney General in charge of the Antitrust Division, and on reasonable notice to a defendant or after the reorganization specified in section I, a BOC, made to its principal office, duly authorized representatives of the Department of Justice shall be permitted access during office hours of such defendants or BOCs to depose or interview officers, employees, or agents, and inspect and copy all books, ledgers, accounts, correspondence, memoranda and other records and documents in the possession or under the control of such defendant, BOC, or subsidiary companies, who may have counsel present, relating to any matters contained in this Modification of Final Judgment; and

2. Upon the written request of the Attorney General or of the Assistant Attorney General in charge of the Antitrust Division made to a defendant's principal office or, after the reorganization specified in section I, a BOC, such defendant, or BOC, shall submit such written reports, under oath if requested, with respect to any of the matters contained in this Modification of Final Judgment as may be requested.

B. No information or documents obtained by the means provided in this section shall be divulged by any representative of the Department of Justice to any person other than a duly authorized representative of the Executive Branch of the United States or the Federal Communications Commission, except in the course of legal proceedings to which the United States is a party, or for the purpose of securing compliance with this Final Judgment, or as otherwise required by law.

C. If at the time information or documents are furnished by a defendant to plaintiff, such defendant or BOC represents and identifies in writing the material in any such information or documents to which a claim of protection may be asserted under Rule 26(c)(7) of the Federal Rules of Civil Procedure, and said defendant or BOC marks each pertinent page of such material, "Subject to claim of protection under Rule 26(c)(7) of the Federal Rules of Civil Procedure," then 10 days' notice shall be given by plaintiff to such defendant or BOC prior to divulging such material in any legal proceeding (other than a grand jury proceeding) to which that defendant or BOC is not a party.

VII

Retention of Jurisdiction

Jurisdiction is retained by this Court for the purpose of enabling any of the parties to this Modification of Final Judgment, or, after the reorganization specified in section I, a BOC to apply to this Court at any time for such further orders or directions as may be necessary or appropriate for the construction or carrying out of this Modification of Final Judgment, for the modification of any of the provisions hereof, for the enforcement of compliance herewith, and for the punishment of any violation hereof.

VIII

Modifications

A. Notwithstanding the provisions of section II(D)(2), the separated BOCs shall be permitted to provide, but not manufacture, customer premises equipment.

B. Notwithstanding the provisions of section II(D)(3), the separated BOCs shall be permitted to produce, publish, and distribute printed directories which contain advertisements and which list general product and business categories, the service or product providers under these categories, and their names, telephone numbers, and addresses.

Notwithstanding the provisions of sections I(A)(1), I(A)(2), I(A)(4), all facilities, personnel, systems, and rights to technical information owned by AT & T, its affiliates, or the BOCs which are necessary for the production, publication, and distribution of printed advertising directories shall be transferred to the separated BOCs.

C. The restrictions imposed upon the separated BOCs by virtue of section II(D) shall be removed upon a showing by the petitioning BOC that there is no substantial possibility that it could use its monopoly power to impede competition in the market it seeks to enter.

D. AT & T shall not engage in electronic publishing over its own transmission facilities. "Electronic publishing" means the provision of any information which AT & T or its affiliates has, or has caused to be, originated, authored, compiled, collected, or edited, or in which it has a direct or indirect financial or proprietary interest, and which is disseminated to an unaffiliated person through some electronic means.

Nothing in this provision precludes AT & T from offering electronic directory services that list general product and business categories, the service or product providers under these categories, and their names, telephone numbers, and addresses; or from providing the time, weather, and such other audio services as are being offered as of the date of the entry of the decree to the geographic areas of the country receiving those services as of that date.

Upon application of AT & T, this restriction shall be removed after seven years from the date of entry of the decree, unless the Court finds that competitive conditions clearly require its extension.

E. If a separated BOC provides billing services to AT & T pursuant to Appendix B(C)(2), it shall include upon the portion of the bill devoted to interexchange services the following legend:

This portion of your bill is provided as a service to AT & T. There is no connection between this company and AT & T. You may choose another company for your long distance telephone calls while still receiving your local telephone service from this company.

F. Notwithstanding the provisions of Appendix B(C)(3), whenever, as permitted by the decree, a separated BOC fails to offer exchange access to an interexchange carrier that is equal in type and quality to that provided for the interexchange traffic of AT & T, the tariffs filed for such less-than-equal access shall reflect the lesser cost, if any, of such access as compared to the exchange access provided AT & T.

G. Facilities and other assets which serve both AT & T and one or more BOCs shall be transferred to the separated BOCs if the use made by such BOC or BOCs predominates over that of AT & T. Upon application by a party or a BOC, the Court may grant an exception to this requirement.

H. At the time of the transfer of ownership provided for in section I(A)(4), the separated BOCs shall have debt ratios of approximately forty-five percent (except for Pacific Telephone and Telegraph Company which shall have a debt ratio of approximately fifty percent), and the quality of the debt shall be representative of the average terms and conditions of the consolidated debt held by AT & T, its affiliates and the BOCs at that time. Upon application by a party or a BOC, the Court may grant an exception to this requirement.

I. The Court may act *sua sponte* to issue orders or directions for the construction or carrying out of this decree, for the enforcement of compliance therewith, and for the punishment of any violation thereof.

J. Notwithstanding the provisions of section I(A), the plan of reorganization shall not be implemented until approved by the Court as being consistent with the provisions and principles of the decree.

APPENDIX A

Bell Telephone Company of Nevada

Illinois Bell Telephone Company

Indiana Bell Telephone Company, Incorporated

Michigan Bell Telephone Company

New England Telephone and Telegraph Company

New Jersey Bell Telephone Company

New York Telephone Company

Northwestern Bell Telephone Company

Pacific Northwest Bell Telephone Company

South Central Bell Telephone Company

Southern Bell Telephone and Telegraph Company

Southwestern Bell Telephone Company

The Bell Telephone Company of Pennsylvania

The Chesapeake and Potomac Telephone Company

The Chesapeake and Potomac Telephone Company of Maryland

The Chesapeake and Potomac Telephone Company of Virginia

The Chesapeake and Potomac Telephone Company of West Virginia

The Diamond State Telephone Company

The Mountain States Telephone and Telegraph Company

The Ohio Bell Telephone Company

The Pacific Telephone and Telegraph Company

Wisconsin Telephone Company

APPENDIX B

PHASED-IN BOC PROVISION OF EQUAL EXCHANGE ACCESS

A. 1. As part of its obligation to provide non-discriminatory access to interexchange carriers, no later than September 1, 1984, each BOC shall begin to offer to all

APPENDIX B—Continued

interexchange carriers exchange access on an unbundled, tariffed basis, that is equal in type and quality to that provided for the interexchange telecommunications services of AT & T and its affiliates. No later than September 1, 1985, such equal access shall be offered through end offices of each BOC serving at least one-third of that BOC's exchange access lines and, upon bona fide request, every end office shall offer such access by September 1, 1986. Nothing in this Modification of Final Judgment shall be construed to permit a BOC to refuse to provide to any interexchange carrier or information service provider, upon bona fide request, exchange or information access superior or inferior in type or quality to that provided for AT & T's interexchange services or information services at charges reflecting the reduced or increased cost of such access.

2. (i) Notwithstanding paragraph (1), in those instances in which a BOC is providing exchange access for Message Telecommunications Service on the effective date of this Modification of Final Judgment through access codes that do not permit the designation of more than one interexchange carrier, then, in accordance with the schedule set out in paragraph (1), exchange access for additional carriers shall be provided through access codes containing the minimum number of digits necessary at the time access is sought to permit nationwide, multiple carrier designation for the number of interexchange carriers reasonably expected to require such designation in the immediate future.

(ii) Each BOC shall, in accordance with the schedule set out in paragraph (1), offer as a tariffed service exchange access that permits each subscriber automatically to route, without the use of access codes, all the subscriber's interexchange communications to the interexchange carrier of the customer's designation.

(iii) At such time as the national numbering area (area code) plan is revised to require the use of additional digits, each BOC shall provide exchange access to every interexchange carrier, including AT & T, through a uniform number of digits.

3. Notwithstanding paragraphs (1) and (2), with respect to access provided through an end office employing switches technologically antecedent to electronic, stored program control switches or those offices served by switches that characteristically serve fewer than 10,000 access lines, a BOC may not be required to provide equal access through a switch if, upon complaint being made to the Court, the BOC carries the burden of showing that for particular categories of services such access is not physically feasible except at costs that clearly outweigh potential benefits to users of telecommunications services. Any such denial of access under the preceding sentence shall be for the minimum divergence in access necessary, and for the minimum time necessary, to achieve such feasibility.

B. 1. The BOCs are ordered and directed to file, to become effective on the effective date of the reorganization described in paragraph I(A)(4), tariffs for the provision of exchange access including the provision by each BOC of exchange access for AT & T's interexchange telecommunications. Such tariffs shall provide unbundled schedules of charges for exchange access and shall not discriminate against any carrier or other customer. Such tariffs shall replace the division of revenues process used to allocate revenues to a BOC for exchange access provided for the interexchange telecommunications of BOCs or AT & T.

2. Each tariff for exchange access shall be filed on an unbundled basis specifying each type of service, element by element, and no tariff shall require an interexchange carrier to pay for types of exchange access that it does not utilize. The charges for each type of exchange access shall be cost justified and any differences in charges to carriers shall be cost justified on the basis of differences in services provided.

3. Notwithstanding the requirements of paragraph (2), from the date of reorganization specified in section I until September 1, 1991, the charges for delivery or receipt of traffic of the same type between end offices and facilities of interexchange carriers

APPENDIX B—Continued

within an exchange area, or within reasonable subzones of an exchange area, shall be equal, per unit of traffic delivered or received, for all interexchange carriers; provided, that the facilities of any interexchange carrier within five miles of an AT & T class 4 switch shall, with respect to end offices served by such class 4 switch, be considered to be in the same subzone as such class 4 switch.

4. Each BOC offering exchange access as part of a joint or through service shall offer to make exchange access available to all interexchange carriers on the same terms and conditions, and at the same charges, as are provided as part of a joint or through service, and no payment or consideration of any kind shall be retained by the BOC for the provision of exchange access under such joint or through service other than through tariffs filed pursuant to this paragraph.

C. 1. Nothing in this Modification of Final Judgment shall be construed to require a BOC to allow joint ownership or use of its switches, or to require a BOC to allow co-location in its building of the equipment of other carriers. When a BOC uses facilities that (i) are employed to provide exchange telecommunications or exchange access or both, and (ii) are also used for the transmission or switching of interexchange telecommunications, then the costs of such latter use shall be allocated to the interexchange use and shall be excluded from the costs underlying the determination of charges for either of the former uses.

2. Nothing in this Modification of Final Judgment shall either require a BOC to bill customers for the interexchange services of any interexchange carrier or preclude a BOC from billing its customers for the interexchange services of any interexchange carrier it designates, provided that when a BOC does provide billing services to an interexchange carrier, the BOC may not discontinue local exchange service to any customer because of nonpayment of interexchange charges unless it offers to provide billing services to all interexchange carriers, and provided further that the BOC's cost of any such billing shall be included in its tariffed access charges to that interexchange carrier.

3. Whenever, as permitted by this Modification of Final Judgment, a BOC fails to offer exchange access to an interexchange carrier that is equal in type and quality to that provided for the interexchange traffic of AT & T, nothing in this Modification of Final Judgment shall prohibit the BOC from collecting reduced charges for such less-than-equal exchange access to reflect the lesser value of such exchange access to the interexchange carrier and its customers compared to the exchange access provided AT & T.

Editorial Note

In the definitive publication cited, i.e., *552 F. Supp. 131 (1982),* the MFJ is preceded by a lengthy document of Judge Greene's Court, titled *Opinion.* It occupies the first 95 pages in the cited publication. While full-length inclusion here would be beyond the scope of this book, the reader should be made aware of the breadth and depth of the judicial inquiry that justified the court's action of unprecedented results for a primary infrastructure industry.

The following few pages reproduce the *Opinion*'s opening statement, directly taken from court transcript dated August 11, 1982. This is followed by a detailed

Contents, specially prepared for this book, as culled from the *Opinion*'s subdivided paragraph headings, spread over 178 pages of court transcript.

4.3.2 Judge Greene's "Opinion," Preparatory for the MFJ

UNITED STATES DISTRICT COURT
FOR THE DISTRICT OF COLUMBIA

UNITED STATES OF AMERICA, Plaintiff, v. AMERICAN TELEPHONE AND TELEGRAPH COMPANY; WESTERN ELECTRIC COMPANY, INC.; AND BELL TELEPHONE LABORATORIES, INC., Defendants.	Civil Action No. 74-1698 **F.ILED** AUG 1 1 1982 JAMES F. DAVEY, Clerk
UNITED STATES OF AMERICA, Plaintiff, v. WESTERN ELECTRIC COMPANY, INC., AND AMERICAN TELEPHONE AND TELEGRAPH COMPANY, Defendants.	Civil Action No. 82-0192
UNITED STATES OF AMERICA, Plaintiff, v. AMERICAN TELEPHONE AND TELEGRAPH COMPANY, et al., Defendants.	Misc. No. 82-0025 (PI)

OPINION

These actions are before the Court[1]/ for a determination
whether a consent decree proposed by the parties is in the
"public interest"[2]/ and should therefore be entered as the
Court's judgment. Over six hundred comments from interested
persons, many of them objecting to various aspects of the proposal, have been received, and the Court has considered briefs
submitted by the parties and others, and it has heard extensive
oral argument. This opinion discusses the principal questions
raised by these interested persons, and it embodies the Court's
decision on the appropriateness of the proposed decree under the
Tunney Act's public interest standard.

The opinion is divided into twelve parts. Part I relates
the history of the litigation and the terms of the proposed
decree. The next two sections contain analyses of two underlying
legal issues -- the standard of review to be applied by the Court
under the Tunney Act (Part II) and the relationship between the
decree and state regulation (Part III). The following section
(Part IV) considers the question whether the divestiture of the

---

1/   A number of prior opinions of this Court deal with earlier
phases of these cases. The principal opinions in that category
are reported at 461 F. Supp. 1314 (D.D.C. 1978) and 524 F. Supp.
1336 (D.D.C. 1981). Other opinions and memoranda may be found at
1982-1 Trade Cas. ¶64,623 (D.D.C. 1982); 1982-1 Trade Cas.
¶64,522 (D.D.C. 1982); 1982-1 Trade Cas. ¶64,521 (D.D.C. 1982);
1982-1 Trade Cas. ¶64,476 (D.D.C. 1982); 1982-1 Trade Cas.
¶64,465 (D.D.C. 1982); 524 F. Supp. 1381 (D.D.C. 1981); 524
F. Supp. 1331 (D.D.C. 1981); 1981-2 Trade Cas. ¶64,203 (D.D.C.
1981); 516 F. Supp. 1237 (D.D.C. 1981); 1981-1 Trade Cas. ¶63,987
(D.D.C. 1981); 1981-1 Trade Cas. ¶63,938 (D.D.C. 1981); 1980-81
Trade Cas. ¶63,711 (D.D.C. 1981); 1980-81 Trade Cas. ¶63,705
(D.D.C. 1981); 1980-81 Trade Cas. ¶63,696 (D.D.C. 1980); 88
F.R.D. 47 (D.D.C. 1980); 498 F. Supp. 353 (D.D.C. 1980); 86
F.R.D. 603 (D.D.C. 1980); 1980-1 Trade Cas. ¶63,244 (D.D.C.
1980); 84 F.R.D. 350 (D.D.C. 1979); 83 F.R.D. 323 (D.D.C. 1979);
and 86 F.R.D. 603 (D.D.C. 1979).

2/   Antitrust Procedures and Penalties Act, 15 U.S.C. §§ 16(b)-
(h) (hereinafter referred to as the Tunney Act). See Part I(C)
and II *infra*. The statute was sponsored by Senator Tunney of
California.

local Operating Companies is in the public interest. Two sections discuss the removal of restrictions from AT&T -- Section V
as a general matter, and Section VI in the context of the provision of information and of electronic publishing services. The
next two sections directly relate to the Operating Companies:
Section VII considers whether the proposed limitations on
Operating Company activities are in the public interest and
Section VIII whether the decree makes adequate provision for
access by intercity carriers to Operating Company networks. Part
IX discusses the issues arising from the division of assets
between AT&T and the Operating Companies; Part X considers
special issues and provisions; and Part XI deals with problems of
implementation and enforcement. Part XII contains the Court's
summary and conclusion.

Box 4.4

CONTENTS
of the Opinion released on August 11, 1982

PART | TITLE

I (A) History of the Litigation
   (B) Terms of Proposed Decree
   (C) Procedures Connected with the Settlement

II   Powers of the Court in this Public Interest Proceeding
   (A) Purpose of the Tunney Act
   (B) Factors to be Considered
   (C) Degree of Deference to the Proposals Submitted
        by Parties

III   Conflict Between the Proposed Decree and State
         Regulation
   (A) General
   (B) Parker vs. Brown
   (C) Avoidance of Unnecessary Conflict with State Law

IV   The Divestiture
   (A) Conditions Necessitating Antitrust Relief
   (B) Effect of Divestiture
   (C) Alternative Remedies
   (D) Effect of Divestiture Upon Other Interests

Box 4.4 (continued)

PART		TITLE
V		Absence of Restrictions on AT&T
	(A)	AT&T Power in the Interexchange Market
	(B)	Interexchange Restrictions
	(C)	Equipment Restrictions
	(D)	Bypass
	(E)	Patent Licensing Requirements
VI		The 1956 Decree and Line of Business Restrictions
	(A)	Data Processing and Other Computer-Related Services
	(B)	Electronic Publishing Services
VII		Restrictions on the Divested Operating Companies
	(A)	Interexchange Service
	(B)	Information Services
	(C)	Manufacture of Equipment
	(D)	Marketing of Customer Premises Equipment
	(E)	Directory Advertising
	(F)	Removal of the Restrictions
VIII		Equal Exchange Access
	(A)	General Principles
	(B)	Exceptions to Equality
IX		Division of Assets
	(A)	Compensation and Transfer of Assets
	(B)	Book Value vs. Market Value
	(C)	Division of Assets and Debts
X		Special Provisions and Concerns
	(A)	Department of Defense Concerns
	(B)	Interests of AT&T Employees
	(C)	Prima Facie Effect of the Decree in Private Litigation
	(D)	Conflict with Federal Regulation
	(E)	Cincinatti Bell
XI		Future Proceedings
	(A)	Deferral of Approval of the Judgment
	(B)	The Court's Continuing Enforcement Authority
	(C)	Status of Third Parties
	(D)	Participation of the Bell Operating Companies
XII		Conclusion

4.3.3 The EC's View of the Situation in the United States (1987)

The perceptive report on the US regulatory situation was prepared by the EC Commission. It appeared as an Appendix to the *Green Paper*. A more informative yet still concise report on the complex regulatory climate that led up to the AT&T divestiture and its aftermath would be difficult to find.

REGULATORY DEVELOPMENTS IN THE US

The "deregulation" process of US telecommunications over the last 25 years has been one of the dominating influences on the world's telecommunications market.

In 1986, an EC fact finding mission reported on the current state of developments in the United States [*Report on the Fact-Finding Mission to the United States,* June 16–27, 1986, Commission of the European Communities]. While this mission investigated a wide range of topics, including existing barriers to European manufacturers on the US market, hereunder only regulatory developments are presented.

I *HISTORY*

Major steps in the developments of US telecommunications have been:

1934: Communications Act. Creation of the Federal Communications Commission (FCC) as the main regulatory agency. The Act determines the legal framework of telecommunications in the United States to this date.

1956: Consent Decree, United States *v.* Western Electric Company, District Court of New Jersey. Following an initial intervention by the Department of Justice, under the Sherman Anti-Trust Act, AT&T was limited to regulated services (mainly the telephone). Its manufacturing subsidiary (Western Electric) was now to work only for the Bell System, a subsidiary of AT&T operating over 90% of the American network.

1959: Above 890 decision, Report and Order 27 FCC 359. The FCC allowed the construction of private networks using micro-wave radio.

1968: Carterfone, 13 FCC 2d 420. The FCC ruled that the Bell system should, in principle, allow equipment not produced by AT&T to be connected to its networks.

1971: Specialised Common Carrier Decision, First Report and Order, 29 FCC 2d 870. A general licence was granted to specialised common carriers, which allowed them to offer switched telecommunications services, connected directly to the existing network of local telephone exchanges, and a large number of such carriers were formed. This was the first step towards developing competition within the network.

1971: Computer Inquiry I, Final Decision and Order 29 FCC 2d 261. After a five year investigation on the increasing interdependence of information and telecommunications technologies, the FCC decided that the integrated office automation systems market should become subject to competition. AT&T, as the regulated operator, was to be allowed to supply these types of services only through a subsidiary separate from its regulated activities.

1976: Equipment Registration Programme, Interstate and Foreign Message Toll Telephone, First Report and Order, 56 FCC 2d 593. The FCC develops procedures to facilitate the opening up of markets for terminals (simplified certification procedures for terminal equipment).

1980: Computer Inquiry II, Final Decision 77 FCC 2d 384. In the light of the convergence between information technology and telecommunications, the FCC updates its 1971 decision. It abandons the earlier distinction between telecommunications and computer services and introduces one between "basic services" and "enhanced services." It deregulates terminal equipment but allows AT&T to enter deregulated markets through an independent subsidiary: "AT&T Information Systems." The separation requirements are known as "structural safeguards."

1982: Modified Final Judgement (MFJ), United States *v*. AT&T, District Court for the District of Columbia. Orders the splitting off of the Bell system regional networks which then represented 77% of the US $150 [billion] of AT&T's capital assets and approximately 50% of its revenue. The new AT&T keeps the long-distance services of the Bell System (under the name "AT&T Communications") and of Western Electric and Bell Laboratories (under the name "AT&T Technologies"). The long-distance network is opened to competition whereas the regional networks remain regulated.

1984: AT&T Divestiture. On 1 January 1984. AT&T divests itself of 22 Bell Operating Companies (*BOCs*). These 22 companies then form themselves into the present structure of 7 Regional Holding Companies (*RHCs*). These RHCs are often referred to by the old name of "BOCs."

The MFJ also imposed restrictions on the business lines that both the divested AT&T and the newly formed RHCs could enter. Thus, AT&T was prevented from providing electronic publishing services (for a period of 7 years) while the RHCs were prevented from providing inter-exchange services, from offering information services and from manufacturing telecommunications equipment.

Generally, the MFJ imposed "*structural separation requirements*" for provision by BOCs or AT&T of competitive "enhanced" services (these services were to be offered through separate subsidiaries).

The MFJ also imposed a requirement on the BOC's to provide "equal access" arrangements to all long distance carriers.

Subsequent to the MFJ, a large number of exceptions ("waivers") to the imposed restrictions were conceded by the District Court of Columbia on a case-by-case basis, in order to allow for practical requirements.

The instability of the regulatory regime thus demonstrated finally led to the FCC's Computer Inquiry III, provisionally concluded in July 1986 [*Third Computer Inquiry,* Report and Order, FCC 86 252]. Computer III replaced the concepts of "structural safeguards" in order to allow the BOCs to offer of integrated services. For this purpose it introduced the concepts of Comparably Efficient Interconnection (CEI) and Open Network Architecture (ONA). (See below).

In February 1987, the *Department of Justice* filed with the District Court of Columbia its *first triennial report and recommendations on the MFJ* which recommended further lifting of restrictions on AT&T and the BOCs.

At this stage, the regulatory situation in the US seems therefore to be *in full flux* and still not stabilised.

II CURRENT SITUATION

1. Regulatory Bodies

Federal Communications Commission: The main regulatory body remains the Federal Communications Commission (FCC). The FCC was created by the Communications Act which gave the FCC regulatory power over all interstate and international ("foreign") communications by "wire or radio." In practice, the FCC regulatory authority is split into three parts dealing with common carriers, broadcasting and cable TV.

The Communications Act directs the FCC to exercise its regulatory authority over interstate (within the US) and foreign telecommunications:

"so as to make available, so far as possible, to all the people of the United States a rapid, efficient, nation-wide, and world-wide wire and radio communication service with adequate facilities at reasonable charges, for the purpose of the national defense, (and) for the purpose of promoting the safety of life and property . . ."

The FCC adds to these objectives the goal of "universal service" derived from the broad wording of the Act.

The role of the FCC has been fundamental in nearly every telecommunications regulation decision in the US and it continues to regulate all interstate and international communications. It also has great influence over intra-state developments within the US.

The FCC continues to regulate AT&T.

State Regulatory Agencies: The individual Bell Operating Companies of the seven Regional Holding Companies are subject to the regulatory authority of the state utility commissions which are responsible for intra-state communication. The BOCs continue to be strictly regulated.

Congress: Congress holds the ultimate authority of legislation. It created the FCC and can control (or at least influence) the decisions of the FCC through the imposition of new legislation, through the influence of congress committees and through control of the FCC budget.

Federal Courts: Decisions made by the FCC can be appealed against in the Federal Courts. The court will review an FCC decision based on firstly deciding whether it has operated within its authority and secondly whether it has fairly considered the evidence presented before it.

Since the AT&T divestiture, a special role is played by the District Court of Columbia.

Justice Department and District Court of Columbia: The Justice Department has substantially influenced developments by its anti-trust suits against AT&T and the consent decrees entered in settlement of the anti-trust suits.

The 1982 settlement (MFJ) has made the District Court of Columbia one of the most important factors. The Court continues to oversee the implementation of the MFJ and therefore exercises a continuing strong regulatory influence.

Federal Agencies: A number of Federal Agencies are closely involved in telecommunications policy formulation, in particular regarding trade questions and international relations. This concerns notably the United States Trade Representative (USTR) and the National Telecommunications and Information Administration (NTIA) in the Department of Commerce, and the Department of State respectively.

2. *Telecommunications Operators*

The present situation of telecommunications supply in the US can be summed up as follows:

Local basic services —no competition; subject to strict regulation by the State Utility Commissions. *Bell Operating Companies*

Long distance basic services	—competition permitted; "dominant carriers" (as determined by the FCC) remain subject to strict regulation under the Communications Act. OCCs (Other Common Carriers) are only lightly regulated ("forebearance" by the FCC) *AT&T* remains the dominant long distance carrier, followed by *MCI and GTE-Sprint* (OCCs).
Long distance enhanced services	—unregulated; full resale of capacity including voice permitted. Several hundred resellers existing.
Local enhanced services	—competition permitted; BOCs will now be allowed to enter this field under the CEI and later, ONA arrangements (Computer III).

The US represents a market size which is more than 5 times larger than any of the individual European countries. Bell Operating Companies (RHCs) are of comparable size with the largest of the European Telecommunications Administrations.

3. *Increase of Resources for Standardisation*

The restructuring of the US telecommunications services market has taken place on the basis of the original Bell System which ensured US-wide network integrity according to specifications set by the Bell Laboratories, part of the fully vertically integrated AT&T (Bell Laboratories— Western Electric—Bell System).

The gradual break-up of the system since 1971 (Specialised Common Carrier Decision, *op. cit.*) and particularly after AT&T divestiture led to a number of disruptions of services, but still largely benefited from the basic homogeneity of the Bell System and AT&T technologies.

Subsequent to the difficulties experienced after divestiture (in particular during 1984), there is now a clear trend to strengthen co-operation between the BOCs, AT&T and industry on standardisation. The BOCs have created BELLCORE on a shared basis and with a total staff of 8,000 highly qualified experts (see *Fact-Finding, op. cit.*) for work on standards and technological development (total annual budget of 920 million US$). At the same time, the intra-US co-ordination structure for preparation of standards has been substantially strengthened (Bellcore—Exchange Carrier Standards Association, ECSA—T1 Committee—ANSI). The approach has been very pro-active, with participation from all industry and carriers.

The US input to international standardisation bodies has been substantially stepped up. The input to CCITT (see ANNEX 5) is now tightly coordinated by the Department of State, taking into account technical, regulatory, and political objectives.

4. *Service Definition Problems*

The US is exposed to the same technological change as Europe, i.e., the convergence of telecommunications and computer technology. The instability and re-definition of service boundary lines therefore is a dominating theme of US deregulation to this date. In the US, boundary lines have been the subject of three rulings by the FCC (Computer I, Computer II and Computer III, see above).

The current distinction by the FCC is still based on *Computer II* (as is the MFJ), though *substantial problems of service definition remain unsolved.*

Under Computer II, the FCC currently distinguishes between two classes of communications services—namely basic and enhanced.

Basic communication is defined as:

a pure transmission capability over a communication path that is virtually transparent to customer-supplied information.

Enhanced communication includes any service beyond basic communications; its definition is:

a service which employs computer processing applications

- to perform protocol conversion,
- to provide the subscriber with additional, different, or restructured information, or
- involving subscriber interaction with stored information.

Protocol conversion, the effect of which is merely to facilitate subscriber information transfer, is currently being reassessed under Computer III in the Supplemental Notice of Proposed Rulemaking (adopted May 15, 1986).

Basic local exchange services are currently the most highly regulated area in the US, with the local telephone company holding a near monopoly on the provision of services within each area, and competition only being allowed for services that cross geographic boundaries, i.e., traffic which flows from one so called Local Access Transport Area, or LATA, to another.

For enhanced services, one effect of the Computer III decision is to force the BOCs to provide Comparably Efficient interconnection (CEI) under which the operating companies will have to offer their basic transmission facilities to allow fair competition amongst all enhanced service providers.

5. *Effects on tariffs*

According to the FCC, deregulation of telecommunications services within the US has driven tariffs closer to costs.

One of the results of this has been to cause tariffs for local service to rise (in real terms) while the more profitable long distance and international service tariffs have fallen.

The FCC has imposed some direct controls on the process of shifting of costs from long distance to local by the imposition of "access charges."

The rise of local tariffs is under close scrutiny by the Congress and subject to approval by the State Utility Commissions. Dominant carriers (e.g. AT&T) must file tariffs with the FCC.

According to public statements by the FCC, competition on long-distance basic services has led to a price decline of approximately 30 per cent since the beginning of 1984. Local rates, with the exception of 1984, have generally increased no faster than inflation. However, according to statements by FCC representatives, in Washington, DC, the last set of telephone rate increases ranged from 25 to 50 percent.

6. *Interconnection Issues*

The interconnection arrangements in the US for voice telephony have undergone substantial changes over the last years, following deregulation by the FCC and the AT&T divestiture.

Initially, the OCCs interconnected their long distance networks with the existing monopoly local telephone networks on a customer basis—i.e., they were connected to subscriber-line terminations on the local exchanges.

Problems with this arrangement were in particular,

—the need for the customer to enter a large number of digits (typically about twenty-two) to make a single call, and often to do so in two different formats (decadic pulses and DTMF);

—the lack of automatic identification of the calling subscriber to the OCC (needed for billing purposes) requiring the subscriber to enter an authority code (with the consequent risk of fraud);

—a technical problem of providing an automatic signal indicating the time at which the called subscriber answered the call; and

—a significant probability of an overall call encountering high levels of transmission loss leading to subjectively unacceptable performance.

Under the MFJ, an "Equal Access" plan was adopted. The Equal Access Plan required that the BOCs provide "non discriminating" access on all their local exchanges for all long distance carriers by September 1986 (and to a proportion of their exchanges by earlier dates).

This equal access provided for customer chosen digits. Typically the customer would dial 10XXX to access their chosen long distance carrier. At the same time, answer supervision and automatic called number identification would be provided to the OCCs.

7. *International Repercussions*

The deregulation process in the United States has had a profound influence on countries outside the US (see main part of Green Paper).

Firstly, the FCC now allows enhanced service providers to own and use satellite systems and to own and use submarine cable capacity (either through the provision of private cables such as the proposed private transatlantic cable PTAT-1 or through the purchase of indefeasible right of users (IRUs) in existing cables).

Secondly it permits (and in many ways encourages) enhanced service providers offering international services to become Recognised Private Operating Agencies (RPOAs).

Thirdly, the FCC takes a more aggressive stance towards international services (see *Regulatory Policies and International Telecommunications*, Notice of Inquiry and Proposed Rulemaking, FCC 86-563, 30th January 1987). FCC and the Justice Department seem to encourage new US entries into the international scene (OCCs, RHCs, private satellite operators).

III *COMPUTER III—COMPARABLY EFFICIENT INTERCONNECTION (CEI)—OPEN NETWORK ARCHITECTURE (ONA)*

1. *Computer III—FCC Objectives for the Enhanced Services Market*

In spite of continuing classification problems, due to the trends towards integration of services and the resulting blurring of boundary lines, the FCC maintained the Computer II classification (basic/enhanced) under Computer III.

While leaving a number of definition issues unresolved. Computer III concentrates on two objectives:

—lifting "structural safeguards" and restrictions from the RHCs and AT&T, in order to allow them integrated services offerings combining basic and enhanced services, with a view to the introduction of ISDN;

—defining the conditions under which the regulated carriers should offer the network infrastructure to competitive enhanced service providers.

2. *Comparably Efficient Interconnection (CEI)*

Computer Inquiry III seeks to replace structural separation by specific requirements for "fair access" by competitors to the basic communications facilities of dominant carriers, which may now offer enhanced services directly.

Structural separation was introduced to counter concern about potential anti-competitive conduct by the dominant carrier, with control over "bottle-neck" local exchange facilities needed by potential competitors.

According to Computer III, the Comparably Efficient Interconnection (CEI) element of Computer III has the twin goals of preventing discrimination and promoting efficiency. It requires carriers to spell out the basic service functions they will offer specifically to support directly competing enhanced communications providers. For the longer term, this commitment is required to take the more general form of an infrastructure for enhanced communications networking—known as Open Network Architecture.

2.1. *Principles of CEI*

CEI seeks to extend the "internal" advantages of the dominant carriers to all enhanced service providers. Thus carriers' enhanced service operations will be free to exploit their basic facilities by locating enhanced functions at switching sites, or employing "trunk-side" interfaces, etc.—provided that comparable facilities are made available to other enhanced communications providers.

The Comparably Efficient Interconnection offered need not be identical, but must be functionally equal and similarly priced. Specifically, the FCC requires that basic service functions utilised by a carrier-provided enhanced service are equally available to others—on an unbundled basis (i.e. individually tariffed), with technical specifications, functional capabilities, quality, and other characteristics (such as installation times and maintenance response) showing no systematic difference from those provided to the carrier's enhanced service.

According to Computer III, examples of the basic service elements anticipated include supervisory signalling, transmission, switching, billing, and network management; as part of a CEI offering a carrier must make available standardised hardware and software interfaces to support the relevant functions, together with related technical information and specifications.

2.2. *Related Competitive Safeguards*

Since Computer Inquiry III is eliminating corporate structural safeguards (separation requirements, i.e. operation via subsidiaries) previously placed on the enhanced communications operations of the dominant carrier organisations, the FCC have specified additional business practice safeguards to accompany the CEI requirements to provide fair access to basic services. The areas addressed are the reporting of non-discriminatory performance, the maintenance of separate accounts for enhanced services (with no cross-subsidy from "monopoly" services), the publication of information on changes in network services, and equal access to customer information arising from the basic carrier network.

Carriers will be required to file quarterly reports with the FCC comparing the service/performance levels provided to their own enhanced service operations with those provided to enhanced service competitors (and their end-customers).

The CEI concept has not had, up to now, tangible effects. AT&T had not filed any CEI plan. By March 1987, only one BOC (Bell South) had filed a CEI plan. A CEI plan is required for each enhanced service to be offered.

3. *Open Network Architecture (ONA)*

3.1. *ONA objectives according to Computer III*

The initial CEI requirements of Computer III call for the filing of CEI plans specific to each proposed new enhanced service offering by a dominant carrier (BOC or AT&T).

In the longer term, the FCC envisages the extension of CEI facilities into a network service infrastructure for enhanced services generally—the *Open Network Architecture* (ONA). Approval of a carrier's ONA plan would obviate the need for repeated CEI approvals of individual enhanced services.

According to Computer III, an Open Network Architecture should reflect the overall design of a carrier's basic network facilities and services to permit all users of the basic network (including the enhanced service operations of the carrier and competitors) to interconnect to specific network functions and interfaces on an unbundled and "equal access" basis. ONA thus should involve a technological implementation which opens service to all vendors and end-users in a manner which makes discrimination by the carrier impossible—and thus is "self-regulating."

ONA must offer "reasonably equivalent" access to competitive enhanced service providers. The FCC has indicated that although it does not wish to restrict technical implementations of ONA, it needs to be satisfied that the general CEI requirements are met. Accordingly it proposes to view more favourably those designs which utilise the same interconnection facilities for the carrier's enhanced service operations as for other enhanced service providers—since the equal functionality and anti-discrimination aspects of such a configuration are more easily evaluated. An ONA design that permits a carrier to integrate its enhanced services within basic service software or hardware, while others' services interconnect in a different manner, must demonstrate nevertheless that CEI requirements are satisfied.

An implementation of ONA is required to provide Basic Service Elements (on a publicly available, unbundled tariff basis) including an initial set of key Basic Service Elements (a range of call control and network supervision primitives as well as connection and transmission functions) that can be used in a wide variety of enhanced services—regardless of whether the carrier's current enhanced service offerings rely on such elements. Any basic element which is incorporated in a carrier's enhanced offering must be provided publicly, and the carrier's enhanced services operations must obtain basic services under the applicable tariffed terms and rates.

3.2. *ONA Planning*

The Computer III ruling requires the dominant carriers (seven BOCs and AT&T) to file Open Network Architecture Plans with the FCC by February 1988.

These plans must demonstrate compliance with CEI and ONA principles and list the initial set of Basic Service Elements to be offered; the ONA facilities must be introduced within one year of the plan's approval.

Subsequently the carrier will not be required to file a service-specific CEI plan prior to any new enhanced service, and will be free from structurally separate subsidiary conditions in providing enhanced services.

However, for any enhanced service which is based on underlying services different from those explained in the approved plan, a carrier must obtain FCC approval for an amendment to the ONA plan to be filed at least 90 days prior to offering the new service.

If any carrier fails to file an ONA plan by February 1988 the FCC intends not to consider any further interim CEI plans from that carrier, effectively suspending its ability to introduce new enhanced services.

It should be noted here that AT&T has clearly stated that it has no intention to file an ONA plan, and has filed a petition for reconsideration with FCC. If the petition is not accepted, AT&T will prefer to provide enhanced services through separate subsidiaries.

IV *RECENT DEVELOPMENTS*

Since January 1987, two further important developments have taken place which could substantially influence future US and international telecommunications development.

In February 1987, the Department of Justice submitted its first triennial report on the implementation of the MFJ (*op. cit.*). In the report, the Justice Department proposes to the District Court of Columbia, to *lift all essential restrictions imposed on the BOCs by the MFJ*. This concerns in particular the provision of information services, inter-exchange (long-distance) traffic and manufacturing of equipment.

Thus, the report largely accepts the conclusions of a major study undertaken for the Department of Justice and made public in the beginning of 1987, which identified the requirement of integrated service offerings (vertical service integration) as a major essential for future telecommunications development [1987 *Report on Competition in the Telephone Industry, The Geodesic Network*, US Department of Justice, Antitrust Division, January 1987]. The report argues that therefore the BOCs should be allowed to offer the full range of services.

If the proposals by the Justice Department are accepted by the Court, this will be a major turning-point in US concepts of telecommunication regulation.

At the same time, the FCC has adopted a Notice of Inquiry and Proposed Rulemaking to examine the interrelationship of the FCC's regulatory policies with the policies of foreign governments [*Regulatory Policies and International Telecommunications*, 30th January 1987, *op. cit.*]

The Notice would establish the US regulatory environment as a virtual bench mark for evaluating the regulatory policies of other countries and for determining the "openness" of foreign markets. For this purpose, the Notice proposes a substantial increase of regulatory control by the FCC on the activities of foreign service providers and manufacturers.

In conclusion, at the beginning of 1987 it seems that US regulatory policies in telecommunications are undergoing substantial change. The trend seems to be moving away from regulation based on service definitions and separation requirements towards allowing the dominant carriers (BOCs and AT&T) freedom for a broad range of activities, in exchange for the definition of clear access conditions under which they will make their facilities and services available to competitors. At the same time, US regulators seem to be becoming more and more concerned with international aspects. [Commission of the European Communities, June 1987.]

4.3.4 Twenty-Five Years of FCC Rule-Making in Review

Between the *Final Judgment* of 1956 and the *MFJ* of 1982, the FCC exerted its regulatory oversight of the telecommunications industry. We can say that the lengthy legal court action and its product, the *MFJ*, are a defeat of the FCC. Because the FCC reports to the United States Congress, the court's drastic solution to the regulatory problems can also be seen as a defeat of Congress's effectiveness in this area of legislation.

Judge Greene's court heard "expert" testimony, confirming a widely held view that the FCC has been ineffective in regulating the giant monopoly of AT&T. Yet the FCC's responsibilities, under the Communications Act of 1934, focus on maintaining an orderly provision of telecommunication services to the public, not on optimizing competitive opportunities for selective users' services. An overriding consideration for the FCC was the objective of "Universal Telephone Service," a policy that encouraged cost averaging so that less affluent subscribers would be served as well as big business accounts.

Against this background, the FCC ventured quite far into what was then uncharted territory of opening up opportunities for new service providers. Landmark cases are the three rulings that, in effect, trimmed AT&T's monopoly in progressive steps. They are colloquially known as: *Carterphone* (1968), *Specialized Common Carriers* (1970), and *Customer Interconnection* (1974).

Excerpts of these FCC decisions are included in the book, The *Telecommunications Deregulation Sourcebook,* edited by Stuart N. Brotman (Artech House, Norwood, MA, 1987).

4.4 USER GROUPS' ORGANIZATIONS

4.4.1 Introduction

The convergence of computer and communication technologies has contributed to the climate of telecommunication reform. Perceptions of potential opportunities for users of novel or expanded classic services have clashed with apparent "foot dragging" on the part of entrenched service providers. A focus on which both service providers and user groups can meet is the urgent need for more pervasive standards. In the business-oriented societies of leading European countries, the fragmented, piecemeal negotiation with each national telecommunication administration for more liberalized access to networks seemed agonizingly slow. Most discouraging has been the recourse to claims of national sovereignty in such decisions, making the chance of international interconnection for novel service applications a distant possibility.

Against this background, some business interests have banded together across European borders, creating organizations for the express purpose of representing users' *transnational standards needs*. In 1974, INTUG (International Telecommunications Users Group) was founded at Brussels; it is now headquartered at London. By 1985, INTUG had achieved recognition by ITU as an important observer status organization, so that ITU and INTUG jointly sponsored an *International Telecommunication User Conference*, at Geneva. This type of conference has since become a biannual event.

The *International Chamber of Commerce* (ICC), from a Paris office, has issued "Policy Statements on Telecommunications and Transborder Data Flow."

Another organization, *EUSIDIC*, appears to have broadened its representation from scientific to more general users of information services. EUSIDIC was founded in 1970 as "European Association of Scientific Information Dissemination Centers." The present name *European Association of Information Services* was adopted in 1977, at a meeting in Berlin (West). EUSIDIC is itself a member of INTUG.

In this section, we present a few, short excerpts from studies, respectively announcements, of these three international user group organizations. We make no attempt to do justice to the detailed work of these organizations; we only call attention to their drive for standards—a drive that has left its mark on CCITT, in particular.

In the United States, large-scale users have generally had less difficulty in seeing their preferences met. However, the advent of ISDN, as documented in Chapter Two, opens very wide angle vistas for users with combinations of telephone, data, visual, and hard copy office services at stake. ISDN is an ideal candidate for close collaboration between potential users and service providers, as well as the manufacturers catering to both. Widespread implementation of ISDN seems to depend on such collaboration, particularly in the harshly competitive market environment of the United States. Service providers' investments are too substantial, and user options too numerous, to encourage self-started, ready-made installations in the manner of cross-country microwave systems, the telephone companies' self-adopted enterprise in the 1950s and 1960s.

Since the founding of INTUG, the organized representation of telecommunication users has been hailed as an enfranchisement of previously ignored partners in standards-setting. However, user groups with special needs have long had representation in the work of ITU's CCIR and CCITT. The following organizations have participated in CCITT Plenary Conferences, with observer status, since 1972 or earlier, except as otherwise noted:

ECMA: European Computer Manufacturers Association
IATA: International Air Transport Association
ICAO: International Civil Aviation Association (1976)
ICC: International Chamber of Commerce
ICS: International Chamber of Shipping (1976)
    International Marine Radio Association (1976)
IPTC: International Press Telecommunication Council
WMO: World Meteorological Organization

These organizations have documented special requirements or criticism of specific CCITT Recommendations, as the case may be, through the same written *Contribution* channels used by regular CCITT members. On occasion, their representatives present at the Plenary Assembly have asked for, and been granted, the right of direct intervention from the meeting floor.

Material descriptive of users' organizations is presented in four short sections, as follows.

4.4.2—INTUG: Announcement of 1989 joint conference with ITU. (See Box 4.5a, b.)

4.4.3—ICC: (International Chamber of Commerce): Front pages of a "Position Paper" (Box 4.6a, b) and a "Report" (Box 4.6c).

4.4.4—EUSIDIC: Survey of Public Data Networks, 1987, front page (Box 4.7a) and first page (Box 4.7b).

4.4.5—North American ISDN Users' Forum (NIU): Charter of February, 1988 (Box 4.8a), followed by two pages of "Objectives" (Box 4.8b) and "Why the National Bureau of Standards" (Box 4.8c).

NIU-FORUM is directed by the Institute for Computer Sciences and Technology of the former National Bureau of Standards (NBS), an agency of the US government under the Department of Commerce, now named the National Institute for Standards and Technology (NIST).

4.4.2 INTUG

Box 4.5(a)
USERCOM 89 Announcement

Box 4.5(b)
USERCOM 89 Agenda

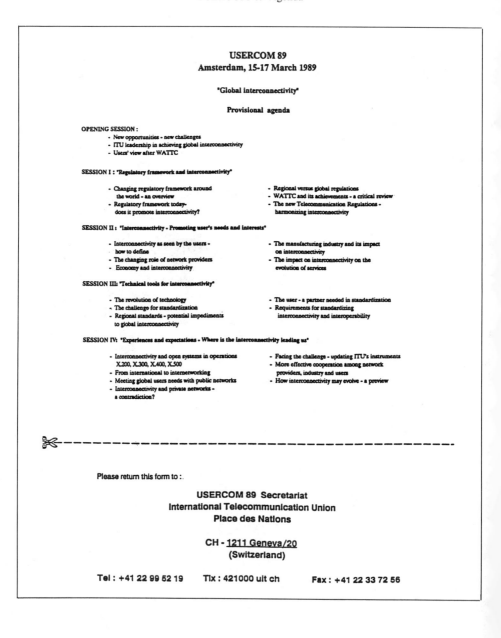

USERCOM 89
Amsterdam, 15-17 March 1989

"Global interconnectivity"

Provisional agenda

OPENING SESSION :
- New opportunities - new challenges
- ITU leadership in achieving global interconnectivity
- Users' view after WATTC

SESSION I : "Regulatory framework and interconnectivity"

- Changing regulatory framework around the world - an overview
- Regulatory framework today- does it promote interconnectivity?

- Regional versus global regulations
- WATTC and its achievements - a critical review
- The new Telecommunication Regulations - harmonizing interconnectivity

SESSION II : "Interconnectivity - Promoting user's needs and interests"

- Interconnectivity as seen by the users - how to define
- The changing role of network providers
- Economy and interconnectivity

- The manufacturing industry and its impact on interconnectivity
- The impact on interconnectivity on the evolution of services

SESSION III: "Technical tools for interconnectivity"

- The revolution of technology
- The challenge for standardization
- Regional standards - potential impediments to global interconnectivity

- The user - a partner needed in standardization
- Requirements for standardizing interconnectivity and interoperability

SESSION IV: "Experiences and expectations - Where is the interconnectivity leading us"

- Interconnectivity and open systems in operations X.200, X.300, X.400, X.500
- From international to internetworking
- Meeting global users needs with public networks
- Interconnectivity and private networks - a contradiction?

- Facing the challenge - updating ITU's instruments
- More effective cooperation among network providers, industry and users
- How interconnectivity may evolve - a preview

✂ -

Please return this form to :.

USERCOM 89 Secretariat
International Telecommunication Union
Place des Nations

CH - <u>1211 Geneva/20</u>
(Switzerland)

Tel : +41 22 99 52 19   Tlx : 421000 uit ch   Fax : +41 22 33 72 56

4.4.3 ICC

ICC POLICY STATEMENTS ON
TELECOMMUNICATIONS AND
TRANSBORDER DATA FLOWS

Position paper N° 2

AN INTERNATIONAL PROGRAMME
FOR HOMOLOGATION/CERTIFICATION OF EQUIPMENT
ATTACHED TO TELECOMMUNICATION NETWORKS

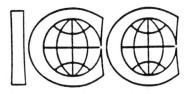

Box 4.6(b)
ICC Position Paper, Contents

CONTENTS

Published in November 1983

The International Chamber of Commerce
38, cours Albert 1er - 75008 Paris - France
Telephone 562 34 56 - Telex 650770

Document N° 373/15 Rev.3

Box 4.6(c)
ICC Report, Title Page

TELECOMMUNICATION STANDARDS

A NEW DIMENSION FOR INTERNATIONAL BUSINESS

Report

Adopted by the Executive Board of the International Chamber of Commerce (ICC) on 2nd December 1986

International Chamber of Commerce
Chambre de Commerce Internationale
38, Cours Albert 1ᵉʳ, 75008 Paris, Tél. 45 62 34 56
Télex 650770, Télégrammes : Incomerc

4.4.4 EUSIDIC

Box 4.7(a)
Survey of Public Data Networks, Title Page

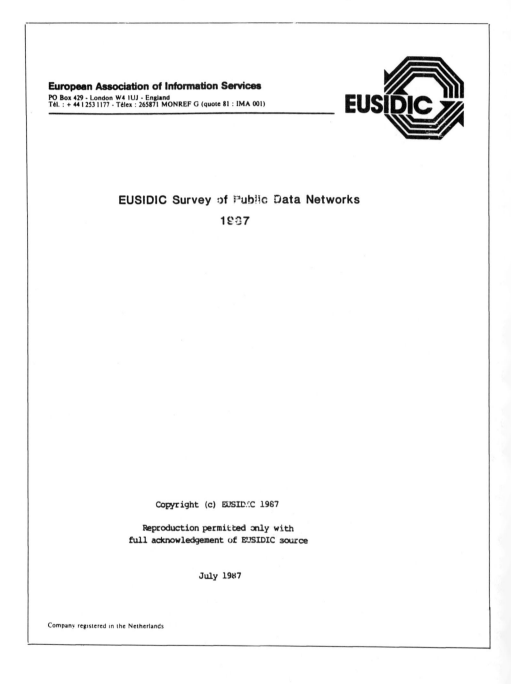

European Association of Information Services
PO Box 429 - London W4 1UJ - England
Tél. : + 44 1 253 1177 - Télex : 265871 MONREF G (quote 81 : IMA 001)

EUSIDIC

EUSIDIC Survey of Public Data Networks

1987

Copyright (c) EUSIDIC 1987

Reproduction permitted only with
full acknowledgement of EUSIDIC source

July 1987

Company registered in the Netherlands

Box 4.7(b)
Survey of Public Data Networks, First Page

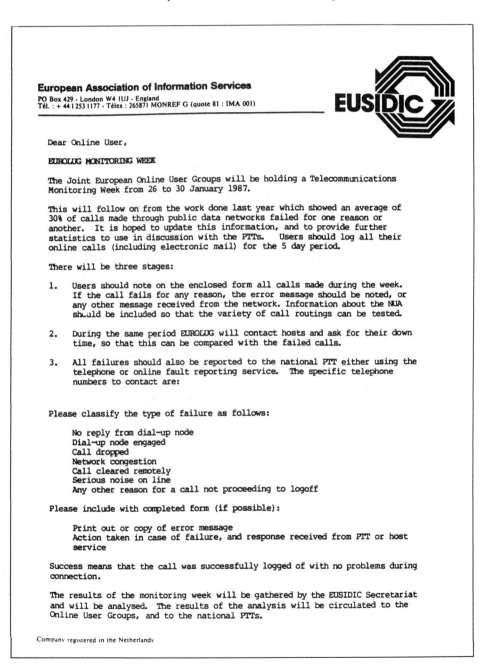

European Association of Information Services
PO Box 429 - London W4 IUJ - England
Tél. : + 44 1 253 1177 - Télex : 265871 MONREF G (quote 81 : IMA 001)

EUSIDIC

Dear Online User,

EUROLUG MONITORING WEEK

The Joint European Online User Groups will be holding a Telecommunications
Monitoring Week from 26 to 30 January 1987.

This will follow on from the work done last year which showed an average of
30% of calls made through public data networks failed for one reason or
another. It is hoped to update this information, and to provide further
statistics to use in discussion with the PTTs. Users should log all their
online calls (including electronic mail) for the 5 day period.

There will be three stages:

1. Users should note on the enclosed form all calls made during the week.
    If the call fails for any reason, the error message should be noted, or
    any other message received from the network. Information about the NUA
    should be included so that the variety of call routings can be tested.

2. During the same period EUROLUG will contact hosts and ask for their down
    time, so that this can be compared with the failed calls.

3. All failures should also be reported to the national PTT either using the
    telephone or online fault reporting service. The specific telephone
    numbers to contact are:

Please classify the type of failure as follows:

    No reply from dial-up node
    Dial-up node engaged
    Call dropped
    Network congestion
    Call cleared remotely
    Serious noise on line
    Any other reason for a call not proceeding to logoff

Please include with completed form (if possible):

    Print out or copy of error message
    Action taken in case of failure, and response received from PTT or host
    service

Success means that the call was successfully logged of with no problems during
connection.

The results of the monitoring week will be gathered by the EUSIDIC Secretariat
and will be analysed. The results of the analysis will be circulated to the
Online User Groups, and to the national PTTs.

Company registered in the Netherlands

4.4.5 North American ISDN Users' Forum

Box 4.8(a) NIU Charter

CHARTER
FOR
NORTH AMERICAN ISDN USERS' FORUM

I. BACKGROUND

Following the National Bureau of Standards' (NBS) congressional mandate to
assist in the development and exploitation of telecommunications standards, the
Institute for Computer Sciences and Technology (ICST) solicited broad industry
contacts to investigate the Integrated Services Digital Network (ISDN), the
development of ISDN conformance testing methodology, and the development of
ISDN implementation agreements. Those responding recognized a paucity of user
representation in the ongoing development of ISDN. Because of the increasingly
urgent need to provide public standardized solutions driven by users, the
participants sought to establish a mechanism that would continuously articulate
user needs, focus on user application profiles, and, in turn, efficiently influence the
implementation of those ISDN applications in a multi-vendor, multi-service
provider environment. The result was the creation of the North American ISDN
Users' Forum.

II. URGENT NEED

To expedite the timely introduction of ISDN user applications and products there is
an urgent need for a strong ISDN user voice. This voice is required to address
many high level concerns over a broad range of ISDN issues as well as to reach
consensus on ISDN implementation agreements. While many of the technical
ISDN issues are being addressed in the ANSI accredited Committee T1, the
power and promise of portable and interoperable ISDN products and applications
will not be realized until ISDN user and ISDN implementation issues are resolved.

III. MISSION

The NORTH AMERICAN ISDN USERS' FORUM (NIU-FORUM) has been
formed under the auspices of the National Bureau of Standards with the following
mission:

To create a strong user voice in the implementation of ISDN and ISDN
applications and to ensure that the emerging ISDN meets users' application
needs.

IV. SCOPE

The NIU-FORUM will hasten the availability of interoperable, conforming ISDN
products and services which meet users' needs. It will operate in conjunction with
established, recognized standards bodies and testing organizations such as the
Committee T1 and the Corporation for Open Systems (COS), respectively. It is

Box 4.8(a) continued

not anticipated that the NIU-FORUM will duplicate efforts currently undertaken in these or other public arenas.

V. OBJECTIVES

The NORTH AMERICAN ISDN USERS' FORUM (NIU-FORUM) was formed to address three principal objectives:

1. To promote an ISDN forum committed to providing users the opportunity to influence the developing ISDNs to reflect their needs;

2. To identify ISDN applications, develop implementation agreements, and to facilitate their timely and harmonized implementation;

3. To solicit user, product provider, and service provider participation in this process.

VI. METHODOLOGY

The NIU-FORUM will focus on ISDN issues of common interest and identify strategies to promote the timely resolution of these issues.

The NIU-FORUM will identify ISDN applications and secure implementation agreements for those application profiles. When specific applications are identified, implementation agreements based upon emerging national and international ISDN/OSI standards will be formulated to promote product development. Standards will be selected for implementation as well as recommendations made as to how the standards will be implemented with the specified options. Implementation agreements for user application profiles will then be passed to conformance testing organizations such as COS. The NIU-FORUM will expedite vendor implementations of the defined requirements by supplying focused input to supplement the work of North American and international standards groups.

VII. ORGANIZATIONAL COMPOSITION AND FUNCTIONS

The NIU-FORUM consists of two workshops, the ISDN Users' Workshop (IUW) and the ISDN Implementors' Workshop (IIW). These workshops meet at regularly scheduled times to fulfill the objectives of the NIU-FORUM. Each workshop establishes its own internal organizational structure, operating procedures and administrative practices. The chairs of these workshops are elected to serve for a term, the length of which will be defined by the respective memberships.

Box 4.8(b)
NIU Forum Objectives

NORTH AMERICAN ISDN USERS' FORUM (NIU-FORUM)

OBJECTIVES:

1.) TO PROMOTE AN ISDN FORUM COMMITTED TO PROVIDING USERS THE OPPORTUNITY TO INFLUENCE THE DEVELOPING ISDNs TO REFLECT THEIR NEEDS;

2.) TO IDENTIFY ISDN APPLICATIONS AND TO FACILITATE THEIR TIMELY AND HARMONIZED IMPLEMENTATION;

3.) TO SOLICIT USER, PRODUCT PROVIDER, AND SERVICE PROVIDER PARTICIPATION IN THIS PROCESS.

Box 4.8(c)
NBS (NIST) Goals

WHY THE NATIONAL BUREAU OF STANDARDS?

NBS GOAL: TO STRENGTHEN AND ADVANCE THE NATIONS SCIENCE AND TECHNOLOGY AND TO FACILITATE THEIR EFFECTIVE APPLICATION FOR PUBLIC BENEFIT.

ASSURE INTERNATIONAL COMPETIVENESS AND THE LEADERSHIP OF U.S. INDUSTRY.

IMPROVE U.S. PRODUCTIVITY, PRODUCT QUALITY AND RELIABILITY

4.5 TELECOMMUNICATION RESTRUCTURING IN THE FEDERAL REPUBLIC OF GERMANY

4.5.1 Background

The government of the Federal Republic of Germany (FRG) has pursued the question of telecommunication planning and policy twice in the span of twelve years. Each time, the formal inquiry was assigned to a specially created, independent commission. Remarkably, from the volatile North American observation point, both commissions were headed by the same person, Professor Eberhard Witte, of the Institute for Organizational Studies at Munich.

The first commission's title-mandate has been translated as "Commission for the Development of the Telecommunication System," abbreviated to *KtK* from its German key words. KtK was set up in early 1974 and presented its report in January of 1976. Its recommendations dealt with nationwide completion of comprehensive telephone and other classic services coverage, and appropriate steps for the development of teleinformatic and broadband services.

The second creation of a special commission was adopted by the federal government on March 14, 1984, but the commission was actually set up a full year later. Its twelve members were selected as follows: five from trade, industry, industry associations and trade unions; three from science; and four representatives of political parties.

At the Commission's first meeting, in April 1985, its mandate was spelled out as given below.

The Government Commission for Telecommunications is to submit a report on the tasks and possibilities of improving the fulfilment of tasks in telecommunications. The report is to be based on the concept of the Federal Government for promoting the development of microelectronics, information and communication technologies.

The objectives to be achieved are the most effective promotion of technical innovation, the development and observance of international communication standards as well as the safeguarding of competition on the telecommunications market. The inquiry should mainly cover the following aspects:

Present and future tasks in telecommunications, consideration being given to both national and international aspects;

scope, limits and structure of Government tasks in telecommunications;

organizational, economic and legal prerequisites for the efficient fulfilment of Government tasks by the Deutsche Bundespost in line with requirements;

framework to be defined by the Government for the fulfilment of private enterprise tasks.

The inquiry is to be based on the fact that pursuant to Articles 73 and 87 of the Basic Law for the Federal Republic of Germany the Federation is responsible for posts and telecommunications and on the principles governing the constitution of the Deutsche Bundespost which are laid down in the Postal Administration Law.

It is expected that the Commission will endeavour to establish the opinions of all social groups concerned with this question and include them in its considerations.

4.5.2 The Commission's Recommendations

The commission published its *Report* on September 17, 1987. Results of its work were presented in two categories: (F) Findings and (R) Recommendations. We omit some of the Findings, but present the forty-seven Recommendations exactly as published. Note the reference to *TELEKOM,* a name given by the commission to the Deutsche Bundespost's telecommunication sector. This new term, which corresponds to the names chosen in France and the United Kingdom, has since been adopted by the German government.

R 1   TELEKOM shall keep its network monopoly as long as it provides leased lines (fixed connections) on fair and competitive conditions and in line with quality and quantity requirements. The Federal Government shall supervise the development of competition. The state of development shall be examined every three years. If the market does not develop satisfactorily, the Federal Government shall permit the establishment of competing networks.

R 2   The existing powers for licensing private telecommunication installations shall be exercised to the largest possible extent.

R 3   Cable links between different premises belonging to one and the same owner with a majority interest in these premises or belonging to one enterprise shall not require a licence if they are exclusively intended for handling gratuitous traffic related to the use of the premises.

R 4   Individual data traffic transmitted at low bit rates via satellite (point-to-point) shall be excluded from the network monopoly. This shall also apply to one-way data distribution (point-to-multipoint).

R 5   The Federal Government may define TELEKOM's infrastructural obligations.

F 10   The infrastructural obligations may refer to the nationwide provision of networks and services, the obligation to contract, the equal treatment of customers, the nationwide application of uniform tariffs as well as measures providing security in the case of disaster and in times of crisis and war.

R 6   Suitable measures such as financial compensation shall enable TELEKOM to meet the infrastructural obligations in the interest of public welfare.

R 7   Measures ensuring that the infrastructural obligations can be met must not lead to unfair competition between TELEKOM and its private competitors.

R 8   The internal transfer prices applied to the use of the network by the different service sectors of TELEKOM shall correspond to the tariffs payable by private competitors for the use of the network.

F 11   Public telephones are components of the network.

R 9   Private enterprises shall be free to operate telephones accessible to the public.

Services

F 12   A distinction is made between the following categories of telecommunication services: monopoly services, regulated services and unregulated services. Several regulatory recommendations have been submitted in this context.

R 10   TELEKOM shall keep its monopoly for the telephone service. All other telecommunication services shall be offered in competition with others.

F 13   Telephone service is understood as meaning exclusively voice communication. The storage or conversion of signals (e.g. voice mail) and the integration of speech into text, image or data communication are excluded from the monopoly.

R 11   The tariffs for monopoly services (fixed connections and the telephone service) shall be subject to approval by the Federal Minister of Posts and Telecommunications in consultation with the Federal Minister of Economics. In principle, tariffs shall be in line with costs. Before giving his approval the Federal Minister of Posts and Telecommunications shall examine whether the tariffs are reasonable.

R 12   Tariff distortions in the telephone service that are mainly due to excessive long-distance tariffs and extended local area tariffs which as a rule do not cover costs shall be gradually eliminated.

F 14   Regulated services are services which TELEKOM shall be obliged to render. These services shall be offered in competition with private enterprises which shall be under no obligation to provide such services.

R 13   The regulated services shall be defined by law or by ordinance having the force of law.

F 15   Unregulated services are not subject to any regulation. They may be offered by both TELEKOM and private enterprises. There is no monopoly or obligation to render such services.

R 14   Private enterprises shall have the right to provide all telecommunication services except the telephone service.

R 15   TELEKOM shall be free to offer unregulated services in addition to the telephone service and the regulated services.

R 16   Neither the suppliers of unregulated services nor the unregulated services as such or their prices shall be subject to registration or approval.

F 16   Since the network monopoly will largely be maintained, private enterprises will in principle only be able to offer their services on fixed and switched connections to be provided on lease by TELEKOM.

R 17   Everybody shall have the right to lease fixed connections (leased lined).

R 18   Private service suppliers shall be permitted to interconnect
—fixed connections and fixed connections
—fixed connections and switched connections
—switched connections and switched connections.

R 19   Usage-sensitive tariffs for fixed connections shall be clearly reduced step by step to promote competition in the network.

Terminal equipment

R 20   The subscriber shall be entitled to have a network termination installed which will allow him to connect any equipment he wishes (plug and socket solution). This shall also apply to the analogue telephone.

R 21   TELEKOM shall not have a monopoly for the supply or maintenance of terminal equipment. This shall also apply to the telephone connected to an ordinary telephone main station.

R 22   The prices of terminal equipment offered by TELEKOM and private enterprises shall not be subject to approval.

R 23   TELEKOM shall enter into competition on the terminal equipment market. It shall be allowed to sell, lease and maintain terminal equipment.

R 24 TELEKOM shall be authorized and enabled to develop software for networks, services and terminal equipment itself.

R 25 TELEKOM requires sufficient research capacity to be able to take an active part in the innovation of networks, services and terminal equipment.

R 26 TELEKOM shall not engage in the production of equipment for the time being.

R 27 The approval office for telecommunications terminal equipment shall be an independent authority reporting directly to the Federal Minister of Posts and Telecommunications. TELEKOM's equipment shall also be subject to approval.

R 28 The approval office shall examine whether the equipment submitted to it causes interference or harm to the network or the communicating parties.

R 29 The Federal Minister of Posts and Telecommunications shall ensure that the approval procedure is simple as regards the administrative requirements, the time required for tests and the costs.

Structural consequences for the Deutsche Bundespost

R 30 The sovereign tasks shall be separated from the entrepreneurial tasks as far as organization is concerned.

R 31 The Federal Ministry of Posts and Telecommunications shall perform the sovereign tasks as an independent ministry.

R 32 The Federal Minister of Posts and Telecommunications shall supervise the performance of the entrepreneurial tasks.

R 33 TELEKOM's budget/economic plan shall be subject to approval by the Federal Minister of Posts and Telecommunications in consultation with the Federal Minister of Finance.

R 34 Posts and telecommunications shall be separate as far as organization is concerned.

R 35 To promote the development of telecommunications, the subsidies paid by TELEKOM to the postal sector shall be reduced step by step over a period of five years. In any case they shall be recorded separately in TELEKOM's budget.

R 36 The telecommunications sector of the Deutsche Bundespost shall remain a public enterprise and its funds part of the special funds of the Federation.

R 37 The official relationship of the members of the Board of Managers of the enterprise to the Federation shall be governed by public law. This shall also apply to the second management level.

R 38 The network, the monopoly services, the regulated and unregulated services and the terminal equipment area shall be managed as separate divisions of TELEKOM with separate budgets/economic plans and separate annual accounts. Any cross-subsidies shall be identifiable as such.

R 39 From the point of view of organization and accounting the divisions responsible for unregulated services and terminal equipment shall be treated in a way effectively preventing the transfer of monopoly profits to the divisions exposed to competition. An auditing company shall determine and certify every year whether or not this requirement has been met.

R 40 TELEKOM may set up subsidiaries under private law for the provision of unregulated services and for any complementary business activities to be able to compete on the market without the constraints of the public budget and service law. Joint ventures of TELEKOM and private enterprises should also be considered.

R 41 Private law shall apply to the legal relations between TELEKOM and its customers.
R 42 To prevent competition distortions TELEKOM should be made liable to pay value added tax instead of the levy payable to the Federation. Initially, this arrangement shall at least be applied to the regulated and unregulated services provided in competition with others and to the terminal equipment area. After an adequate transition period, it shall also be applied to monopoly services.
R 43 After the change-over from the levy payable to the Federation to value added tax, TELEKOM shall be liable to pay all other taxes like any other corporation.
R 44 Concerning the appropriation of profits, the application of company law is considered convenient.
R 45 Pension reserves shall only be set up for pension obligations entered into after 1 January 1987.
R 46 The regulation concerning the maximum number of staff positions, the incentive systems, the payment of bonuses for particularly difficult work and the financial conditions applicable to the recruitment of staff shall be made more flexible and more closely related to performance.
R 47 The budgeting of personnel costs for the different divisions and decentralized organizational units will give TELEKOM greater flexibility in the deployment of staff.

[Commission for the Development of the Telecommunication System, Federal Republic of Germany, March 1984]

4.5.3 Implementation of German Restructuring

In 1988, the Ministry of Posts and Telecommunications set about to translate the commission's recommendations into detailed steps. Putting TELEKOM on a liberalized basis involves rearranging the postal sector for which the commission had no mandate. Since late 1988, the ministry's (i.e., the federal government's) plan for complete implementation has made its way through the parliamentary political process. A final version became law, after approval by Upper and Lower Houses, in May 1989. The organizational separation illustrated in Figure 4.2 took effect July 1, 1989.

   We should make clear to the reader that separation of TELEKOM from Postal Services and Postal Bank is made possible only by a coordinating board of directors, composed of the board chairmen of the three separate business organizations. The reconstituted ministry exercises oversight over all three by virtue of its exclusive responsibilities in "sovereign and jurisdictional tasks." One result of the multiplication of management decision centers, from one Bundespost Ministry in the past to nine chiefs or boards is an increase in staff positions. The government defends this as a price worth paying if the TELEKOM sector is to be freed from the constraints of postal service as a not-for-profit social commitment, while keeping unified

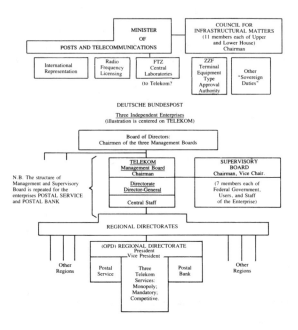

Figure 4.2 German Bundespost Structure after July 1, 1989.

the constitutionally mandated upper-level responsibilities. The jealously guarded prerogatives of the German states (Länder) also contribute to the dispersed upper management control structure. At the upper level, the Minister must endure a "Council for Infrastructural Matters." Half of the council's membership is drawn from the Bundesrat (the Upper House), which speaks for the particular interests of the German Länder.

4.6 REGULATORY DEVELOPMENTS IN THE UNITED KINGDOM***

4.6.1 Regulatory Body

Primary regulatory authority lies with the Department of Trade and Industry (DTI), which is responsible for drafting legislation and for issuing licences for the operation of telecommunications systems. However, a range of regulatory and advisory powers are vested in the Office of Telecommunications (OFTEL), which is an independent body directly responsible to Parliament. [*British Telecommunications Acts 1981 and 1984.*]

***This section gives the text of an Appendix to the Green Paper, originally distributed June 30, 1987.

4.6.2 Telecommunications Operator(s)

Following the privatisation in 1984 of British Telecom (the former monopoly telecommunications carrier), 14 organisations are now licensed as Public Telecommunications Operators (PTOs):

—British Telecommunications plc (BT), which is a company with 51% private ownership, 49% government ownership;†
—Mercury Communications Limited (Mercury), privately owned.

Both these companies are licensed to run nation-wide fixed networks.

—RACAL Vodafone
—Telecoms Securicor Cellular Radio Ltd (Cellnet) } only for mobile cellular radio telephone systems
—City of Kingston Upon Hull: a fixed network only for its own area
—9 cable operators, full range of telecommunication services and cable TV in their franchise areas.

[Licence granted by The Secretary of State for Trade and Industry to British Telecommunications under Section 7 of the Telecommunications Act 1984]
[Licence granted by The Secretary of State for Trade and Industry to Mercury Communications Limited under Section 7 of the Telecommunications Act 1984]
[Licence granted by The Secretary of State for Trade and Industry to Racal—Vodafone Limited under Section 7 of the Telecommunications Act 1984]
[Licence granted by the Secretary of State for Trade and Industry to Telecoms Securicor Cellular Radio Ltd (Cellnet) under Section 7 of the Telecommunications Act 1984]
[Licence granted by the Secretary of State for Trade and Industry to Kingston upon Hull City Council under Section 7 of the Telecommunications Act 1984]

4.6.3 The Current Situation with Regard to Equipment and Services

Most telecommunications services are provided in competition by BT and Mercury. BT is likely to be the only carrier offering country-wide residential, basic telecommunications services for the foreseeable future, but Mercury now provides services in most of the main business centres and in areas where it can do so cost effectively, and is starting to operate a national digital switched network with interconnection with the BT network. It also competes with BT on those international routes to which it is able to obtain access—a limited number at present. A number of other service providers supply mobile radio and radio paging services on a competitive basis, and telecommunication services and cable TV are provided by the cable operators.

---

†It is UK government policy to sell its residual shareholdings in privatised companies. In the case of BT, undertakings were given in 1984 when the 51% was sold, that there would be no further sales before April 1988.

Major services available in the UK are as follows:

VOICE: Public switched telephone network (BT and Mercury); Mobile telephone network (cellular radio); (Telecoms Securicor Cellular Radio Ltd (Cellnet) and Racal Vodafone).

DATA: Data transmission services over the PSTN; Non-switched leased lines (analogue and digital); Packet switched network.

TEXT: Telex network (BT and Mercury); Teletex; A number of electronic mail services, the largest of which is one run by BT; Facsimile (BT); Videotex (BT, Prestel).

VIDEO: BT offers two videoconferencing services; Cable: a number of cable TV networks are operated by private companies, mainly using coaxial networks.

RADIO-PAGING: BT and several other private operators.

The UK has by far the largest number of "value-added" services of any of the European countries (see below).

With regard to terminal equipment supply, there has been no monopoly since 1984 and any equipment other than pay phones (for the time being), provided it has been approved, can be bought from private suppliers. OFTEL is now responsible for approval. It relies upon evaluation carried out by the British Approvals Board for Telecommunications (BABT), an independent private sector body, and to a diminishing extent by BT.

4.6.4 Current National Trends and Discussion on Regulatory Issues

A significant degree of liberalisation has taken place since the Telecommunications Act of 1981. This has entailed some re-regulation which has affected not only the terminal market but has also brought about major changes in the conditions for the use of the network in the UK.

Public Networks

As a result of the Telecommunications Act of 1981 the telecommunications operations of the Post Office were split off into a separate organisation, British Telecom, and the power to license networks was given directly to the Government, thus paving the way for competition in network services. BT only held a consultative role with respect to the licensing of telecommunications operators, although it had limited powers to grant licences under a general authority issued by the Secretary of State.

The Act was followed three years later by the Telecommunications Act of 1984 which served to increase the range of liberalisation in the UK. This Act changed BT's status from that of a public to a private company, removed BT's exclusive privilege to run telecommunications systems and required BT to operate under a licence, which set out its rights and obligations [*British Telecom Licence, op. cit.*]. The terms of the BT licence state, amongst others, that:

—universal service is obligatory;

—tariff increases for a basket of basic services are regulated (consumer price index minus 3 percent);

—BT is obliged to provide interconnection for licensed systems;

—no undue price discrimination is allowed;

—OFTEL has the power to prevent cross-subsidisation of BT equipment supply and network operations.

A similar licence was granted to Mercury Communications. Both companies were placed in a new category of telecommunications operator which was created, known as Public Telecommunications Operator (PTO—a telecommunications operator providing public services which enjoys a privileged position in return for accepting a specific series of obligations). The government made it clear that it was not intending to license any further PTOs which could provide basic fixed network services before 1990 at the earliest, in order to limit the amount of competition while Mercury established its infrastructure and while BT adapted to the new competitive climate. There is thus now a duopoly operating in the provision of national public networks in the UK.

Other PTOS comprise the two operators of public cellular radio telephone networks, and cable companies offering local network services including in some cases voice telephony in conjunction with Mercury or BT.

Under the Act of 1984, OFTEL was created as an independent regulatory body for overseeing the sector.

Private Networks

With regard to private networks (that is, networks made up from lines leased from the PTOs), following the 1981 Act the government announced that it intended to issue a licence to permit the provision of "value added" services. It stated that the provision of simple resale of excess capacity on leased lines would be prohibited until at least July 1989. (Simple resale service has a legal definition—not all forms of resale are precluded). In practice, Value Added Network Services (VANS) can be provided over the public network as well as over private networks.

A license for VANS operation was issued in 1982 under the 1981 Telecommunications Act [*General Licence* under Section 15 (1) for telecommunications systems used in providing value added network services, October 1982]. It remains the current VANS licence at the time of writing, although a new licence was due to be published in early 1987 (see below). The licence permits any person, including the Public Telecommunications Operators to run what is known as an "applicable system" which provides "value added" telecommunications services. In order to satisfy this "value added" term, the messages conveyed must fulfil one or more of the following criteria: they must be stored; or the code, content, format or protocol of the messages must be acted on significantly; or they must be multi-addressed. These criteria are used to differentiate "value-added" services from 'basic' services (with minor exceptions—for example where the messages passed relate solely to the licensee.)

The licence requires that where a connection is made between a VANS network and a public network, the apparatus within the VANS network must be 'approved' and the connection between the VANS network and any other network can only be made by a Public Telecommunications Operator. For international traffic, the VANS system must only be used to pass messages to or from persons outside the UK over leased lines where those messages relate only to the affairs of the person on whose sole behalf the circuit has been leased. To date some 180 service providers have registered under this licence, although there are effectively only a limited number of VANS networks operating on a national basis.

The UK government has found the distinction between "basic" and "value-added" services extremely difficult to maintain, with the result that the area has been under continual review. In 1985 a consultative document proposing a new category of "Managed Data Network Services" was issued in an attempt to allow basic conveyance (with no "added value") for data messages. However the new distinctions proved to be difficult to define and the Government was persuaded that a simple and more comprehensive licensing regime was required. Accordingly, a revised licence has been issued in February 1987 [*Draft Class Licence for Value Added and Data Network Services,* Department of Trade and Industry, July 1986; final version released February 1987]. It covers two different types of operations. Firstly, there are telecommunications operators who provide value added or data services for profit. In this case, either value added services or simple conveyance of data services can be provided. Secondly, there are telecommunications networks run to support a non-telecommunications business activity. In this case "basic" services can also be run under the terms of the licence (i.e. voice and telex services) provided the operator does not charge for these services.

Within the VADS licence there are a number of conditions that apply to Major Service Providers, that is to say, operators having a total turnover in excess of £50 million per year or a telecommunications business turnover in excess of £1 million per year. These include a prohibition on predatory pricing, unfair cross-subsidisation of services provided to users outside the operator's group, and so on. Major Service Providers also have to register with OFTEL and pay a licence fee. In addition, they have to provide access arrangements in compliance with OSI standards. Over international leased lines VANS may be provided, as may basic data services where these are provided within closed user groups. International VADS may be provided within closed user groups which have a common business interest in an area other than the provision of telecommunications services.

The draft Class Licence gives no general definition of "value-added service" or "basic conveyance."

Under the VADs Class Licence, overseas providers will implicitly be required to operate their licensed service from a UK site, although there is provision for special bilateral arrangements between the UK and foreign PTTs.

In-house private networks have also been the subject of a new licensing regime, quite apart from the VANS/VADS issue. Prior to 1984 private networks were controlled by BT. They are now controlled by the companies or organisations which operate them. A license is now required to allow the operation of private in-house networks whether or not connected to the public switched network [*Branch Systems General Licence (BSGL),* 1984].

In order to overcome a number of deficiencies in the licence and to bring it more into line with the proposed new VADS licence. The UK Government has recently issued a revised Branch Systems General Licence. The major change involves the relaxation of the conditions which relate to the conveyance of traffic which has arrived from, or is destined for, the PSTN within a private network. Where networks can meet certain technical requirements related to speech call quality it is proposed that they should now be permitted to carry PSTN traffic without restriction within their own network. The licence also changes the classification of equipment deemed to be call routing apparatus, clarifying the permitted use of international leased lines.

In addition to the BSGL and VADS licences, individual licences for the operation of networks that would not otherwise comply with one of the existing licences are available. The main criteria is that licences will be granted except where the main predictable effect of the licence would be the diversion of revenue from the Public Telecommunications Operators. For example a Temporary Licence has been granted to Reuters Ltd to run certain telecommunications systems.

Terminal Equipment

The de-regulation process has had a significant effect on supply of the terminal market. Following the 1981 Act, the almost complete monopoly on the supply of customer premises equipment which BT once held has been gradually relaxed, so that essentially all equipment, with the exception of payphones (for the time being), may now be purchased from private suppliers.

Future Liberalisation

The UK Government has announced that it does not intend to permit the provision of simple resale services before July 1989. It also announced that it did not intend to licence operators other than BT and Mercury to run national public networks until November 1990 at the earliest. The position will then be reviewed. [Commission of the European Communities, June 1987.]

4.7 REGULATORY DEVELOPMENTS IN JAPAN‡

4.7.1 History

Since the early 1950s, domestic telecommunications services in Japan have been provided by the Nippon Telegraph and Telephone Corporation ("NTT"), whilst all of the international services were provided by Kokusai Denshin Denwa Company Ltd ("KDD").

NTT was established in 1952 as a public corporation and KDD was formed in 1953 as a private company.

Between them, these two companies took over most of the responsibilities previously assumed by the Ministry of Communications. The remaining responsibilities were then combined with postal functions into a new Ministry entitled the Ministry of Posts and Telecommunications ("MPT").

---

‡This section gives the text of an appendix to the Green Paper, originally distributed June 30, 1987.

With technological developments taking place, there was increasing pressure to introduce a relaxation of the monopoly held by NTT and KDD in their respective fields of operation. Thus in 1971, the MPT proposed a variety of amendments to the existing law [The Public Telecommunications Law] that would permit the telephone network to accommodate new business services, e.g., VANs operations. Previously, the provision of third party services was a function reserved for the monopoly operators.

4.7.2 The New Telecommunications Laws

In 1985, Japan started to deregulate its telecommunications industry.

Two new laws were introduced which were planned to bring about a process of deregulation and liberalisation within the Japanese telecommunications industry, the results of which it was hoped will last at least to the end of the century [*The Telecommunications Business Law and the Nippon Denshin Denwa Kabushiki Kaisha Law ("NTT Law")*]. The laws, however, also leave considerable room for manoeuvre in the future.

The changes occurring are, in some ways, similar to those occurring in the USA and UK. These changes have the overall objectives of reducing the cost of communications and stimulating the development of new telecommunications and information services.

There are two major aims of these laws:

—to introduce competition into the domestic and international telecommunications markets in the provision of both services and facilities; and
—to transform the dominant domestic operator (NTT) from a state owned monopoly to a privately owned competitive company.

The two new laws came into effect on 1 April 1985.

The new laws have:

—authorised a liberalised use of telecommunications facilities;
—ended the domestic telecommunications monopoly of NTT;
—caused the restructuring of NTT as a private corporation prepared to participate in a competitive marketplace; and
—allowed the possibility of allowing competition with KDD in the international marketplace.

In the light of the Computer II definition problems in the US the Japanese government has attempted to avoid the US "basic" *versus* "enhanced" distinction of Computer II which it saw as unworkable. Instead they opted for a "facilities providers" *versus* "service providers" distinction.

These two classifications are described as follows.

1. *Type I Operators*

Type I operators are regulated operators who own and operate their own transmission facilities. Type I operators remain subject to prior approval by the MPT. Type I applications are judged by the MPT to ensure:

—it will conform to the demands of the area being served;
—it will not result in over capacity in any particular area;

—that the business plan proposed is both "reliable and feasible";

—that the operator is both technically and financially qualified; and

—that it is "appropriate for the sound development of telecommunications in general."

Both NTT and KDD are established by the new law as Type I operators.

In the meantime, the MPT has authorised 5 additional new facility based competitors.

Three of these new Type I operators plan terrestrial networks (one using microwave transmission, the second, optical fibre laid along the roads and the third, optical fibre alongside the railway lines), whilst the other two intend to build networks based on satellite technology.

2. *International Type I Operators*

Whilst KDD remains as the dominant international telecommunications operator, the MPT is likely to issue a second licence for international operations. At present there are two bidders for this licence:

—a consortium (called ITJ) of the largest Japanese trading houses (Mitsubishi, Mitsui and Sumitomo) and others (and assisted by KDD itself); and

—a consortium (entitled KDTK) consisting principally of Cable and Wireless and C Itoh, but also including Toyota Motors, Pacific Telesis, Fujitsu, NEC and a number of others, with assistance from the international arm of NTT.

In order to ensure that the dominant operators do not unfairly use their position to influence other parts of the market, the MPT issued guidelines in August 1986 restricting the involvement of NTT in international ventures to less than 10% capital share (and similarly KDD's involvement in national ventures).

3. *Type II Operators*

Type II operators are all other telecommunications operators and are less regulated. In effect these are operators providing enhanced (or value added) services who do not own their own transmission facilities.

The Telecommunications Business Law does not restrict Type II services to non-voice only, but there may be a de-facto limitation to data services. There are restrictions on the use of NTT circuits for voice resale (although other Type I operators can lease NTT circuits to serve places not served directly by their own transmission capabilities). It is not yet evident whether the MPT will ease these restrictions on resale.

Under the 1985 law, Type II operators are divided into unregulated (small scale) "General" Type II providers and more regulated "Special" (large scale) Type II providers.

However, since the introduction of the new law, the MPT has more or less disregarded the division between the "Special" and the "General" categorisation. In fact the MPT has so expanded the scope of the unregulated General Type II category that there would now seem to be little need for new entrants to register under the Special Type II category.

In order to be classified as a "Special" Type II operator, an operator must satisfy four criteria as follows:

—the operator must serve all the customers who request service "Universal service";

—there must be no preference or discrimination between customers;

—the operator must publish his tariffs; and

—the service must be accessed through the public telephone network.

Furthermore, any operator with more than 500 exchange lines must be classified as a Special Type II operator (although there is no limit to the number of customers who can be served through these 500 lines).

Regarding tariffs, General Type I operators have considerable freedom in the tariffs they charge, Special Type I operators do not have this freedom.

There are at present over 200 Type II operators providing a wide variety of different services.

4.7.3 Role of the MPT

As well as licensing Category I operators, the MPT also has a number of general supervisory powers over type I and Special type II operators, including:

—being able to specify a date by which a particular Type I operator must commence the provision of services;

—a requirement to approve the technical standards of a Type I operator before the commencement of services (this includes general technical standards as well as security and interconnection standards);

—approval of changes to the services offered by a Type I or Special Type II operator; and

—approval of Type I operator tariffs (these are assessed to ensure that they are cost based, although it is not entirely clear exactly what this means in practice).

Great influence is however exerted on the MPT by the Ministry of International Trade and Industry (MITI) which represents [the users' groups] and the government trade policy interests.

4.7.4 Results of the New Laws

Difficulties have been encountered in maintaining the scheme due to problems in maintaining a clear distinction between Type I and Type II licences.

Type I carriers are pressing to be allowed to offer Type II services without being bound by the regulations of a Type I carrier, e.g. [not] having to obtain prior tariff approval. In particular, NTT wishes to offer Type II services through a subsidiary which means that new regulations will be required to prevent cross-subsidisation.

A further blurring of the distinction between Type I and Type II services may arise because Type II services are likely to be subclassified into voice and data services in order to allow NTT to retain its tariff restrictions on resale of voice services. Hence, Type II entities will not be allowed to offer voice store and forward systems utilising NTT leased lines, although voice mailbox services may well be allowed to utilise public switched network services.

Thirdly, the absence of clear service-related distinctions between type II activities, e.g. between "resale of pure transmission," "protocol conversion services," and "hybrid service" is likely to complicate greatly any effort to apply Japanese domestic regulatory categories to Japanese international services.

Fourthly, if the restrictions on voice resale are removed, then the effect of the necessary tariff changes for NTT services would cause price reductions on domestic services, thereby possibly jeopardising the plans of the new Type I operators.

4.7.5 Effect of the New Laws on NTT

Initially, under the new law, the whole of NTT was owned by the Government. However the intent of the Government is to sell up to two-thirds of NTT.

NTT has largely accepted that the changes are inevitable and has started to adapt to the new regulatory environment.

To assist in this process NTT has set up a number of separate subsidiaries to provide all services other than the basic switched telecommunications services.

One of the major problems to be faced by NTT is that of tariffs, and introduction of a system of cost allocation that will allow it to adopt a tariff structure fairly reflecting the cost of provision of the various services. Under the new law, the arrangements for overseeing the tariffs of NTT has changed from the Diet (the Parliament) to MPT.

A review of the restructuring of NTT is expected to take place in 1988. [Commission of the European Communities, June 1987.]

Chapter Five
Consequences of Reform and Market Pressures

5.1 INTRODUCTION

In this book we focused first on a trend toward more definitive, more binding, and more universal standards. Then, in Chapter Three, a taxonomic analysis supports the conclusion that the actual market result of standards is a national variable. The documentation of Chapter Four shows that reform of regulatory policies also varies from country to country. Yet overshadowing and perhaps rendering national variances obsolete in one world subregion is the bold initiative of the EC bureaucracy. It has already fostered some unified European standards in fifteen years of effect on CEPT, as reported in Section 5.3.

Given such divergent but comparably powerful pressures, how have standards-makers and their institutional forums responded? Answers to this question are provided in the present chapter. The US setup in the aftermath of AT&T divestiture is documented first. Next, we focus on Europe's CEPT and its responses to EC demands.

Consideration of national, regional, and worldwide standards activities brings into view a coherent superstructure, with imposing control over choices available to global information interchange. The newly formulated view of a standards suprapower illuminates this writer's outlook to the future, as given in the concluding sections.

5.2 STANDARDS-MAKING IN THE POST-DIVESTITURE UNITED STATES

5.2.1 A Positive-Sum Game Among Adversaries?

In *Collaboration without Coercion*, this writer likens successful international agreement-making to a positive-sum game [1]. Business competitors can agree on common standards when expected gains of an enlarged, homogeneous market outweigh the narrow opportunities available in separate, uncoordinated market segments.

Under this concept, borrowed from game theory, the game's total outcome exceeds the net sum of players' individual stakes. Exploitation of the radio frequency spectrum has been a positive-sum game so long as worldwide collaboration maximizes every user's access and protection from harmful interference. The radio spectrum's selective limitations also supply examples of the positive-sum game's inapplicability. The conventional entertainment and news type of radio broadcasting station assignment offers such an example. The radio transmission band available for assignment has been standardized for many years; the radio receiver supply industry offers consumer products that are only useable for this band; and a hope for new frequency allocations in the future with similar household user, mass market potential is almost zero. Consequently, at any given location in developed countries, the band is filled to capacity with radio station transmissions authorized a good many years ago. Moreover, in spite of the ITU's CCIR technical committee efforts and periodic World Administrative Radio Conferences dedicated to reduction of mutual interference, stations cause interference to each other's reception in most parts of the world, particularly after dark when radio propagation extends over larger areas. Thus, here is an example of international collaboration having met a zero-sum game: if a new station wishes to be granted transmission rights, it can expect so only at the expense of an existing station's demise. In truth, the game has a negative sum, when we take into account the fact that satisfaction of all applicants will surely reduce the net availability of undisturbed receptions to much less than it is under tightly controlled assignment to a few early entrants. In the absence of tight control, usually by a government agency, competing station entrepreneurs attempt to drown out each other's transmissions by using more powerful equipment. This is indeed what happened before the US government created the Federal Communications Commission (FCC), with power to grant, withdraw, or withhold station authorization. Prior to this game-restricting action, there had been "bedlam on the airwaves" [2].

Focusing now on the publicly offered telecommunication *common carrier* services (e.g., telephone, telegraph, telex, data communications), standards-making among competing service providers and their suppliers has benefited from the positive-sum game model for two self-evident reasons: market growth and protected positions.

First, consider the beneficial effect of a continuously growing market for telecommunication services and supporting products. That compatibility throughout networks increases the utility for most users has become axiomatic. The addition of a new user anywhere in the world increases the pool of available contacts for every other user, provided that all are accessible under compatible technical and operational standards. Hence, compatibility increases the world market's growth rate, as compared to obstacle conditions of uncoordinated networks. So long as the number of users increases while services offered increase in diversity, market growth is a certainty. Thus, collaboration on standards benefits all participants in the game. A clear proof of this axiom's persuasiveness is the impatient, persistent demand for accelerated standardization of innovative features or devices made by venturesome users and their suppliers.

The second reason for the traditional effectiveness of the positive-sum game model is the absence of hostile competition in protected markets. The service providers have had exclusive franchises in their respective territories. Even in the competition-oriented United States, after the break-up of AT&T's vertically integrated monopoly, with respect to local telephone service, the derisive old slogan still holds: "It's the only telephone company in town." Worldwide, the administrations of European countries among each other and their counterparts elsewhere have retained sovereign rights in their respective service territories over implementation of any standard to which they had mutually agreed. Competitive interests entered the collaborative process only by way of the manufacturers.

Most manufacturing companies had—and many still have—a protected market position in their respective countries. The German Bundespost would buy equipment only from German suppliers; the French PT&T bought only from French suppliers; the UK Post Office bought from British suppliers, long known as the "ring"; and so on. Thus, competitive rivalry in CCITT study groups has seriously disturbed agreement-making for only two special reasons. In one scenario, a new equipment standard positions one country's manufacturers ahead by several years before other countries' suppliers are able to offer a comparable product. In this case, a national service provider might succumb to the lure of foreign-made equipment that offered unique advantages at the time.

In another, related scenario, a manufacturer may fear impairment of its export potential in the world market if the agreed standard derives directly from a leading, competing supplier country.

In cases on record, manufacturers' competitive concerns have obstructed a single world standard because some government administrations put protection of national industries ahead of the greater benefit of worldwide compatibility. From that point of view, the game becomes zero-sum, at best: "my agreement benefits someone else by as much as I will lose." This short-sighted view discounts the eventual, larger total market that is open to all suppliers of compatible equipment.

In the United States, both the national network service and equipment markets were forcibly thrown open to competition through FCC rule-makings and federal court actions since the mid-1970s (see Chapter 4). Whereas the principle was determined by a few landmark cases, its application is an ongoing preoccupation of the entire telecommunication industry and cognizant government agencies. The driving force for continued competitors' posturing as adversaries is the perception of a zero-sum game. As an example, MCI emerged as a major long-distance carrier only when the company succeeded in taking away customers previously served by AT&T. In addition, MCI obtained large transfer payments from AT&T, adjudged by the courts as a remedy for past restrictions on interconnection [3]. Although the long battle of MCI *versus* AT&T is in some ways an extraordinary case, our perception of a zero-sum game mentality is not. Indeed, the entire FCC regulatory procedure is designed around a legalistic system of adversaries fighting over the same property. This is so, whether the arena is broadcasting station licensing or the fairness of common carrier tariffs. Under this procedure, one applicant is granted a right denied to another. There is no room for a positive-sum game.

An exception to this rule is the FCC's long-held, quasi-Solomonic compromise on competition between satellites and transoceanic cables. Confronted with satellite operators' demands for total denial of planned and future cable installations in the early 1970s, the FCC allowed balanced, parallel expansion of both types of facilities. This action can be best understood in terms of the positive-sum game concept. The FCC was able to forecast spectacular expansion of overseas communication traffic. With some twenty years' hindsight, we can now ascertain that simultaneous availability of satellite and cable circuits had driven the usage growth rate higher than it would have been over one facility. Abundant, alternative, high quality circuits have prevented congestion and black-outs due to link failure. Users were able to place overseas calls with expectations like those of the best local connections. However, this remarkably successful FCC balancing act has been the exception in regulatory history.

Given the powerful zero-sum game perception fostered among competitors in the United States, how has adoption of standards been organized since AT&T divestiture? We can reply with an unequivocal affirmation of the positive-sum game principle: standards collaboration in the fragmented United States works, and it works well. Several good reasons can be named for this favorable outcome. First, the FCC stayed out of standards-making, thereby removing the advocate-adversary setting. Second, worldwide collaborative procedures in CCITT study groups and in ISO-IEC technical committees have a strong, model influence on participating national committees. Third, the standards-compelling issues, such as nationwide ISDN or "smart" network terminals, each promise greater market prospects for all contenders if compatibility is assured.

The next sections focus on the details of US standards activities in the current environment.

5.2.2 Standards Committee T1

This committee was created to fill the void left by the break-up of the Bell System, previously the source of standards for the US telecommunication industry. Preparations during 1983 climaxed in the new committee holding its first meeting in early 1984. Thus, T1 began to function exactly at the time when the AT&T divestiture was to be fully implemented, January 1984.

Our description of the committee's background, composition of membership, and goals is reprinted from an article authored by T1's inaugural chairman (Box 5.1). This is followed by a committee organization diagram (Figure 5.1) and a statistical summary of the membership affiliation (Box 5.2); both sets of information correspond to the status as of the first quarter of 1989.

The T1 committee structure as of 1989 is shown in Figure 5.1.

Box 5.1

Standards Committee T1—Telecommunications, by Ian M. Lifchus. Reprinted by permission of *IEEE Communications Magazine,* v. 23, n. 1, January 1985, © 1985 IEEE. (This reprint is limited to the text on the first two and beginning of third pages [pp. 34–35 and 36 of the original that ends on p. 37].

Standards Committee T1— Telecommunications

Ian M. Lifchus

ECSA-sponsored and ANSI-accredited, T1 works to provide a standards-setting forum

Introduction

STANDARDS FOR TELEPHONY in the United States have evolved over a period of many years, with the former Bell System taking a leading role in their formulation. Utilizing the broad resources of its vertically integrated corporate structure, the Bell System developed internal standards which it shared with the Independent Telephone Companies and manufacturers in various Bell-United States Telephone Association (USTA) forums. These standards were widely used in the industry and resulted in a uniformity of telecommunications facilities across the country. However, the corporate restructuring which resulted from the Second Computer Inquiry and the Bell System divestiture has changed the standards-setting process in the United States and has initiated a new era of broadly based industry participation.

It has been widely recognized in industry and government that consensus standards and procedures are needed in order to preserve the integrity of nationwide telecommunications and to facilitate the interconnection and interoperability of carrier services. The response to this challenge has been the establishment of an independent standards committee, known as "T1," which provides a public forum for developing interconnection standards for the national telecommunications system. Committee T1 is sponsored by the Exchange Carriers Standards Association (ECSA) and is open in membership to all interested parties. As of June 1984, T1's membership includes 90 exchange carriers, interexchange carriers, resellers, manufacturers, vendors, government agencies, user groups, consultants, and liaisons. To ensure that standards projects undertaken within T1 represent an industry consensus, T1 has been accredited by the American National Standards Institute (ANSI). The name T1, not to be confused with the well-known T1 transmission system, is attributed to ANSI's coding of standards committees: T for telecommunications and 1 for the first such ANSI entity.

Industry Initiation and Participation

The ECSA is both a trade association of exchange carriers and the sponsor of an independent standards committee, T1. At the time that ECSA was formed and T1 was conceived, the Federal Communications Commission (FCC) was requesting public comments regarding the vehicle for post-divestiture standards making. As an organization representing more than 95% of the telephone subscribers in the United States, the ECSA mirrored the concern expressed in the FCC's inquiry.

Box 5.1 (continued)

In August 1983, ECSA recommended to the FCC that a public standards committee be established which would be open in membership and use the same ANSI procedures as countless other existing standards committees. Though ANSI develops model procedures for standards setting, it does not actually sponsor standards activities. While ANSI coordinates standards activities, it views the responsibility of sponsorship as belonging to elements of the industry which implement the standards. Consequently, the ECSA advised the FCC that it was prepared to sponsor an ANSI-affiliated committee and provide the secretariat and administrative functions in support of the committee's work.

The principles which underlie ANSI's model procedures are:

- Openness—participation is open to all parties who indicate that they are directly and materially affected by the standards activity;
- Due Process—equity and fair play to assure all interested parties of their right to express a viewpoint and, if dissatisfied, to appeal; and
- Balance—the opportunity for all parties to participate without dominance by any single interest.

ANSI approval of proposed standards is intended to verify that these principles have been followed in the approval procedure and that a consensus of those affected by the standard has been achieved. ANSI coordination among standards committees is intended to ensure that national standards needs are identified and met without conflict in their requirements or unnecessary duplication.

By October 1983 it was apparent from other responses to the FCC that the ECSA proposals had the overwhelming support of the telecommunications industry. Therefore, in November 1983 ECSA announced its intention to establish Committee T1 and invited the public to join T1 and identify standards projects. On February 2, 1984, T1 held its first meeting with 79 inaugural member organizations.

Following ANSI practices, committee members are classified by their principal interest in order to determine whether a cross section of affected interests are involved in the process. Four broad-interest categories were defined: 1) exchange carriers, 2) interexchange carriers and resellers, 3) manufacturers and vendors, and 4) general interests, which includes government agencies, consultants, user groups, and liaisons with other committees. The T1 membership, as of its June 19, 1984 meeting, is categorized in Table I.

The committee structure provides for a number of specialized technical subcommittees. Membership procedures allow for organizations to join specific subcommittees without requiring membership in the full committee. In addition, all meetings are open to the public. Therefore, the number of organizations participating in T1 exceeds the figures shown in Table I. Most major companies and government agencies involved in telecommunications are represented in T1, including two Canadian interexchange carrier organizations. As T1's membership continues to expand, it becomes increasingly apparent that the Committee's principal asset is the broad representation of its participants. This membership base gives T1 the support it needs to provide an effective focal point for the telecommunications industry.

T1's Scope and Goals

T1's broadly based membership provides it with an end-to-end network perspective which is reflected in its mission

TABLE I
T1 MEMBERSHIP
(As of 6/19/84)

• Exchange Carrier Interests	18
• Interexchange Carrier and Reseller Interests	21
• Manufacturing and Vendor Interests	37
• General Interests	14
	90

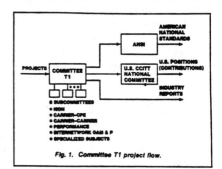

Fig. 1. Committee T1 project flow.

statement: "Committee T1 develops standards and technical reports related to interfaces for U. S. networks which form part of the North American telecommunications system. T1 also develops positions on related subjects under consideration in various international standards bodies. Specifically, T1 focuses on those functions and characteristics associated with the interconnection and interoperability of telecommunications networks at interfaces with end user systems, carriers, and information and enhanced service providers. These include switching, signaling, transmission, performance, operation, administration, and maintenance aspects. Committee T1 is also concerned with procedural matters at points of interconnection, such as maintenance and provisioning methods and documentation, for which standardization would benefit the telecommunications industry."

The organizational interfaces described in the above scope are illustrated in Fig. 1. Projects flow into T1, where they are addressed within a structure of technical subcommittees. Projects intended to yield candidate American National Standards will flow to ANSI and its Board of Standards Review. In addition, T1's work program will also include liaison projects related to continuing work in international forums, such as the International Telegraph and Telephone Consultative Committee (CCITT). T1 expects to formulate industry positions on CCITT-related topics and submit these to the Department of State's U.S. National Committee for CCITT. A third path which is available is for the presentation of industry reports. These reports may represent the consensus output of a subcommittee, which may precede the development of an industry standard or an opinion which would not necessarily result in a standard.

T1 Committee Structure

The T1 structure features a main committee, an Advisory Group, and six Technical Subcommittees. Each subcommittee establishes Working Groups, as needed, to address specific projects. All elements of T1 are subordinate to the main committee. The committee establishes the organizational structure, elects officers, approves standards projects, and approves candidate standards for submission to ANSI.

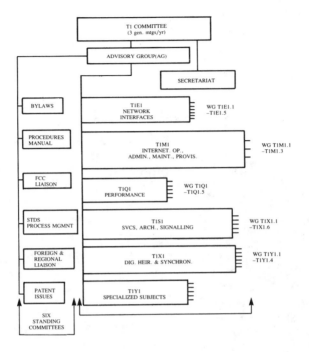

Figure 5.1 Organization of the T1 Committee.

Box 5.2
T1 Statistics

30	Carrier Voting Members:
	19 Exchange Carriers
	11 Interexchange Carriers
	(includes CNCP and Telecom Canada)
2	Exchange Carrier Observers
	(Alltel; NTT America, Inc.)
11	Interexchange Carrier Observers
	(includes Canadian, Japanese, UK Carriers)
17	General Interest Voting Members
17	General Interest Observers
42	Manufacturer Voting Members
	(includes essentially all major domestic and foreign telecommunication equipment suppliers represented in the US)
59	Manufacturer Observers
89	TOTAL VOTING MEMBERSHIP
178	GRAND TOTAL MEMBERSHIP

The text of the committee's *List of first Standards* (Box 5.3), released November 1988, completes this section.

Box 5.3
First List of Standards (Reprinted from *Telecommunications—Committee T1 Standards Newsletter.*
© 1988 ECSA

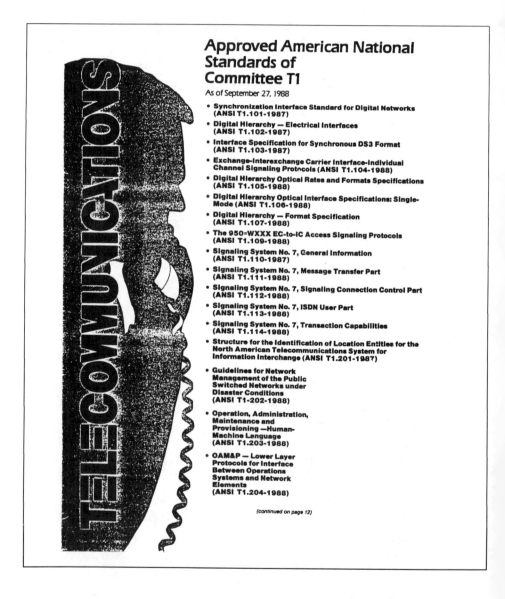

Approved American National Standards of Committee T1

As of September 27, 1988

- **Synchronization Interface Standard for Digital Networks** (ANSI T1.101-1987)
- **Digital Hierarchy — Electrical Interfaces** (ANSI T1.102-1987)
- **Interface Specification for Synchronous DS3 Format** (ANSI T1.103-1987)
- **Exchange-Interexchange Carrier Interface-Individual Channel Signaling Protocols** (ANSI T1.104-1988)
- **Digital Hierarchy Optical Rates and Formats Specifications** (ANSI T1.105-1988)
- **Digital Hierarchy Optical Interface Specifications: Single-Mode** (ANSI T1.106-1988)
- **Digital Hierarchy — Format Specification** (ANSI T1.107-1988)
- **The 950=WXXX EC-to-IC Access Signaling Protocols** (ANSI T1.109-1988)
- **Signaling System No. 7, General Information** (ANSI T1.110-1987)
- **Signaling System No. 7, Message Transfer Part** (ANSI T1.111-1988)
- **Signaling System No. 7, Signaling Connection Control Part** (ANSI T1.112-1988)
- **Signaling System No. 7, ISDN User Part** (ANSI T1.113-1988)
- **Signaling System No. 7, Transaction Capabilities** (ANSI T1.114-1988)
- **Structure for the Identification of Location Entities for the North American Telecommunications System for Information Interchange** (ANSI T1.201-1987)
- **Guidelines for Network Management of the Public Switched Networks under Disaster Conditions** (ANSI T1-202-1988)
- **Operation, Administration, Maintenance and Provisioning —Human-Machine Language** (ANSI T1.203-1988)
- **OAM&P — Lower Layer Protocols for Interface Between Operations Systems and Network Elements** (ANSI T1.204-1988)

(continued on page 12)

Box 5.3 (continued)

Standards

(continued from page 1)

- Representation of Places, States of the United States, Provinces and Territories of Canada, Countries of the World and Other Areas for the North American Telecommunications System for Information Interchange (ANSI T1.205-1988)
- Digital Circuit Loopback Test Line for Digital Exchange and PBXs (ANSI T1.206-1988)
- Digital Processing of Voice-Band Signals — Algorithm and Line Format for 32-kbits/s ADPCM (ANSI T1.301-1987)
- Interface Between Carriers and Customer Installations — Analog Voicegrade Switched Access Lines Using Loop-Start and Ground-Start Signaling (ANSI T1.401-1988)
- Network Performance Standards — 32 kbits/s ADPCM Tandem Encoding Limits (ANSI T1.501-1988)
- System M-NTSC TV Signals —Network Interface Specifications and Performance Parameters (ANSI T1.502-1988)
- ISDN Basic Access Interface for Use on Metalic Loops for Application at the Network Side of NT, Layer 1 Specification (ANSI T.601-1988)

12

- Network Performance Parameters for Dedicated Digital Service—Definitions and Measurement Methods (ANSI T1.503)
- Performance Parameters for Packet Switched Data Communication Service (ANSI T1.504)
- Advanced Digital Program Audio Services Analog Interface and Performance Specifications (ANSI T1.505)
- ISDN Signaling Specification for Application at the User-Network Interface, Layer 2 Specification (ANSI T1.602)
- Minimal Set of Bearer Services for ISDN Primary Rate Interface (ANSI T1.603)
- Minimal Set of Bearer Services for ISDN Basic Rate of Interface (ANSI T1.604)

Draft American National Standards of Committee T1 in Final Approval at ANSI

- ISDN Signaling Specification for Application at the User-Network Interface, Layer 2 Specification (ANSI T1.602)
- Formerly ANSI T1.402-ISDN Basic Access Interface for S and T Reference Points — Layer 1 Specification (ANSI T1.605)

Draft American National Standards of Committee T1 in Public Review at ANSI

- The DS4NA Fourth Hierarchical Level (ANSI T1.108)
- Test Line Access (ANSI T1.207)
- Digital Processing of Voice-Band Signals—32 kbits/s ADPCM Line Format Standard (ANSI T1.302)
- Digital Processing of Voice-Band Signals—Algorithm for 24, 32 and 40 kbit/s ADPCM (ANSI T1.303)
- Carrier to Customer Installation DS1 Metallic Interface Specification (ANSI T1.403)
- Customer Installation-to-Network, DS3 Metallic Interface Specification (ANSI T1.404)

First List of Standards

A glance at this list (Box 5.3) conveys a good sense of the committee's early priorities.

Note the T1.110 series of Signalling System No. 7 standards, which relate the applicable CCITT Series-Q Recommendations (as referenced in the Chapter Two) to the North American network. In addition, there is yet a third level of standards needed: the equipment specifications that will ensure suppliers' compliance with CCITT T1 requirements. Appropriate product standards are provided by Bellcore rather than T1. Refer to our later section devoted to Bellcore.

The three-level build-up of CCITT–ECSA-T1–Bellcore is an example of the complex structure needed for worldwide standards to become effective in national networks.

5.2.3 Bellcore, Old "Standards Bearer" by a New Name

Divestiture of the Bell Operating Companies from AT&T deprived them of the central engineering and standardizing services provided by the combination of AT&T headquarters, Bell Laboratories, and Western Electric. Yet the BOCs need coordinated engineering so that separate service territories add up to a reasonably homogeneous national network (see map shown in Figure 5.2). This need has been filled by creation of a new organization, Bell Communications Research. Bellcore's staffing and competence were ready-made by virtue of the transfer of experienced people from AT&T's payroll.

Figure 5.2 Map of the Regional Bell Holding Companies' Service Areas (as Shown on Title Page of the *Catalog of Technical Information*). Copyright © 1984 Bellcore, Reproduced by Permission.

Bellcore's central guidance is particularly important with regard to equipment procurement from competing manufacturers and vendors. The MFJ expressly forbids the BOCs from entering into manufacturing (a restriction that has been challenged, but not removed as of mid-1989). Particularly where equipment for new services (e.g., ISDN) and new facilities (e.g., optical fiber systems) is required, the BOCs depend on Bellcore for standard specifications.

Such specifications are drawn up by an interactive process between Bellcore and the supplier industry. The process involves the preparation of preliminary, generic requirements by Bellcore in the form of a Technical Advisory (TA). The TA is reviewed by the Regional Bell Holding Companies (RBHCs) before release to industry. Bellcore's Information Exchange Management organization distributes the TA to the industry, announces its availability in the "Bellcore Digest of Technical Information," and solicits written comments from interested parties during what is called the open comment period, usually lasting two to three months.

During this period, a Technology Requirements Industry Forum (TRIF) is often held, at which the TA is formally presented by the authors in an open forum. Questions can be addressed on the spot. Optionally, at the request of interested parties, meetings with Bellcore can be arranged to discuss the proposed requirements in greater detail.

After the comment period expires, Bellcore may revise the TA, taking all comments and questions into consideration. The revised TA is reviewed again by the regional companies and, if approved, is issued as a Technical Reference (TR). It is defined as a stable collection of proposed generic requirements, representing Bellcore's view of the needs of a typical regional company. This method of obtaining vendors' interaction on requirements is followed for network equipment modifications to provide for such things as new switching features or transmission facilities.

Interactions among Bellcore, regional company, and vendor for formulating Bellcore's proposed generic requirements, appear to benefit all three parties. Vendors are given the opportunity to comment on requirements, to identify areas of concern, and to raise issues. Bellcore and the regional companies formulate stable, generic requirements that have had the benefit of industry input before being issued.

Bellcore Technical References comply with international, ANSI, and industry standards. The TRs interpret these standards for the use of the BOCs and detail the features, options, and interfaces required. In addition, uniformity of physical construction and environmental requirements is obtained. Equipment reliability allocations are specified so that overall services can meet their providers' objectives. Software is required to be produced according to certain standards for language, format, and structure. The overall thrust is to create a practical multivendor procurement process. Because the BOCs represent a majority of the local exchange carriers in the United States, Bellcore's TRs become a strong unifying force for the equipment used by the telephone industry.

In summary, the structure of the standards process is such that international standards (mainly those of CCITT) establish the broad interfaces and service descriptions. Committee T1 standards superimpose the US interfaces, operating structures, and operating procedures. Bellcore TRs provide specifications for equipment and its performance.

Bellcore offers their standards, specifications, and reports for sale to the general public. Ordering information is given in a 290-page *Catalog of Technical Information*, from which front pages are reproduced in Box 5.4. The carefully worded "Notice" warrants close reading. It reveals the independence of judgment and decision-making left to users of Bellcore's guidance.

The reader may notice also reference to the monthly publication *Digest of Technical Information*. Bellcore recommends subscription, mainly for purposes of updating the catalog, but also for timely news about the regional companies, forthcoming TRIFs, *et cetera*.

Box 5.4

Bellcore *Catalog of Technical Information*. © 1984 Bellcore. Reproduced by Permission. (The reprinted pages are taken from the catalog's 1988 edition.)

CATALOG OF TECHNICAL INFORMATION

NOTICE

This Catalog, all publications listed in it, their prices and availability are subject to change without notice. Bellcore (Bell Communications Research, Inc.), expressly disclaims all liability to anyone arising out of the use of or reliance upon any information set forth in this catalog or in any publication listed herein, or the unavailability of any listed publications. No representation or warranty, expressed or implied, is made with respect to the availability, accuracy, or utility of any information set forth in this catalog or in any publication listed herein.

Bellcore makes no representation or warranty, expressed or implied, with respect to the sufficiency, accuracy, or utility of any information or opinion contained herein. Bellcore expressly advises that any use of or reliance upon said information or opinion is at the risk of the user and that Bellcore shall not be liable for any damage or injury incurred by any person arising out of the sufficiency, accuracy, or utility of any information or opinion contained herein.

No publication listed herein is to be construed as a suggestion by Bellcore, or any other company to any manufacturer to modify or change any of its products nor does any publication represent any commitment by Bellcore, any divested Bell Operating Company (BOC), any Regional affiliate thereof, or any other company to purchase any product or service whether or not it conforms to requirements, criteria, specifications, or other features or functions or information described in any publication listed herein.

Readers are specifically advised that each Regional Company or BOC may have needs, requirements, specifications, or criteria different from those of any other company. Therefore any person interested in obtaining any BOC or Regional Company's actual needs, specifications, requirements, or other information should communicate directly with that Company.

Certain publications listed in this Catalog and offered by Bellcore were prepared prior to the divestiture of the former Bell System (January 1, 1984) and may contain terminology that is now obsolete. In such instances, there being no revision presently available, Bellcore continues to offer those pre-divestiture publications in their existing format at this time.

Box 5.4 (continued)

DESCRIPTION OF BELLCORE TECHNICAL PUBLICATIONS

POST-DIVESTITURE DOCUMENTS

Technical Advisories (TAs)
These publications are documents describing Bellcore's preliminary view of **proposed** generic requirements for products, new technologies, services, or interfaces. TAs are interim documents, that are offered on a no-charge basis (See TA title listing in this catalog).

Technical References (TRs)
These publications are the standard form of Bellcore-created technical documents representing Bellcore's view of proposed generic requirements for products, new technologies, services, or interfaces.

Special Reports (SRs)
These may contain more general, non product-related technical information that has been released to the telecommunications industry by Bellcore.

Science and Technology (STs)
These documents convey to the telecommunications industry highly technical information based on research work performed by Bellcore.

PRE-DIVESTITURE DOCUMENTS

These are publications now offered by Bell Communications Research, Inc. (Bellcore), that were prepared prior to the January 1, 1984 divestiture of the former Bell System, and may contain terminology and reference information that is now obsolete. There being no revision presently available, Bellcore will continue to offer these pre-divestiture publications in their existing format. As appropriate, these documents may be revised and reissued by Bellcore as either Technical Advisories (TAs), Technical References (TRs), Special Reports (SRs), or other document types.

Compatibility Bulletins (CBs)
These Technical Advisories (TAs) (NOT TO BE CONFUSED WITH PRESENT BELLCORE TAs), provided network planning information and compatibility or interface specifications. They were prepared and released by AT&T (pre-divestiture) through the then United States Independent Telephone Association's (now USTA) Equipment Compatibility Committee and Subcommittee on Network Planning.

Information Publications (IPs)
These publications, more general in scope, comprised a collection of non product-specific, non-technical requirements that covered a wide variety of subject areas, such as forecasts, documentation manuals, general reliability guidelines, etc. Many of the former IPs have been revised and released by the Regional Companies.

Technical Descriptions (TDs)
Prepared and released by AT&T (pre-divestiture) as a result of FCC Tariffs filed by the then Bell System, these documents provided a guide for designers, manufacturers and consultants of customer-provided equipment.

Technical References (PUBs)
These publications described the technical engineering requirements for products in the areas of network interfaces, engineering and maintenance support, distribution products, communications protocols and general documentation guidelines.

General information inquiries regarding Bellcore documents may be directed to:

District Manager
Information Exchange Management
Bellcore
445 South Street, Rm 2K-122
Box 1910
Morristown, N.J. 07960-1910

Order forms and instructions for requesting Bellcore documents can be found at the end of the Bellcore section.

Box 5.4 (continued)

CONTENTS

Box 5.4 (continued)

CONTENTS (Continued)

5.2.4 Telecommunications Industry Association (TIA) Standards for User Terminals, Cables, and General Hardware

The Electronic Industry Association (EIA) has long provided standards utilized extensively throughout electronics manufacturing to ensure product consistency. These standards are created by more than 250 committees dealing with consumer, military, and industrial products, components, and microelectrics. More than 300 general standards have been generated for various products. EIA is accredited by ANSI, similar to T1 described earlier; thus, EIA Standards can become US National Standards.

In the areas of interest to this writing, EIA's Information and Telecommunications Technologies Group (ITG) has become a major provider of voluntary industry standards. Standards are drafted by committees, sponsored by the sections within the group's division. These committees operate under EIA legal guides, monitored by EIA's general counsel and special rules administered by EIA's engineering department. The rules and procedures are carefully designed to permit full participation in the standards effort by ITG members and nonmembers as well as users and government representatives, while complying with standards of conduct needed to protect against violations of the law.

EIA standards have been created for the telephone industry for such products as:

- telephones;
- key systems;
- private branch exchanges (PBXs);
- mobile radiotelephones; and
- fiber optics.

On April 29, 1988, the US Telecommunications Suppliers Association (USTSA) merged with the EIA's ITG to create a new organization, the Telecommunications

Industry Association (TIA). It serves as the telecommunications sector of EIA, and works in concert with EIA industry groups and divisions to further overall electronics industry goals and objectives. Four divisions of TIA focus on development of new technical standards and the gathering of market data: Fiber Optics, User Premises Equipment, Mobile Communications, Network Equipment.

The Fiber Optic Division currently has 48 member companies, 24 of which are members of USTSA. There are four sections organized according to product lines and two separate engineering subcommittees (on components and systems), with a total of 14 subcommittees consisting of 253 company engineers.

The work of the division centers around its two engineering standards committees, which identify fiber optic test procedures for components and systems. The division also participates in, and funds, international standards activities in fiber optics. The International Electrotechnical Commission (IEC) and CCITT are the two organizations in which the division's influence and technical expertise have been most productive.

The four sections of the division work to define the market, remove trade impediments, and promote industry growth. The division will be examining its section structure to see if an issue-oriented subdivision may be more meaningful.

The User Premises Equipment Division (UPED) is governed by its own board of directors, which is open to one representative from each member company in the division. There are two sections in this division: Residential Communications (chaired by David Carter of AT&T) and Business Communications (chaired by Linda Johnson, IBM). UPED's principal activities are in national regulatory and legislative matters, standards formulation, and market data gathering. The division works closely with the FCC staff. UPED and its sections also sponsor several engineering committees involved in writing voluntary industry standards for product performance and compatibility. These programs are carried out through EIA's engineering department.

The Mobile Communications Division has three active sections. The Cellular and Common Carrier Radio Section and the Land Mobile Radio Section deal with issues generally regulated by the FCC's Common Carrier Bureau and Private Radio Bureau, respectively. Members of the Personal Communications Section are primarily interested in issues related to cordless telephones and personal radio systems and equipment. The division is actively involved in FCC allocation of radio spectrum, development of standards for digital cellular phones, and proposals for a mobile satellite system.

The Network Equipment Division has sections for Satellite Communications, Fixed Point-to-Point Communications, and Circuit and Packet Switching. Activities of these sections include monitoring FCC proceedings on rural telephone and multiple address systems, updating standards for antenna towers, and monitoring developments in ONA.

5.2.5 State Department Controls US Interaction with CCITT

Because ITU is an intergovernmental organization, its technical committees, CCITT and CCIR, operate under the umbrella of a treaty instrument, the ITU *Convention*. Hence, the work of the CCIs is supported by national administrations, specifically authorized by the respective governments for such purposes. In the many countries where the telecommunication administration is an agency of government, its delegates speak and act directly on behalf of their respective governments. In the United States, by contrast, a government agency must represent US interests to CCITT and CCIR; this role is performed by the Department of State. The responsibility is centered in State's *Bureau of International Communications and Information Policy* (CIP), headed by a presidentially appointed official with ambassadorial rank. Within CIP is placed the *Office of Technical Standards and Development* (TSD), the continuation of a long established group of technically qualified, career officials. This office oversees U.S. participation in the work of CCITT. The director, currently Earl Barbely, is *ex officio* chairman of the US CCITT National Committee. This committee has the status of an *Advisory Committee,* at the discretion of an Executive Order of the president. Any organization may register for committee membership; there are no dues but neither any obligations. Yet this committee serves as State's only forum for coordination, screening, and occasionally rejection of the US telecommunication industry's inputs to the work of CCITT study groups. The reader must understand that membership in the US CCITT National Committee is not contingent on an organization's direct participation in CCITT's work. This latter membership, registered at the ITU's Geneva headquarters, entails a considerable annual monetary contribution, assessed to help defray the administrative and mailing costs. Open to service providers and industrial-scientific organizations under the Convention's provisions, this registration entitles the member to regular receipt of all study group documentation for which it has registered. Such direct membership in CCITT must have State's approval. It provides the base for the organization's intent to attend study group meetings under its own name.

The Department of State's control over US-CCITT standardization efforts may be understood by separating two categories: "affairs of state" and "common purpose group," as explained in Chapter Three, *supra*. Formal conferences at which some issues are decided by vote are affairs of state by definition. For these occasions, a US delegation is constituted and headed by a State Department employee or a designated employee of an appropriate US government agency (e.g., the FCC). In the case of CCITT, the quadrennial Plenary Assembly is such a formal conference. Inasmuch as the task of the PA is predominantly policy decision-making, delegation membership of service providers is intentionally held to a minimum. One PA routine task is the approval of the study groups' Reports, which are then published as Recommendations. Each Report is introduced by the chairman. Therefore, a US national who holds study group chairmanship is expected to be present, although he may not have been made a member of the delegation. Approval of the thousands of pages, cumulatively submitted by the study groups, is viewed as a "rubber stamp" procedure because there is much other business for the PA to transact. On this remaining business, the national delegation could suffice with very few industry advisors because their concerns should have been integrated with an official US position developed prior to the PA's meeting. Indeed, the State Department usually calls at least one preparatory meeting of its above-mentioned National Committee for the sole purpose of preparing an agreed position for a PA. The issues include anticipated rearrangement of study groups, approval of next period's study program, appointment of study group chairmen and vice-chairmen, the CCITT director's and secretariat's problems with processing the paperwork, and relations with other organizations (e.g., ISO and IEC).

Now, consider CCITT's ongoing business in standardization. It is conducted by the various study groups during the period between PAs, through the medium of face-to-face meetings, supported by documentation distributed by mail to all registered participants in a particular study group's work. The documentation consists of Contributions, sent in by members in reply to a specified Question, and of Reports on the outcome of meetings. In this manner, a study group's last meeting before the next PA produces a set of Reports for submission to it, as previously indicated.

Traditionally, all of this study group activity has been viewed as exchange of proposals and subsequent agreements among technical experts, designated to collaborate at an informal, common-purpose group level. Exceptions have been recognized in study groups concerned with international tariff standards, and in other groups where telecommunication service standards "encroach," so to speak, on national regulatory territory. As regards the United States, until the break-up of AT&T, only some CCITT study groups were clearly in the regulatory domain, one on tariffs, the others dealing with service standards affecting record carriers. The latter category, particularly classic telegraph and telex service, was overseen by US government agencies as a jealously guarded competitive business. We must also understand that international agreements on telegraph and related service standards have historically been very detailed and binding. By contrast, equivalent international standardization in the telephone field has been more flexible, except for such rigid requirements as numbering plans and mutual recognition of service signals. AT&T's people brought a lifetime of experience toward solution of these problems to the respective CCITT study groups; they were the only recognized and respected partners for international agreements. The entry of COMSAT (Communications Satellite Corporation) into the US side of international telephone connections raised the possibility of dissenting voices regarding some technical standards. However, because COMSAT had been authorized as a "carrier's carrier," the technicalities of end-user-oriented telephone service remained in the purview of organizations providing the national network distribution service. AT&T and COMSAT developed a *modus vivendi,* which offered COMSAT's interest in transmission standards favorable to satellite circuits a fair chance when US participation in CCITT study groups was involved. Thus, US government people rarely saw a need for injecting their arbitration and coordination authority into the CCITT work, concerned with telephony.

This long period, during which US government avoided control over CCITT nonregulatory activity, is now coming to an end. The new emphasis on competition in domestic and international services necessitates that a governmental official oversee the fair consideration of all diverse proposals and opinions before a "contribution" may proceed in the name of the United States. National Committee practice so far has kept a channel open for submission to CCITT of a contribution in the originating company's name, provided that no US committee member maintains a valid objection.

In fairness to historical fact, the trend toward more governmental control began some years before the AT&T divestiture, for the same reasons that caused the AT&T break-up. Government was drawn into the computer-communications interface, overlap, and terminal device specifications problem areas, where numerous, diffuse competitive interests tend to clash before agreements are reached. Thus, the work of CCITT study groups covering these fields slipped into the purview of governmental oversight for US participation. Data Transmission (SG XVII), Data Communication Networks, (SG VII), and Telematic Services and Terminals (SG VIII) are in this category. As soon as ISDN developed toward definitive Recommendations, the US National Committee established a Joint Working Party, chaired by a knowledgeable member of the NTIA (National Telecommunications and Information Administration) Institute of Telecommunication Sciences (ITS).

As of 1988, there were still nine CCITT study groups entrusted to a member of AT&T headquarters staff as chairman of the corresponding US National Committee Study Group, labelled "C." In early 1989, the State Department announced a reorganization that assigned three "heavyweight" study groups to regulatory status. They are: SG II, now encompassing all services; SG XI, Signalling and Switching; and SG XVIII, ISDN. Remaining under nongovernmental US CCITT (Committee) Study Group chairmanship are: SG V, Protection Against Electromagnetic Effects, and SG VI, Outside Plant, which have rarely received a contribution from the United States; SG IV, Maintenance; SG X, Programming Languages; SG XII, Telephone Transmission Quality; and SG XV Transmission Systems. These last four study groups have indeed received a very high level of attention by AT&T and its spinoff, Bellcore; little evidence of US competitors' contributions is on record.

Before concluding this section, we must make clear that the US CCITT National Committee nowadays is the last stop for US *draft Contributions that have already been approved by Committee T1*. This prior coordination has not prevented controversial discussion at US National Committee or its study groups' meetings, but it has minimized such occurrences.

5.3 THE EUROPEAN SOLUTION: FROM CEPT TO TRAC AND ETSI

5.3.1 CEPT—Conference of European Post and Telecommunications Administrations: Structure[1]

CEPT was founded on June 26, 1959 in Montreux, Switzerland. It is open to all European Postal and Telecommunications Administrations. It now comprises 26 European countries: all the Member States of the European Community and of EFTA,* together with Turkey and Yugoslavia, and several small states.

CEPT regulations are set out in the founding Act of the Conference. Only the most essential points are laid down, in line with the desire of the organizers to retain maximum flexibility. It is stipulated in the Act that only European Postal and Telegraph Administrations belonging to member countries of the Universal Postal Union (UPU) or the International Telecommunication Union can be members of CEPT.

CEPT is independent of all political and economic organizations and carries out its activities along the lines laid down in the Universal Postal Convention and the International Telecommunication Convention.

Since 1969, CEPT has been a conditional member of the UPU. This status permits CEPT to participate as a single unit in the various meetings of the union. This conditional membership applies only to the postal activities of CEPT.

5.3.2 Objectives

The aim of CEPT is the development of relations between member administrations and the harmonization and practical improvement of their administrative services and techniques. Its tasks are as follows:

- the accomplishment of work and development of services of common interest;
- exchange of information and officials;
- study of questions concerning the organization, technical aspects and functions of services;
- simplification and improvement of postal services and telecommunication; and
- common examination of proposals presented to the congress and conferences of the international postal and telecommunication organizations.

---

[1]The text of this section incorporates the material of an appendix to the EC *Green Paper*, 1987.

*The countries of the European Free Trade Association.

5.3.3 Organization

The Plenary Assembly is the supreme body of CEPT. It deals with questions concerning structure and management of the organization, and is competent in all questions related to posts and telecommunications, especially those elements common to both.

The Plenary Assembly meets periodically, generally every two years, for an Ordinary Session. It can also meet for an Extraordinary Session, subject to the agreement of two-thirds of its members.

In the course of plenary sessions, CEPT nominates a member administration to organize the following Ordinary Session. This *Managing Administration* assumes the presidency and secretarial duties as of the end of the current term. It prepares the following session and guarantees CEPT's continuing work between sessions.

The Managing Administration is assisted in its task by a permanent secretarial staff, situated in Bern, Switzerland, called the Liaison Office.

Two different commissions deal with posts and telecommunication, respectively. These organizations have special responsibility for questions concerning service provision, technical aspects, and tariffs. The vast domain covered by these two commissions has given rise to the appointment of numerous committees and study groups to study specific topics.

The committees of the Telecommunication Commission are as follows:

- Co-ordination Committee for Satellite Telecommunications (CCTS);
- Co-ordination Committee on Harmonization (CCH);
- Commercial Action Committee (CAC); and
- Liaison Committee for Transatlantic Telecommunications (CLTA).

The complete organization (committees and study groups) of the Telecommunications Commission is given in Figure 5.3 and Box 5.5.

5.3.4 Relations Between CEPT and the European Community

Formal relations between CEPT and the EC began in March of 1975, by way of a "Communication of the EC Commission." This was the first request for *harmonization* of telecommunication standards. CEPT's response was prompt: it created a new committee *CCH* at the plenary session of Málaga-Torremolinos in April of the same year. *Com CCH* and its working groups became very active during the ensuing years; however, progress toward *de facto* harmonization was negligible due to entrenched national protectionism and insistence on sovereignty.

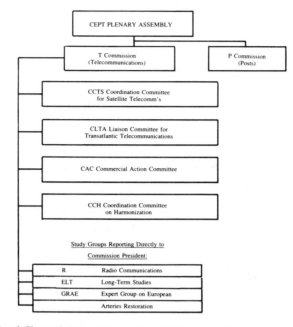

Figure 5.3 Organizational Chart of CEPT (1988; before ETSI was in full operation).

Slowly and steadily, the central bureaucracy of the EC acquired more politi power and with it a greater influence over CEPT at its top level, the ministers posts and telecommunication of the member governments. Applying pressure at t level climaxed in a "Memorandum of Understanding" (MOU), establishing a fraı work of cooperation between the EC and CEPT. The MOU was signed in July 19 It now serves as the platform for the plans of action proposed in the Green Pap

The basic idea of the agreement is that CEPT annual working programs the relevant decisions regarding priorities and schedules are to take into account particular requirements of the Commission, assisted by the Senior Officials Gr on Telecommunications (SOG-T).

The aims of this cooperation are:

- to adopt a common interpretation of international standards; and
- to allow the same or compatible services on an international basis.

The following subjects have been included in the agreed program:

(a) Terminals and user interfaces, relating to the Council Directive on the mu recognition of type approval [86/361/EEC];

(b) ISDN (narrowband) networks and services, in line with the EC's recent I ommendation in this area [86/659/EEC];

Box 5.5
Organization of CEPT

Study Groups of CCH		*Designation*
GSM	Mobile Services	T/GT 10
TE	Terminal Equipment	T/GT 11
TM	Transmission and Multiplexing	T/GT 12
NA	Network Aspects	T/GT 14

These four Study Groups have been transferred to ETSI, the new European
Telecommunication Standards Institute (see the immediately following section in this book).

Study Groups of CAC		*Designation*
Tg	Telegraph Operations and Tariffs	T/GT 1
Tph	Telephone Operations and Tariffs	T/GT 2
TTVS	Television and Sound Transmission	T/GT 4
PGT	General Tariff Principles	T/GT 5
SF	Services and Facilities	T/GT 7
SG	Statistics and Management	T/GT 13

According to the EC Commission's staff report on Telecommunications, CEPT Committee
CAC is leading in the implementation of goals of harmonization at the customer level. Four
high-priority projects are mentioned:

1. MDNS, Managed Data Network Services, such as are now offered in the United States by
   IBM, EDS, and Geisco;
2. Europe-wide Packet-Switched Services, currently a patchwork;
3. Pan-European Videoconferencing;
4. A European "Green Number" service, also known as Freephone, equivalent to the "800"
   number service in North America. CCITT has a recommendation, but country-by-country
   offering so far has not been uniform enough to enable worldwide through-dialing of such
   numbers.

(c) IBC (Integrated Broadband Communications) networks and services, relating
to the RACE program (R&D in Advanced Communication Technologies for
Europe); and

(d) Mobile communications, in line with the Commission's proposed Recommendation and Directive.

Working programs of CEPT regarding standardization have been agreed since
1985 with the Commission and EFTA, with which CEPT has reached a similar agreement. CEPT specifications have the status of Recommendations, which are not mandatory for telecommunication administrations or any other bodies.

The CEPT decided on request of the Commission to study the possibility of working out a "family" of specifications which could be made binding on its members. These are known as *NETs* (Normes Européennes des Télécommunications). To reach this goal, a MOU has been prepared to bind the signatory countries to compulsory acceptance of these specifications. An important application is the type approval of telecommunication terminals which can henceforth be obtained once only, yet recognized by all MOU signatories.

By February 1987, fifteen countries had signed this memorandum, namely the twelve EEC member states plus Sweden, Finland, and Norway.

Implementation of this memorandum has resulted in the creation of a new body, the Technical Recommendations Application Committee (TRAC), Figure 5.4. Its task is to determine a list of NETs to be worked out on a basis of unanimity, and to adopt, under a qualified majority system, the final decision to transform and to publish, as a NET, the work carried out by CEPT technical groups and approved as a recommendation by the Telecommunications Commission.

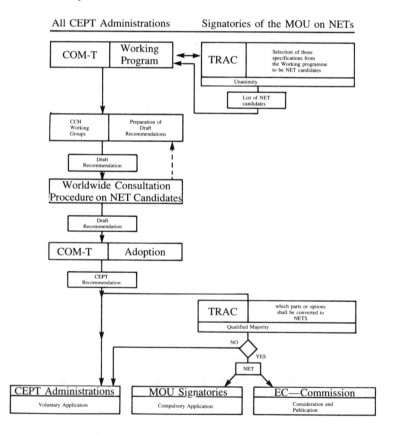

Figure 5.4 Conversion of CEPT Standards to NETs.

NETs can be subdivided into three categories:

(a) those generally valid for all equipment (administrative, security norms, *et cetera*);
(b) those valid for certain types of equipment (interfaces between terminals and networks); and
(c) those that are specifically valid for particular types of terminals (teletex, facsimile, *et cetera*).

The NETs will not contain any clauses which may restrict competition. They will be subject to public debate.

In addition, an agreement has been reached between CEPT, CEN, and CENELEC to avoid overlap in the work of the three bodies, which might otherwise occur, given the increasingly indistinct boundary line that exists between telecommunication and information technology.

5.4 EUROPEAN TELECOMMUNICATIONS STANDARDS INSTITUTE (ETSI)

5.4.1 Genesis of a Regional Powerhouse

This new European institute is a direct implementation of EC *Green Paper* recommendations. The founding decision was made at a meeting of CEPT Directors-General in September 1987. The decision was formally adopted at a follow-up meeting in London, January 1988. The position of the institute's director was immediately opened to Europe-wide applications. By the summer of 1988, Diodato Gagliardi of Italy had been selected to head ETSI. The director's post is limited to five years; three-year extension is possible, at the option of ETSI's supreme body, the General Assembly.

The choice of Dr. Gagliardi as inaugural director is most auspicious. He has twenty-five years of experience in CCITT and CEPT collaborative work. At the time of the EC *Green Paper,* Gagliardi was head of CEPT committee CCH (i.e., the forerunner of ETSI). In prior years, he had become vice-chairman, then chairman, of CCITT SG XV (transmission systems). In 1980, he presided over the CCITT Seventh Plenary Assembly. In 1984, he ran for Director of CCITT, but lost to Theodor Irmer of Germany in the final ballot. Indeed, Irmer and Gagliardi, with quite different national backgrounds and personalities, have in common a supreme competence and self-assurance. These two men, now heading the two most significant organizations in telecommunication standardization, have worked their way up the traditional government monopoly career ladder, starting from modest engineering assignments. Both have mastered the transition to a more competitive, politically-charged environment. If Gagliardi will not make ETSI effective, nobody can.

5.4.2 How ETSI Makes Regional Standards Go All the Way

Need for an ETSI became compelling after EC headquarters realized that neither CCITT nor CEPT standards have the power to eliminate nonconformance in the marketplace. Institutional arrangements were needed by which specified classes of standards may acquire supranational status. CEPT's harmonization committee (CCH) had opened up an avenue in that direction, but the parent organization's top decision-makers could not disregard their respective national prerogatives.

Meanwhile, the information processing industry's manufacturers and vendors in Europe had taken steps toward common equipment standards. The many competing companies had been brought together through CEN and CENELEC (see reference of Chapter Two *supra*). In the field of computers and related terminals, CEN and CENELEC "Norms" began to make a Europe of interworking equipment a reality. Thus, a harsh spotlight was put on telecommunication administrations and their suppliers for not opening network services and equipment to a matching, definitive standardization. We should remember that CEN and CENELEC, both interacting with worldwide ISO and IEC, made standardization easier because majority vote would decide a controversial issue. CCITT and CEPT, however, aim for a more harmonious, unanimous acceptance of their standards. In the final analysis, the goal of binding, supranational standards is not compatible with unanimity. Thus, the road that led to ETSI also led European telecommunication out of the paradise of an infrastructure industry built on voluntary collaboration.

Now that ETSI is in place and operational, Europe boasts a complete, controlling standards superstructure for the "Information Age." Service options and user terminals, all made accessible through "Open Networks," can become portable, as it were. The structure is illustrated in Figure 5.5. Noteworthy is the central, coordinating role of ITSTC (Information Technology Steering Committee). It was formed in 1985 by CEPT, CEN, and CENELEC.

How soon and how effectively the ambitious goals of this multiorganizational structure will be accomplished is a question that cannot be answered at this time. Much depends on steady, popular support for the European Community concept and its broad-gauge implementation by 1992. However, the momentum for the telecommunication sector is now assured by the very independence of the standardizing organizations.

The neatly balanced structure shown here is not protected from pressure groups. The following European organizations were created in parallel with the CEPT-CCH-ETSI gestation period for the purpose of having a hand in standardization:

- EWOS—European Workshop for Open Systems,
- EMUG—European Manufacturer Users Group,
- SPAG—Standards Promotion and Application Group (comprising twelve big manufacturers in the EC).

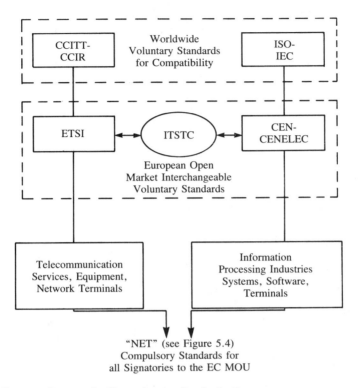

Figure 5.5 European Structure for Comprehensive Standardization

This list is not exhaustive and excludes the many national organizations that pursue similar goals through corporate membership in ETSI or one of the above-listed groups.

5.4.3 ETSI's Organization and *Modus Operandi*

This section reproduces most of ETSI *Rules of Procedure,* from an edition datelined Copenhagen, November 10, 1988. A few articles have been omitted, as is indicated by the words "not reproduced." Where we have omitted only certain paragraphs of a numbered article, this is indicated by "text suppressed." Our comments on certain provisions are also clearly identified in brackets or italics.

The Rules of Procedure reveal a very mature stage of collaborative enterprise. The Europeans who drafted and approved this document have clearly put a common objective above national pride, as may be seen in the choice of English as the sole language for final documents. Weighted voting is another concession to the real world, quite distinct from ITU's procedures under United Nations "one state, one vote" rules. In ETSI, those who have most to contribute, and also the most to gain or lose, have a correspondingly greater control over the outcome. In ITU's technical committees, voting is avoided, as stated before; by their active participation, the "heavyweights," in effect, control the outcome. A list of ETSI's technical committees (*circa* 1989 status) follows at end of this section (Box 5.6).

Box 5.6
Technical† Committees Established by ETSI Technical Assembly
(status: *Circa* 1989)

Code Name	*Field of Standardization*	Chairman's Nationality
ATM	Advanced Testing Methods	Italy
BT	Business Telecommunications	Norway
EE	Equipment Engineering	Switzerland
GSM	Special Mobile Group	Sweden
HF	Human Factors	Germany
†IPR	Intellectual Property Rights	
†ISM	ISDN Standards Management	Germany
NA	Network Aspects	UK
PS	Paging Systems	Spain
RES	Radio Equipment and Systems	Germany
SES	Satellite Earth Stations	France
SPS	Signalling, Protocols, Switching	Sweden
†SRC	Strategic Review Committee	France
TE	Terminal Equipment	UK
TM	Transmission and Multiplexing	France

Author's Note: Blank space in last column indicates chairmanship not known to this writer at time of publication.

†IPR, ISM, and SRC are Special Committees, established apart from the Technical Committees with clear-cut standards drafting assignments.

TABLE OF CONTENTS
RULES OF PROCEDURE OF THE EUROPEAN TELECOMMUNICATIONS STANDARDS INSTITUTE (ETSI)

PREAMBLE

These Rules of Procedure must be read in conjunction with the Statutes of the European Telecommunications Standards Institute, hereinafter referred to as the Institute.

ARTICLE 1—MEMBERSHIP

1.1 Conditions for membership, observer status and counsellor status

1.1.1. Administrations, public network operators, manufacturers, users including private service providers offering services to the public and research bodies who belong to a country falling within the geographical area of the CEPT and who demonstrate their interest in European standardisation efforts in the field of telecommunications, may become members of the Institute. National and European organisations concerned with telecommunications may also become members of the Institute.

1.1.2. In relation to membership, definitions of administrations, public network operators, manufacturers, users, private service providers, research bodies and organisations are given in Annex 1. [not reproduced].

1.1.3. Membership of the Institute cannot be obtained by:
   —supranational organisations such as EEC and EFTA,
   —organisations from outside the geographical area covered by the CEPT or
   —worldwide organisations.

1.1.4. Members may participate individually or grouped in a national or European† basis.

National organisations which combine the functions of national administrations and network operators, may apply for membership in both of the two categories provided that each membership is separately represented.

1.1.5. Members of the Institute have the right to participate directly in the work of the Institute by attending meetings of the two Assemblies and by allocating experts to the Technical Committees and by proposing experts to the Project Teams.

1.1.6. The Institute may have observers.

Observer status may be obtained by European organisations entitled to become members, but who do not wish to do so, and by European organisations concerned with telecommunications who are not entitled to become members.

Non-European organisations concerned with telecommunications may be invited to participate as observers in the Technical Assembly and in the meetings of the Technical Committees.

Observers may attend the meetings of the two Assemblies of the Institute with the right to speak but without the right to vote.

1.1.7. The counsellors mentioned in paragraph 11.3 of the Statutes of the Institute may attend the meetings of the two Assemblies with the right to speak but without the right to vote. [*See* 3.2 below.]

1.2 Admission to membership [text suppressed]

1.3. Withdrawal and expulsion [text suppressed]

ARTICLE 2—STRUCTURE

The Institute shall consist of:

a. A General Assembly
b. A Secretariat
c. A Technical Assembly
d. Technical Committees
e. Project Teams

---

†Throughout this document, "European" means from a country falling within the geographical area of the CEPT.

ARTICLE 3—GENERAL ASSEMBLY

3.1. The General Assembly shall comprise representatives of members of the Institute which may be grouped in national delegations.

3.2. Representatives from the EEC and EFTA shall have a special status as counsellors.

3.3. Representatives from organisations concerned with telecommunications may, by invitation, attend meetings of the General Assembly as observers.

3.4 The primary function of the General Assembly is to make decisions on the management of the Institute. Voting procedures are described in paragraph 12.2., with the exception of the approval of the annual budget and financial statements for which the voting procedures described in paragraph 12.3. shall apply.

3.5. The General Assembly's functions shall be:
- —to elect its Chairman and Vice Chairman
- —to determine the general policy of the Institute
- —to adopt the internal Rules of Procedure of the Institute and any subsequent modifications to them and to decide upon disputes arising from their applications.
- —to adopt amendments to the Statutes
- —to decide upon transferring the headquarters
- —to appoint and to dismiss the Director and the Deputy Director
- —to rule on questions concerning membership and observer status
- —to decide upon the voluntary dissolution of the Institute
- —to adopt the annual budget and approve financial statements
- —to approve the annual report
- —to appoint an auditor annually and to determine the annual remuneration of the auditor.

3.6. Upon the proposal of the Director of the Institute the General Assembly shall examine how to solve any possible disputes arising in the Technical Assembly which are not of a technical nature.

3.7. The General Assembly shall meet at least twice a year in ordinary session. [Additional text suppressed.]

ARTICLE 4—DIRECTOR AND DEPUTY DIRECTOR

4.1. The Director, assisted by the Deputy Director and their staff, shall be responsible for: the assigning of resources; preparation of work schedules and priorities; and relationships with external bodies, all within the framework of guidelines laid down by the General Assembly, and decisions taken by the Technical Assembly.

4.2. The Director, assisted by the Deputy Director, shall be responsible for:
- —the co-ordination of the activities of the Technical Committees and Project Teams
- —the administration of public enquiry on draft standards
- —the day-to-day administration of the staff
- —the recruitment of staff [or] experts
- —giving an account of the management and finances of the Institute to the General Assembly
- —presenting annually the balance sheet for the approval of the General Assembly
- —communicating regularly to the Chairmen of both Assemblies important information within their areas of responsibility

—putting progress reports to both Assemblies
—promotion of the work of the Institute outside and shall be responsible for putting detailed proposals to both Assemblies on:
—the fully costed annual programme of work
—the preparation of the annual budget.
The Director shall be the legal representative of the Institute. He shall hold Chief Executive authority in all matters, apart from those which are expressly reserved for the General Assembly and the Technical Assembly in the Statutes, to manage and administer the affairs of the Institute.

4.3. The Director shall be responsible for the practical organisation of the meetings and work of the General Assembly and the Technical Assembly and shall provide any support required during their meetings.

4.4. The term of office of the Directorship and of the Deputy Directorship should not exceed 5 years, extendable by one further term not exceeding 3 years.

The post of Director or Deputy Director, when vacant, or when the term of office of the current Director or Deputy Director is due to expire, shall be advertised publicly.

The General Assembly shall decide upon the appointment of the Director using the voting procedure set out in paragraph 12.2. from a shortlist of candidates presented to it by the Chairman.

The General Assembly shall decide upon the appointment of the Deputy Director using the voting procedure set out in paragraph 12.2. from a shortlist of candidates presented to it by the Director.

ARTICLE 5—SECRETARIAT [suppressed in its entirety].

ARTICLE 6—TECHNICAL ASSEMBLY

6.1. The Technical Assembly comprises the members of the Institute.

Representatives from the EEC and EFTA shall have a special status as counsellors.

Representatives from organisations concerned with telecommunications may, by invitation, attend meetings of the Technical Assembly as observers.

Individuals of special eminence in the field of telecommunications [or] standardisation may also be invited to become special observers.

6.2. The Technical Assembly is the highest authority within the Institute for the production and approval of technical standards, elaborated by itself (and its technical bodies) or other technical bodies.

6.3. The Technical Assembly's functions shall be:
—to elect its Chairman and Vice Chairmen
—to give guidance to the Director on the work to be undertaken and indicate the priorities and give its views on proposals from other sources (EEC, EFTA, CEPT, etc.)
—to approve the costed annual work programme unanimously, noting the resources required and approve the associated timetable
—to decide upon the creation or cessation of Technical Committees and Project Teams and approve their terms of reference
—to adopt, according to the provisions of Article 14, draft standards submitted to it by the Technical Committees
—to vote at intermediate stages of the preparation of draft standards in the Technical Committees where it has not been possible to arrive at a timely consensus

—to ensure that a public enquiry has been carried out after preparation of the draft standards by the Technical Committees and before approval by the Technical Assembly
—to approve other forms of output of the Institute such as reports, specifications and recommendations as may be decided by the Technical Assembly
—to approve work undertaken under the special voluntary account.

6.4. Voting is described in paragraph 12.2.

6.5. The Technical Assembly shall meet at least twice a year and may meet on other occasions for special meetings. [Addition text suppressed.]

ARTICLE 7—CHAIRMANSHIP AND VICE CHAIRMANSHIP OF THE GENERAL ASSEMBLY AND TECHNICAL ASSEMBLY

7.1. The General Assembly and Technical Assembly each elect their own Chairman and Vice Chairmen using the voting procedure of paragraph 12.2.

7.2. The Chairman and the Vice Chairmen shall be elected for two years. The Chairman or Vice Chairmen may be elected for one further consecutive term only. [Additional text suppressed.]

ARTICLE 8—TECHNICAL COMMITTEES

8.1. The Technical Committees of the Institute will provide a forum for consensus building among European technical experts in developing relevant new standards. They will also be the focus of harmonising a European view for worldwide standards organisations particularly for CCITT and CCIR. They shall consist of experts from members of the Institute meeting as required on an ad hoc basis. With the approval of the Technical Assembly a Technical Committee can involve participants who are not members of the Institute.

8.2. The Technical Committees shall submit proposals for draft standards to the Technical Assembly for approval, after examination of the proposals made by the Project Teams and any Sub Committees. The Technical Committees shall endeavour to reach consensus. If no consensus can be reached, the Chairman of the Committee can decide to take an indicative vote amongst the members of the Committee. After this vote, if it is still not possible to reconcile diverging opinions all alternative opinions shall be submitted to the Technical Assembly for decision.

8.3. The Technical Committees may appoint their own officers and designate their rapporteurs.

8.4. Technical Committees shall keep the Secretariat regularly advised of their activities for the information of members of the Technical Assembly.

8.5. Subject to any directions from the Technical Assembly, Technical Committees shall be free to organise themselves.

8.6. The meetings of the Technical Committees shall be hosted on a voluntary basis by members of the Institute and costs of attendance shall be borne by the organisations of each attendee.

ARTICLE 9—PROJECT TEAMS

9.1. The Project Teams of the Institute created by the Technical Assembly for well defined tasks and limited time periods will consist of small numbers of experts specifically chosen for their competence and their availability for the tasks entrusted to them.

9.2. The Teams shall be disbanded when their tasks are completed—unless fresh or further tasks are given to them. The Teams shall submit draft documents to a Technical Committee for peer group consensus forming before submission to the Technical Assembly, but the Technical Assembly may also specify they be submitted directly via the Director.

9.3. Members should be advised regularly by the Director of progress of work of the Teams.

9.4. Subject to any directions from the Technical Assembly, Project Teams may be free to organise themselves.

ARTICLE 10—FINANCIAL YEAR

The financial year of the Institute shall commence on January 1 and end on December 31.

ARTICLE 11—FINANCE

11.1. The budget voted annually by the General Assembly shall comprise:

11.1.1. The common operating costs (salaries, expenses and other emoluments, costs of premises, etc.) of the Secretariat.

11.1.2. The costed work programme, which has been agreed unanimously by the Technical Assembly. This would cover the costs of Project Teams whose work is included in the agreed programme; and a contingency fund to meet the costs of urgent work that must be undertaken, which arises between meetings of the General Assembly.

11.1.3. A special voluntary account to cover the costs of all other work undertaken and not covered by 11.1.2, which the Technical Assembly has agreed can be undertaken.

A special "language account" to cover the costs of interpretation in French and German in the Technical Assembly and translation into French and German of the approved standards. [Additional text suppressed.]

ARTICLE 12—VOTING

12.1. Principles

In all bodies of the Institute, members shall endeavour to reach consensus.

National weighted voting (using procedure A) shall apply in both the General Assembly and the Technical Assembly subject to

—in the General Assembly, individual voting (using procedure B) shall apply to the approval of the annual budget and financial statements,

—in the Technical Assembly, approval of the costed work programme shall be unanimous.

Voting procedures shall be reviewed after a period of two years from the adoption of the Memorandum of Understanding between CEPT Telecommunications Administrations to establish a European Telecommunications Standards Institute on 15 January 1988.

12.2. Procedure A—National weighted voting

Weighted voting by national delegations as stipulated in Annex 4 shall apply. The views of operators, manufacturers, users and research bodies shall be taken into account by delegations in arriving at a view on how their votes are cast.

12.3. Procedure B—Individual voting

Each member shall have an individual vote. The aggregate votes of none of the type of members defined in Article 6 of the Statutes‡ shall exceed 35% of the total votes cast. The

---

‡Administrations; public Network Operators; manufacturers; users, including private service providers offering services to the public; and research bodies.

percentage of votes needed to approve a proposal shall be 71% of the total votes cast except where the Rules of Procedure provide otherwise.

12.4. Care should be taken to protect minority rights.

12.5. Under the voting procedure described in paragraph 12.2., the vote of each national delegation shall be cast by the head of the national delegation.

12.6. An applicant Administration member whose country is not included in the list of allocations of weightings (Annex 4) shall be consulted first by the Chairman of the General Assembly as to the size of the weighting applied for. The Chairman shall then obtain the views of the other members of the Institute, after which he shall obtain the views of the Chairman of TRAC, who will have similarly consulted the signatories of the TRAC, with a view to ensuring there is consistency in the weightings allocated by both the Institute and TRAC.

The Chairman shall subsequently put a proposal before a meeting of the General Assembly for an allocation of weighting to the applicant Administration, and for a consequential amendment to Annex 4. Voting will be in accordance with procedure A subject to the majority vote required being 75% of the total weighted votes cast.

ARTICLE 13—QUORUM AND PROXY VOTING

13.1. In any meeting of the General Assembly and the Technical Assembly, the quorum of those present or represented required for voting under the procedure described in paragraph 12.2. shall consist of at least 50% of the total number of weighted votes given in Annex 4.

The quorum of those present or represented required in the two Assemblies for voting under the procedure described in paragraph 12.3. shall consist of at least 50% of the members.

13.2. A member unable to attend a meeting of the General Assembly or the Technical Assembly may give its vote to another member to cast as a proxy vote provided it has notified the Chairman of that Assembly in advance. No member may cast more than one proxy vote.

ARTICLE 14—ELABORATION, APPROVAL AND IMPLEMENTATION
OF STANDARDS

14.1. Elaboration

Standards approved by the Institute shall be known as ETS (European Telecommunications Standards).

ETS (and I-ETS mentioned in Article 14.5.) shall be elaborated within the fields set out in Article 3 of the Statutes of ETSI which include:

(a) telecommunications terminal equipment including interfaces to networks,
(b) areas common to telecommunication and information technology according to decisions made by the ITSTC or common to telecommunications and broadcasting, or
(c) areas which embrace the telecommunications networks themselves and other areas such as radio communications.

14.2. General

Each national delegation shall inform the Director and the relevant Counsellor in writing of the recognised national standards organisation or organisations having the exclusive responsibility for carrying out the establishment of the national position for the vote, and the standstill and the transposition requirements referred to in this Article, together with their rules which govern how these functions are carried out. Any member shall have the right to inspect a copy of these rules held by the Director and bring to the attention of the General Assembly any problems arising from their application.

14.3. Standstill Period

From the date the Technical Assembly decides that ETSI should produce a standard on a specific matter with its defined scope and for the duration, not generally exceeding 15 months, the Technical Assembly sets down as being required to prepare and adopt that standard, the organisations identified in Article 14.2. shall not publish a new or revised national standard which is not completely in line with an ETS or EN in existence or in preparation on the specific matter in question or take any other action which could prejudice the harmonization intended.

14.4. Public Enquiry

Before a Technical Committee according to Article 8.2. or the Director according to Article 9.2. submits a draft ETS for approval to the Technical Assembly a public enquiry should have been carried out for this draft. The administration within ETSI for this public enquiry shall be the responsibility of the Director. In the ETSI Member Countries the public enquiry shall be carried out by the organisations referred to in Article 14.2. Moreover for a draft ETS which is intended to become a NET a worldwide public enquiry shall be carried out under the responsibility of the Director. Any comments received during the time set shall be given due consideration in an appropriate Technical Committee.

14.5. Approval Procedure**

An ETS shall be approved by the weighted voting procedure of Article 12.2. The vote shall be taken by correspondence except where the Chairman of the Technical Assembly decides that the vote is to be taken at a meeting announced thirty days beforehand. The procedure of Article 14.4. and this procedure may also be applied to documents coming from other organisations (eg. CCITT or CCIR recommendations).

In the event that a standard is not approved, then the votes of EC members only shall be counted: if 71% of the total votes cast by the EC countries are in favour of the proposed draft standard and at least 8 countries are in favour, then it shall be adopted as a European Telecommunications Standard in the European Community and other countries which have voted in favour.

The Technical Assembly may decide in a specific case that a limited period of application is to be associated for a draft standard either because the standard represents a provisional solution for a more advanced standard coming later or that the standard is immature and requires some period of trial. In such cases a standard shall be approved by the above procedures but designated as an "Interim" European Telecommunications Standard or I-ETS.

14.6. Transposition Arrangements

When ETSI has approved an ETS on a specific matter then on an agreed date set by the Technical Assembly the organisations mentioned in Article 14.2. shall ensure that all conflicting national standards on that specific matter are withdrawn. They shall refer interested parties enquiring about standards on that specific matter to where copies of the relevant ETS can be obtained.

**Author's Note: Weighted voting is an important procedural difference from ITU, where the one member, one vote rule prevails. However, CCITT and CCIR normally do not submit their Recommendations to voting approval; hence, the customary preamble "the CCITT . . . *unanimously* decides," *et cetera* found in the opening paragraph of most Recommendations.

The organisations referred to in Article 14.2. shall be entitled to publish and market the texts of ETS and I-ETS according to a format specified by ETSI.

14.7. Worldwide Telecommunications Standardisation

The activities of the Institute shall build upon worldwide standards, existing or in preparation, and furthermore will contribute to the production of harmonised new worldwide standards in the same fields.***

Members of ETSI shall support within worldwide organisations the promotion of ETS as the basis of worldwide recommendations and standards.

The Technical Assembly shall be responsible for approving arrangements for the promotion of ETS as described above.

In addition members of ETSI shall support common positions for worldwide organisations (e.g. CCITT and CCIR) which have been adopted by the Technical Assembly.

ARTICLE 15—RELATIONSHIP OF THE INSTITUTE TO OTHER BODIES

15.1. Standards which have been identified by TRAC as candidate NETs shall be transmitted to this external body for consideration by that Committee for possible adoption as a mandatory standard given legal force.

15.2. The Institute should play its part in supporting EWOS in developing proposals for OSI functional standards in ways to be determined by the ITSTC.

15.3. The Institute and the other European standards bodies shall co-ordinate viewpoints via the ITSTC thus consolidating the views of the major industrial and networking operators throughout Europe, and facilitating the long term integration of standardisation activities.

ARTICLE 16—TRANSITION PERIOD

A transition period, as short as possible, shall be allowed for the orderly transfer of CEPT's technical pre-standardisation and standardisation work to the Institute. During this period a committee comprising the Director, the Deputy Director, the Chairman and Vice Chairmen of the Technical Assembly, the Chairman and Vice Chairmen of CCH, the Chairmen of CR and CAC, the Chairmen of the CCH Working Groups, the Chairmen of GMR, SF and RES, the Chairman and Vice Chairman of TRAC and the manager of the CCH Permanent Secretariat shall be established to ensure close co-ordination between the Institute and CEPT.

In particular, this committee shall draw up a plan within the first six months after the inaugural General Assembly for the orderly transfer from CEPT to the Institute of relevant activities and appropriate Working Groups, taking into account the importance of ensuring continuity of work and avoiding duplication. Any differences of view shall be presented to the Technical Assembly or General Assembly as appropriate for resolution.

ARTICLE 17—REVIEW OF ACTIVITIES

An evaluation of the operations of the Institute, including the Rules of Procedure, should be made by early 1990 by the members. In preparation for this, the Director shall present a report to the members on the activities of the Institute since its creation.

***Author's Note: The goal stated in the first paragraph seems to be in potential conflict with the priority of ETSI's standards claimed later.

ARTICLE 18—OFFICIAL LANGUAGES

18.1. The official languages of the General Assembly shall be English, French and German. Subject to the provisions of paragraphs 18.2. and 18.3. below, the official documents such as the annual report shall be published in English, French and German.

18.2. The official language of the Technical Assembly shall be English. Simultaneous interpretation in French and German shall however be provided and the costs of the interpretation shall be covered by a special "language account". The costs of the special "language account" shall be met by contributions from the member Administrations having agreed to share those costs.

Draft-standards and standards (ETS) and all other documents shall be approved and published in English.(*)

18.3. The working language in the Technical Committees and the Project Teams shall be English. Documents produced by Technical Committees and Project Teams shall be in English.*

18.4. Once a standard (ETS) has been approved by the Technical Assembly and published in English as an official standard, it may be translated into French and German and published equally as an official standard. The costs of the translation shall be covered by the special "language account".

ARTICLE 19—LITIGATION [text suppressed]

ARTICLE 20—AMENDMENTS TO THE RULES OF PROCEDURE [not reproduced]

ANNEX 1 [not reproduced]

ANNEX 2—CONTRIBUTION TO THE COMMON OPERATING COSTS

25 unit-class	Germany (Fed. Rep. of)
	France
	Italy
	United Kingdom
18 unit-class	Spain
10 unit-class	Austria
	Belgium

---

*Author's Note: ETSI's language policy is the most remarkable in the history of international organizations. Agreement on English as the sole official documentation language is in direct contrast with ITU policy applied to CCITT and CCIR study group documentation and eventual, formal publication. This policy was set when English and Spanish joined French, originally the only language of published documentation. On occasion, the Spanish delegate at a CCITT meeting has gone so far as to hold up proceedings while, as he announced, he was looking for a text under discussion in Spanish translation where it appeared on a different page number. The CCITT Secretariat has been made to labor under extraordinary pressure to "align" translations so that the equivalent texts would appear on exactly identical pages in three languages. Obviously, the Francophone and Spanish-speaking ETSI members want none of this.

	Denmark
	Finland
	Greece
	Ireland
	Norway
	Netherlands
	Portugal
	Sweden
	Switzerland
	Turkey
	Yugoslavia
1 unit-class	Cyprus
	Iceland
	Luxembourg
	Malta
1/2 unit-class	Liechtenstein
	Monaco
	San Marino
	Vatican City

ANNEX 3 [not reproduced]

ANNEX 4—NATIONAL WEIGHTED VOTES

1. The percentage of votes needed to approve a proposal shall be 71% of the total votes cast (rounded up to the nearest whole number of votes), if not otherwise provided.
2. Allocation of weightings shall be as given below in order to determine the result:

France	10
Germany (Fed. Rep. of)	10
Italy	10
United Kingdom	10
Spain	8
Belgium	5
Greece	5
Netherlands	5
Portugal	5
Sweden	5
Switzerland	5
Austria	3
Denmark	3
Finland	3
Ireland	3
Norway	3
Cyprus	2
Iceland	2

Luxembourg	2
Malta	2
Monaco	1

[ETSI, 1989.]

5.5 CCITT RESPONDS TO CRITICISM

Worldwide clamor for increased standardization output has put pressure on CCITT's study group work. Criticism focuses particularly on the four-year period between release of formally approved Recommendations. While ITU's budget has been held down by its governing Administrative Council, the ever-growing flood of standards-preparatory documentation seems to beg for increased funds if the approved output is to keep pace. Consider the growth in page counts of CCITT Plenary Assembly books:

Seventh PA Yellow Book (1980)	6,000 pages
Eighth PA Red Book (1984)	10,000 pages
Ninth PA Blue Book (1988)	19,400 pages

(Page total rounded off; Blue Book publication in progress during 1989).

These statistics tell only part of the story. The frequency and intensity of meetings have also increased. So has attendance increased by many poorly informed participants, an encumbrance for the small permanent staff.

In considering these realities *versus* demands on CCITT, this writer perceives several contradictions. The first is in the incessant demand from user groups and some vendors of innovative equipment, in particular, for faster and more definitive CCITT standardization when economic "prove-in" of new systems or services requires a market experimentation period. Most important is feedback from selective applications, which can cause considerable modification of a proposed standard. In fact, in the bygone days of the integrated Bell System, no new service or new Western Electric product ever became a "system standard" until after exhaustive field trials and subsequent modifications in the responsible engineering departments. If this path proved unavoidable in a one-company, noncompetitive environment, how much more critical would it be to arrive at an acceptable standard among hotly competing parties?

The second contradiction is in restricting funds for CCITT work while expecting much expanded output. The decisions for financing CCITT activities are made by jaundiced-eyed representatives of the industrialized nations' governments; their numerically stronger administrative partners that represent less developed countries prefer funding priorities to benefit assistance to developing countries. Thus, citizens of the same countries that keep a tight string on the CCITT purse, paradoxically, fault the organization for not giving them standards at the rate desired by the developed markets.

The third paradox is in unprecedented, liberal spending of manufacturers', vendors', and consultants' man-hours and travel costs for conferences, symposia, and seminars focused on standards, while a handful of companies supply the few people capable of creating standards agreements.

Against this confusing background, the CCITT Ninth Plenary Assembly, Melbourne, November 1988, had two lines of reform to consider. One focused on streamlining of study group programs in adjacent or overlapping specializations. This is not new; a careful examination of the study group structure had become traditional, since the late 1960s. Several, now vacant, study group numbers bear witness to past consolidations (e.g., numbers XIII, XIV, and XVI). However, past streamlining was limited to agreements developed during the PA's crowded meeting days. This time, in 1988, the PA had the benefit of a *Special Group "S" Recommendations*, prepared during the preceding three years.

As a result, the post-1989 study group structure reflects several improvements, as shown in the juxtaposition of the study group tables before and after the Ninth PA (see Box 5.7). Most significant is the step taken toward a unified concept of *telecommunication* services. Until then, the traditional separation of telegraph operations and engineering practices from those for telephone had prevailed. Yet digital systems facilitate transmission and switching of electronic bit streams that can represent many types of superimposed messages. The proposition of ISDN carries this capability to the point where the same networks become conduits for a panoply of services. Taking note of these developments, the Ninth PA was able to merge all service-definition tasks into SG I. Questions on network operations, regardless of service carried, are assigned to SG II. Further, SG XVIII, which had controlled all digital systems standardization since 1972, would henceforth concentrate on ISDN only. Digital switching will continue to be pursued by SG XI and digital transmission by SG XV, as has been the practice for some years. The difference now is that SG XVIII will leave them free from potential overlap.

The Ninth Plenary Assembly's other reform action is laid down in three Resolutions. The lowest numbered, Resolution No. 2 [Box 5.8], which previously provided for *provisional* approval of new or revised Recommendations, was completely recast to encourage definitive, final approval at any time between Plenary Assemblies. Trade publications have hailed this change as an important step toward a more timely release of standards. However, as the terse 1968 edition shows, accelerated approval has a twenty-year history. The procedure has been used, particularly in the circulation of new or revised Series X: Data Networks Recommendations. If the new procedure, which assures approval without resubmission to the next PA, will, in practice, speed up the output remains to be seen.

Two other Resolutions address the critical pressures on CCITT performance in two ways. Resolution No. 17 appeals to the higher powers of the ITU Plenipotentiary Conference in May–June of 1989. Its text, reproduced in Box 5.9, is self-explanatory. Resolution No. 18, reproduced in Box 5.10, establishes an *ad hoc* group under CCITT's umbrella, with the mandate to submit a report for action by the next (i.e., Tenth PA), likely to meet in 1992.

Box 5.7 (a)
CCITT Study Groups with Significant Name Changes
(Name in brackets was used in the 1985–1988 period)

	Designation	Title
COM I	Study Group I	Services [Definition, operation and quality of service aspects of telegraph, data transmission and telematic services, e.g., facsimile, teletex, videotex]
COM II	Study Group II	Network Operation [Operation of telephone network and ISDN]
COM IV	Study Group IV	Maintenance [Transmission maintenance of international lines, circuits, and chains of circuits; maintenance of automatic and semiautomatic networks]
COM XI	Study Group XI	Switching and Signalling [ISDN and telephone network switching and signalling]
COM XV	Study Group XV	Transmission Systems and Equipment [Transmission systems]
COM XVIII	Study Group XVIII	ISDN [Digital networks, including ISDN]

Note: Study Groups III, V, VI, VII, VIII, IX, X, XII, XVII did not change. They are listed in Box 5.7(b).

Box 5.7 (b)
Study Groups Continuing Unchanged, 1989–1992

Designation		Title
COM III	Study Group III	Tariff and accounting principles
COM V	Study Group V	Protection against electromagnetic effects
COM VI	Study Group VI	Outside plant
COM VII	Study Group VII	Data communications networks
COM VIII	Study Group VIII	Terminals for telematic services
COM IX	Study Group IX	Telegraph networks and telegraph terminal equipment
COM X	Study Group X	Languages for telecommunication applications
COM XII	Study Group XII	Transmission performance of telephone networks and terminals
COM XVII	Study Group XVII	Data transmission over the telephone network
CMTT‡		Television and sound transmission

‡Joint CCIR-CCITT Study Group administered by the CCIR.

Box 5.7 (c)
Special Autonomous Groups
(These three groups produce tutorial handbooks on subjects of particular interest to developing countries. They do not make standards.)

Designation	Title
GAS 7 (continued)	Rural telecommunications
GAS 9 (continued)	Economic and technical aspects of transition from an analogue to a digital network (case study of a global network)
GAS 12 (new for 1989)	Strategy for the introduction of new nonvoice telecommunication services in developing countries

Note: Other CCITT Groups not shown in detail are: World Plan Committee and four Regional Plan Committees; four Regional Tariff Groups.

Box 5.8

CCITT Resolution No. 2 (IXth Plenary Assembly, Melbourne, 14–25 November 1988)

RESOLUTION No. 2

Approval of new and revised Recommendations
between Plenary Assemblies
(Melbourne, 1988)

The CCITT,

considering

     (a)   that rapid changes in technology and telecommunication services make it desirable for an accelerated procedure to be used for the approval of new and revised Recommendations between Plenary Assemblies;

     (b)   that use of this procedure should be encouraged to reduce the work-load on Plenary Assemblies;

decides

     that the approval of new and revised Recommendations between Plenary Assemblies may be sought from Members in accordance with the following rules:

1.   **Prerequisities**

1.1   Upon request of the Study Group Chairman the Director of the CCITT shall explicitly announce the intention to seek to apply the approval procedure set out in this Resolution when convening the meeting of the Study Group. He/she shall include the specific intent of the proposal in summarized form. Reference shall be provided to the report or other documents where the text of the draft new Recommendation or the draft revised Recommendation to be considered may be found.

     This information shall also be distributed to all Members.

     The invitation to the meeting as well as the advice on the intended use of this approval procedure should be sent by the Director of the CCITT so that it shall be received, so far as practicable, at least three months before the meeting.

1.2   Approval may only be sought for a draft new Recommendation within the Study Group's mandate as defined by the Questions allocated to it in accordance with Article 58, No. 326 of the Nairobi Convention. Alternatively, or additionally, approval may be sought for amendment of an existing Recommendation within the Study Group's mandate, unless the text of that Recommendation specifically excludes application of this procedure.

1.3   Where a draft Recommendation (or revision) falls within the mandate of more than one Study Group, the Chairman of the Study Group proposing the approval should consult and take into account the views of any other Study Group Chairmen concerned before proceeding with the application of this approval procedure.

Box 5.8 (continued)

1.4   In the interests of stability, revision of a Recommendation approved during a given study period should not normally be put to this procedure again during the same study period unless the proposed revision complements rather than changes the agreement reached in the previous version.

2.   Requirements at the Study Group's meeting

2.1   After debate at the Study Group's meeting the decision of the Delegations to apply this approval procedure must be unanimous (but see 2.3).

2.2   This decision must be reached during the meeting upon the basis of a text available in its final form to all participants at the meeting. Exceptionally, but only during the meeting, delegations may request more time to consider their positions. Unless the Director of the CCITT is advised of formal opposition from any of these Delegations within a period of six weeks after the last day of the meeting, he shall proceed in accordance with section 3.1.

2.3   A delegate may advise at the meeting that his/her delegation is abstaining from the decision to apply the procedure. This delegation's presence shall then be ignored for the purposes of 2.1 above. Such an abstention may subsequently be revoked, but only during the course of the meeting.

3.   Consultation

3.1   Within one month of a Study Group's final decision to seek approval, the Director of the CCITT shall request Members to inform him/her within three months whether they approve or do not approve the proposal.

        This request shall be accompanied by reference to the complete final text in the three working languages of the proposed new Recommendation of the proposed revised Recommendation.

3.2   The CCITT Secretariat shall also advise RPOAs, SIOs and IOs participating in the work of the Study Group in question that Members are being asked to respond to a consultation on a proposed new Recommendation or proposed revised Recommendation, but only Members are entitled to respond.

3.3   If 70% or more of the replies from Members indicate approval, the proposal shall be accepted.

        If the proposal is not accepted it shall be referred back to the Study Group. Subject to further consideration in the Study Group, the proposal may be submitted again for approval, either using the procedure set out in this Resolution (including the prerequisites in section 1 above) or through the Plenary Assembly according to section I.12 of Resolution No. 1.

3.4   Those Members who indicate disapproval are encouraged to advise their reasons and to indicate possible changes in order to facilitate further consideration by the Study Group.

4.   Notification

4.1   The Director of the CCITT shall promptly notify the results of the consultation by Circular-letter.

Box 5.8 (continued)

The Director of the CCITT shall arrange that this information is also included in the next available ITU Notification.

4.2   Should minor, purely editorial amendments or correction of evident oversights or inconsistencies in the text as presented for approval be necessary, the CCITT Secretariat may correct these with the approval of the Chairman of the Study Group.

4.3   Any comments received along with responses to the consultation shall be collected by the CCITT Secretariat and submitted to the next meeting of the Study Group or to the relevant Special Rapporteur for consideration.

4.4   The Secretary General shall publish the approved new Recommendations or revised Recommendations in the working languages as soon as practicable, indicating, as necessary, a date of entry into effect.

RESOLUTION No. 2

Provisional Recommendations

(Mar del Plata, 1968)

The International Telegraph and Telephone Consultative Committee

decides that:

1. If the necessary authority is granted by the Plenary Assembly, a Study Group meeting may decide that the procedure for provisional approval be applied to a draft Recommendation.

2. In cases of urgency a Study Group meeting may decide that the procedure for provisional approval be applied to a draft Recommendation. Such a decision shall be taken by unanimous agreement between the administrations and recognized private operating agencies represented at the meeting of the Study Group, both in respect of the Recommendation and the need for urgent approval.

3. The C.C.I.T.T. Secretariat shall then request the administrations of countries Members of the I.T.U. to inform it within three months whether they approve the provisional adoption of the draft Recommendation concerned. The Recommendation shall be provisionally adopted if, within this time limit, a simple majority of favourable replies is received provided that more than half of the members of the Study Group concerned have replied.

4. Definitive adoption will be a matter for the following Plenary Assembly.

Note – For the purpose of this Resolution, use of the term "Member" should not be read as having any implications for the customary practice of each country in dealing with CCITT matters. It should be further noted that Article 11 of the Nairobi Convention, Nos 86 and 87, states that administrations of all Members of the Union are, of right, members of the CCITT.

Box 5.9

CCITT Resolution No. 17 (IXth Plenary Assembly, Melbourne, 14–25 November 1988

RESOLUTION No. 17

Pre-eminence of CCITT in world-wide telecommunications standardisation

(for the attention of WATTC and the consideration of the Plenipotentiary
Conference via the Administrative Council)

The IXth CCITT Plenary Assembly, Melbourne, 1988,

considering

(a) the accelerating pace of development of telecommunications
technology which is shortening product life cycles and increasing the range and
diversity of new services and applications and the speed with which they become
feasible;

(b) the high priority accorded by Member countries of the ITU to
investment in telecommunications systems and services and the strong desire
which exists for this investment to be based upon CCITT Recommendations;

(c) the need for timely and reliable CCITT Recommendations to assist
all Member countries in the balanced development of their telecommunications
infrastructure;

(d) that the updating of CCITT Resolution No. 1 of the IXth Plenary
Assembly gives a formal basis for a number of immediate and useful practical
changes in Study Groups' working procedures;

(e) the need for CCITT to manage its expanding work-load effectively
and efficiently taking full account both of resource constraints which affect
the Union as a whole and the quality and universality of the results of the
CCITT's work;

(f) the need for CCITT to work effectively with national and regional
standardization activities in particular through working to comparable time-
frames;

(g) the need for CCITT to examine closely its appropriate relations
with other international standardisation bodies, including in particular the
CCIR, ISO and IEC in order to reflect properly the implications of increasing
convergence of technologies;

(h) the need for CCITT to maintain its pre-eminent position in the
field of world-wide standardisation for telecommunications.

noting that

1. the consequences of CCITT's failing to keep well abreast will be that
the coordinated development of new world-wide systems and services will be
delayed, and the cost of their introduction will be increased through lack of
economies of scale which affects all Members but particularly developing
countries;

2. for CCITT to be fully responsive to the rapid changes in the world
telecommunications environment now in train it must work with the maximum
flexibility and be able to make timely adjustments as and when necessary to its
procedures and working methods;

Box 5.9 (continued)

<u>observing that</u>

the periods of time between CCITT Plenary Assemblies and Plenipotentiary Conferences of the Union are such that rapid changes to working procedures for the CCITT as currently set out in the Convention are very difficult to achieve;

<u>requests the Administrative Council</u>

<u>to convey to the Plenipotentiary Conference, Nice, 1989 an invitation to endorse</u>

the importance of the CCITT's maintaining its pre-eminent world-wide position in telecommunications standardisation through its Recommendations and the need, in order to ensure this, for the CCITT to give priority to:

- modernisation,

- flexibility,

- efficiency,

in the organisation and working methods, and

- cooperation

in the production of high quality Recommendations;

<u>and to request the Plenipotentiary Conference</u>

when it reviews the International Telecommunication Convention, Nairobi, 1982

- to consider what changes may be needed to enable the CCITT to do what is necessary in a timely way to maintain its pre-eminent position;

- to note in particular Resolution No. 2 of the CCITT Plenary Assembly, Melbourne, 1988, and take the appropriate steps so that the CCITT can achieve immediate improvements in its performance.

Box 5.10

CCITT Resolution No. 18 (IXth Plenary Assembly, Melbourne, 14–25 November 1988 [revised text])

SOURCE: WORKING GROUP ON CCITT WORKING METHODS AND STRUCTURE
TITLE: FUTURE EVOLUTION OF THE CCITT WORKING METHODS AND STRUCTURE

RESOLUTION No. 18

FUTURE EVOLUTION OF THE CCITT WORKING METHODS AND STRUCTURE

Box 5.10 (continued)

The IXth Plenary Assembly of the CCITT, Melbourne, 1988
considering
(a) that there is general agreement regarding the need for the future evolution towards a functional CCITT Study Group structure;
(b) that with the development of ISDN many aspects of the traditionally separate voice and non-voice services are likely to be drawn closer together;
(c) that related CCITT studies should take into account such growing commonality of service provision;
(d) that the work of the CCITT will increasingly need to take account of the needs of broadband/broadcast services and that increasing liaison with CCIR for these and other converging areas will be required;
(e) that there is continuing pressure to increase the efficiency of working in CCITT Study Groups and to reduce costs without prejudicing the quality and universality of the results of the CCITT's work;
(f) that any proposed reorganization must take account of the needs of both developed and developing countries;
(g) that the relations between the CCITT and other relevant bodies inside and outside the ITU should be taken into account including harmonization of the respective work programmes to the extent possible;
(h) that the working methods of CCITT Study Groups may be affected by the structure of the Study Groups and that this should be taken into account;
(i) that the further evolution of CCITT organization and working methods may be affected by the decisions of WATTC-88, as well as those of the Plenipotentiary Conference;

resolves

1.   to establish an ad hoc Group, open to all administrations, RPOAs and scientific and industrial organizations participating in the work of the CCITT for the purpose of continuing studies related to the working methods and structure of CCITT and CCITT's relations with other relevant bodies within and without the ITU;

2.   that the principal task of the Group will be to develop specific proposals designed to ensure that the CCITT continues to maintain its pre-eminent world-wide position in telecommunications standardization. The Group's work should be based on the need for the CCITT to give priority to the following principles:

—modernization,
—flexibility,
—efficiency, in organization and working methods,
—cooperation, in the production of high quality Recommendations

the Group should, amongst any other issues it may consider relevant, develop proposals on future Study Group structure having regard to the issues on this subject left open by Special Study Group 'S' for consideration after the IXth Plenary Assembly as in AP IX-1, Annex C;

the Group should review all existing Resolutions, Series-A Recommendations and other relevant texts with a view to improving further the efficiency of CCITT working methods. In its work, the Group should take account of relevant decisions of, and instructions from, the

Box 5.10 (continued)

Plenipotentiary Conference, as well as the results of the IXth Plenary Assembly, including in particular the discussion of the IXth Plenary Assembly on the question of relation of Study Group chairmen and vice-chairmen.

3.   that the ad hoc Group should complete and publish its work one year before the Xth Plenary Assembly, so that administrations may consider its proposals in advance of the Plenary Assembly;

4.   that Study Groups should take the ad hoc Group's proposals into account in preparing Questions for the 1993–1996 study period;

5.   that the ad hoc Group should report to the Xth Plenary Assembly. This report may take into account comments on the proposals of the ad hoc Group received after the proposals are published;

instructs

the Director of the CCITT to solicit contributions and convene a first meeting of the ad hoc Group at an appropriate time soon after the Plenipotentiary Conference. The ad hoc Group should elect its Chairman and Vice-Chairman(men) at that first meeting.

REFERENCES

1.   G. Wallenstein. *International Telecommunication Agreements,* Binder One, Part One: "Collaboration without Coercion." Dobbs Ferry, NY: Oceana Publications, 1976. The subtitle of Part One is "The ITU as a Model for Worldwide Agreement-Making."

2.   Cited in: W. K. Jones, *Regulated Industries,* Brooklyn: Foundation Press, 1967. The citation appears in ch. 10; p. 1023.

3.   The acronym *MCI* is derived from the company's original, full name Microwave Communications, Inc. It reflects the company's beginning as a "specialized common carrier," authorized under the FCC's microwave station assignments. The first MCI radio system, providing service between Chicago and St. Louis, became operational in 1972. The company has since pursued competitive challenges to AT&T and some other common carriers, through pleadings for interconnection before the FCC and cases in the courts of law. In the 1980s, MCI emerged as a major, general-purpose, long-distance carrier, having abandoned reliance on microwave transmission. By 1989, MCI had absorbed the record carrier operations of WUI (Western Union International) and RCA Globecom (Global Communications, Inc.). The company now offers a wide range of national and international long-distance services.

Chapter Six
Conclusions

6.1 OUTLOOK FOR COMPETITION IN WORLD MARKETS

Henceforth, committee-approved standards are intended to exert control over the computer-communication markets. That economic objective is stated unequivocally in the ETSI enabling papers of the EC. No equivalent North American policy statement, related to the T1 Committee's function, seems to exist. However, T1's participating enterprises have no doubts about the economic make-or-break value of the standards in which they collaborate. Moreover, the rationale for creating T1 responds directly to the procompetitive intervention of US government agencies and courts. Viewed worldwide, in Japan as well as in nonindustrialized countries, the competitive evaluation of one standard over another has always controlled economic decisions for telecommunication. For these many countries, a limited choice among a few, firmly entrenched regional standard families will replace the case-by-case negotiation of the past.

The emerging competitive scenario may be likened to a three-ring megacircus, as illustrated in Figure 6.1. Network service providers and resellers are interlocked with equipment suppliers, as both sectors interlock with users of services. The standards committees provide the arena, stage management, and props, including figurative camels, dogs, and white elephants. The spectators are government decisionmakers, accompanied by technical staff, expert witnesses, advisory economists, and lawyers. The significance of the spectators' metaphor is in ushering in a diminished role of governmental authorities. These spectators may applaud or hiss a standards-controlled market performance, they may even leave the venue in protest, yet the show will go on. Further, the reduced role of national governments in standards may force faster, more effective liberalization of *transborder data flow* than the prestigious OECD (Organization for Economic Cooperation and Development) has been able to achieve so far [1].

In short, competition in major regional markets is possible for all who partake of the respective regional standards; competition in other, worldwide markets will

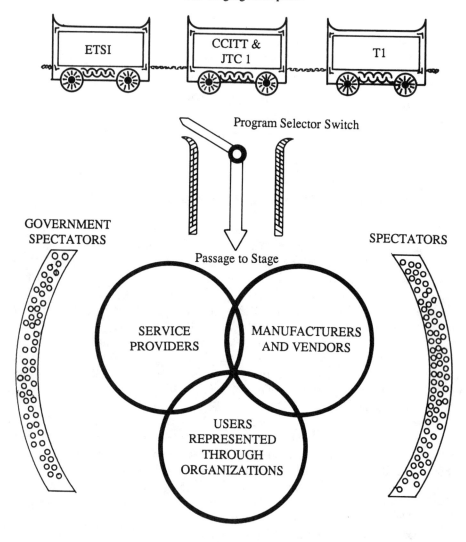

The Staging Enterprises

ETSI

CCITT & JTC 1

T1

Program Selector Switch

GOVERNMENT
SPECTATORS

SPECTATORS

Passage to Stage

SERVICE
PROVIDERS

MANUFACTURERS
AND VENDORS

USERS
REPRESENTED
THROUGH
ORGANIZATIONS

Figure 6.1 Scenario for Standards-Centered Competition—a Three-Ring Circus.

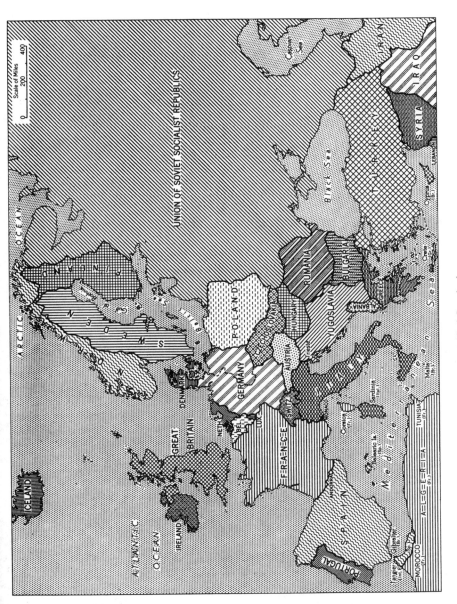

Figure 6.2 Map of CEPT's Europe Committed to Unified Standards.
Outline map of Europe used by permission of Rand McNally © 1951, 1954, 1961.

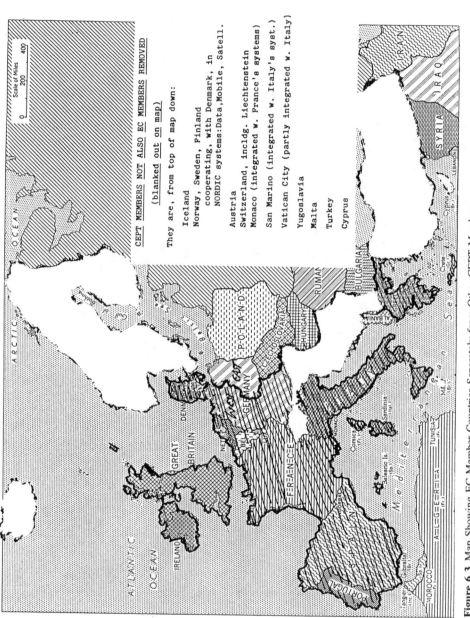

Figure 6.3 Map Showing EC Member Countries Separately from Other CEPT Members.

CEPT MEMBERS NOT ALSO EC MEMBERS REMOVED (blanked out on map)

They are, from top of map down:

Iceland
Norway, Sweden, Finland
    cooperating, with Denmark, in
    NORDIC systems:Data,Mobile, Satell.

Austria
Switzerland, incldg. Liechtenstein
Monaco (integrated w. France's systems)

San Marino (integrated w. Italy's syst.)
Vatican City (partly integrated w. Italy)

Yugoslavia

Malta

Turkey

Cyprus

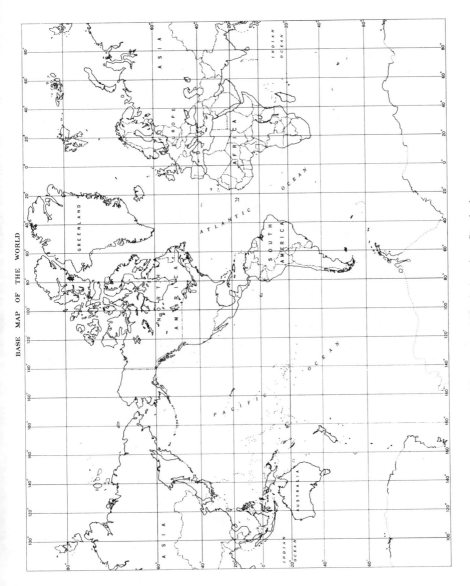

Figure 6.4 World Influence Zones of European and North American Standards.

be controlled by a given country's adherence to one or another regional standard. The reader may refer to a map of Europe for a visual impression of ETSI's domain, as marked in Figures 6.2 and 6.3. We have ventured farther with a map of the world (Figure 6.4), marked in a broad-brush manner to indicate the probable standards preference in most parts of the world. As seems evident, the CEPT-ETSI source will carry much of the world outside North America.

The power of standards has an additional, competitive result for the US market. It is thus far the only market open to unrestricted competition, and the largest market until Europe's 1992 target has been achieved. The world's most powerfully competing telecommunication manufacturers have subsidiaries in the United States. These subsidiaries participate in T1 Committee standards activities as a matter of right. Their parent companies thus can be involved in North American as well as their home countries' respective regional standards. This enviable position on two fronts could have been reciprocated by leading US companies if they had maintained their subsidiaries of many years' standing in Europe. By a remarkable, and surely not coincidental, corollary to the FCC and Court administered fragmentation of the US telecommunication industry, both ITT and GTE corporations have sold their foreign-based subsidiaries to European competitors, Alcatel and Siemens, respectively. These sales included substantial operations *in* the United States, so that Alcatel and Siemens acquired a much broader based presence in North America than they had before. Thus, telecommunication standards for the United States appear to be, again, in the care of AT&T, joined on many occasions by Bellcore, which began as an AT&T spinoff. The other major North American country, Canada, may continue to work in concert with the United States in standards-making. A plausible reason would be the important supplier position held by Canada's Northern Telecom, a company also well represented in Committee T1.

The European presence in the North American market offers an opportunity for future mergers of new standards proposals, so that, in time, some ETSI and T1 standards may become identical. The two standards committees have already established "observer" status liaison, enabling both to have "early warning" of forthcoming actions. Yet for years to come, some basic and pervasive differences will persist. We mention the deep-set divergence of digital system hierarchy standards, recorded side by side in the CCITT G.700 series. The spread of North America's T1 derived system technology is now so universal that a very large number of competing equipment suppliers have an investment in its permanence. In whatever different forms ISDN will eventually be adopted in the United States, the networks used will employ the T-carrier family of systems, not the European counterpart. The US business elite has been made well aware of this ISDN framework (Box 6.1).

With due allowance for such deeply rooted standards differences, the long-run outlook is for increasing worldwide compatibility. As shown earlier, that objective is best attained by *a priori* standards agreements, before large, competitive investments are made. This trend, taken together with the concentration of manufacturing

Box 6.1
Changed Business Perspective of Digital Systems from 1958 to 1988
(as reflected in *Fortune* magazine)

November 1958	Francis Bello, feature writer, describes long-term importance attached to new PCM carrier systems development. His source is *Bell Laboratories*. The article titled "Tomorrow's Telephone system", is one of two devoted to the Bell Labs.
November 1988	A "special insert" paid-advertising section explains and extolls the wide-ranging applications of ISDN. This time, credit for preparing the nontechnical text is given to a consulting company. The supporting advertisements promote several, strongly competing supplier organizations, US and foreign. AT&T, still enfolding Bell Labs but divested of local service companies, is now just one company among many vying for ISDN users' favor in US market.

capabilities in the hands of a few giant firms, foreshadows a kind of cartelization of the telecommunication network supply business. When all suppliers cite the same standards, which include performance, maintenance, and test routine specifications in great detail, purchasers are hard-pressed for valid criteria with which to select one from among other competitors. It seems, to this writer, to be an ideal setup for mutual accommodations of market share, aided in many cases by strong regional or national incentives for *a priori* preferences. If US government leaders alone persist in pursuit of free-market, anticartel policies, the US market might appear like a throwback to outdated, colonialist "open door" mercantilism of Europe's empire-building era.

The opposite possibility, namely that of opening markets to free, international competition anywhere in Europe and Asia, as in the United States, seems more remote than ever. The justification for this writer's pessimistic view in this regard is to be found precisely in the regional-to-worldwide unification of standards. During the long years when standards were used as barriers to trade, they were convenient instruments of protection for national industries. Europeans have since agreed to remove barriers among each other, but not to non-Europeans. This writer cannot predict what other policy tool will replace the convenience of nonconforming standards. What can be predicted, however, is sustained popular, political pressure in all industrialized countries outside North America for protection from overseas competition.

For reasons expounded in the preceding paragraphs, a state of "benign" cartelization with worldwide membership is probably the best compromise among conflicting regional and national ambitions. The result would at least minimize the potential for colonial status of one, large, free-market country.

6.2 OUTLOOK FOR THE NONINDUSTRIALIZED COUNTRIES

Developing countries expect to gain from the emergence of firm, finely detailed standards that acquire a power to which all telecommunication service partners and suppliers submit. An approved, common reference for all administrations has been seen as the basis for safe planning and procurement, helping those who lack intellectual and financial resources. Without question, a developing country's position as a client or licensee will improve.

Yet there is an offsetting, negative aspect. The greater concentration of standards-making efforts, coupled with increasing complexity of the actual standards, makes active participation of experts from a developing country less useful than before. Thus, aspirations of gradual accession to the "club" of standards-makers cannot be realized in the foreseeable future. Perpetuated dependency on decisions of the same, few industrialized leaders may not sit well with representatives of developing countries. Because they cannot influence the standards, alternative avenues for satisfying their aspirations must be found. This conclusion seems to foretell more, rather than less, bloc voting for Resolutions focused on developing country needs, at every major ITU conference. Such a trend can only disaffect the principal industrialized country representatives, with a possible decline in ITU effectiveness as worldwide standards coordinator. The history of CEPT's growth, climaxing in ETSI, gives some indication of rallying around regional institutions, free from the troublesome divergences of ITU's diffused membership. These potentially negative aspects cloud the outlook for ITU's future preeminence in standardization.

The reader must be clear that the author describes a dilemma for ITU, not a negative view of the role of developing countries. Their legitimate needs and concerns with regard to planning, designing, financing, installing, and maintaining telecommunication infrastructures are not in question. Rather, the ITU's acceptance of responsibility for programs and projects of development assistance needs to be critically reexamined. The combined pressures of technical assistance and standardization have proved too heavy for reconciliation within one organization. These two tasks should be separated from the top down, so that each can staff and spend without encroachment on the other. Indeed, many developing countries' representatives in ITU, individually speaking, recognize the conflict between the two tasks. Only during voting on Resolutions, budgets, and other administrative decisions, does bloc posturing of the UN General Assembly prevail over individual insight. This posture and voting pattern perpetuates and aggravates ITU's dilemma.

6.3 LEARNING TO PLAY THE SUPRAPOWER GAME

For telecommunication business oriented companies, preoccupation with standards in the purview of national and international committees becomes a high-level, central management task. Personnel assigned to this work preferably should have experienced engineering decisions made in the presence of adverse market activities, or comparable career setbacks. These persons will expect to be known as "Mr. or Mrs. Standard" of their respective companies to make their voices heard in committee. Continuity is of great importance in this work for two reasons. First, the company's interests are ill served by temporarily assigned people, who lack opportunity and incentive for familiarity with the particular issue under consideration. Second, collaborative committee work is an intensely human task, where mutual acquaintance and tolerance count as much as personal expertise.

Beyond steps taken by company management, the study of standards and standardization needs to be established in the programs of colleges and universities. The orientation is cross-disciplinary, as is the case with telecommunication management and policy programs now offered by some universities. Focus on the standards process, structure of standards organizations, and entire families of existing standards requires full concentration through courses and problem solving. An effective standards course program may be comparable in depth and length of study time to the learning of a foreign language.

In fact, the comparison to language is quite appropriate, considering the special terminology developed by and for computer and communications technology. CCITT Recommendations and the standards of other bodies employ specialized vocabularies, some that are themselves standardized, yet others that are arbitrary, *ad hoc* creations for the convenience of the drafting committees. In the latter category, are acronyms, condensed citations of two, three, or four word compound expressions. Acronyms are usually introduced near the start of a Recommendation, but rarely redefined in later documentation. The CCITT *Red Book* of 1984 listed 1740 such acronyms on 23 pages of its "Index," volume X!

In a class apart from acronyms are the special "languages" for specification-descriptive and computer programming purposes developed by CCITT. In the latest (1989 *Blue Book*) edition, these language standards occupy seven facsicles, averaging close to 200 pages each, which represents a respectable reading load for the serious student.

In conclusion, we may state that a firm or entrepreneur that is ignorant of the standards has no business in the telecommunication market. That caveat is more decisive than it has been for a long time, before standards acquired suprapower status. Henceforth, continuous awareness of changes and additions is a prerequisite for sustained, if not enlarged, market position. Fortunately, a kind of *glasnost* has come into being with telecommunication reforms, so that every interested company or person can now share the information processed and published by committees. There is a cost of sharing, either through paid participation in the respective committee, as in CCITT and US T1, or through selective publication purchase, as with Bellcore's "Catalog of Technical Information." Standards-making is expensive; it needs to be financed by its collaborators and beneficiaries in partnership.

6.4 CONCLUDING SUMMARY

A quarter-century of relentless technological drive has created visions of a wonderland of unlimited computer-communication opportunities. Actual progress in worldwide telecommunication service coverage, quality, and diversity of options has been impressive by any past measure. Simultaneously, computer service and terminal offerings have proliferated to the point where the smallest office uses some of them—at least, in the industrialized countries. Yet with all this progress, the computer-communication marriage seems to lag far behind. The available networks are not "open" to a great variety of optional and competitive applications; the most innovative terminals do not necessarily interface smoothly at network terminations. The multiservice promise of ISDN arrives via a patchwork of partial implementations. What steps can be taken to accelerate computer-communication integration in the marketplace?

Answers to this question have been sought first in one major government policy area: reform of the service monopolies. In one country after another, and in the European Community's coming unified market, the provision of telecommunication services has been opened up to allow greater freedom for computer-communication. Yet this forceful opening accentuates the service providers' and their networks' lagging in another policy area: standardization. So, the advocates of regulatory reforms have a new target: more, and more timely, standards. One worldwide and several regional committees are under pressure to meet this challenge. That the most extraordinary committee standardization performance can satisfy every demand of all parties with a stake in the market is doubtful. What becomes clear, however, is that these very pressures enhance the powerful positions occupied by the committees. Henceforth, standards is computer-communication's "name of the game." Play it by their rules or lose it! That is our message.

ANNOTATED REFERENCE TO CHAPTER SIX

[1] *Transborder Data Flows,* Proceedings of an OECD Conference, December 1983, Hans-Peter Gassmann, ed., Amsterdam: Elsevier Science Publishers, 1985.
The Organization for Economic Cooperation and Development (OECD), founded in 1960 and formally established in 1961, is a convention type of intergovernmental organization (IGO). Its stated aims are economic growth in member countries, development of the world economy, and "expansion of world trade on a multilateral, nondiscriminatory basis in accordance with international obligations."
In pursuit of these goals, OECD has set up a committee and a division on Information, Computer and Communications Policy (ICCP). An ICCP working party on Transborder Data Flows has been exploring political, legal, and eco-

nomic aspects of international data communications. Prior to the above-cited conference, the working party had obtained proposals for a policy declaration in favor of *free flow* from two respected, academic sources. These proposals were flatly rejected by OECD and have apparently remained unpublished under OECD imprimateur. OECD's member governments apparently continue to invoke the sovereign nation-state's prerogatives with regard to inflow and outflow of data.

Glossary of Acronyms and Abbreviations†

Acronym or Abbreviation	Definition	Region or Country of Origin
AIM	Advanced Information in Medicine in Europe	EU
ANSI	American National Standards Institute	US
AT&T	American Telephone and Telegraph Company	US
Bellcore	Bell Communications Research	US
BOC	Bell Operating Companies	US
BT	British Telecom	UK
CAC	Commercial Action Committee	EU
CADDIA	Cooperation in Automation of Data and Documentation for Imports/Exports and Agriculture	EU
CCH	Coordination Committee on Harmonization	EU
CCIF	International Telephone Consultative Committee	ITU
CCIR	International Radio Consultative Committee	ITU
CCIT	International Telegraph Consultative Committee	ITU
CCITT	International Telegraph and Telephone Consultative Committee	ITU
CEI	Comparably Efficient Interconnection	US
CEN	European Committee for Standardization	EU
CENELEC	European Committee for Electrotechnical Standardization	EU
CEPT	European Conference of Posts and Telecommunications Administrations	EU
CMV	Joint Group on Vocabulary (or Terminology)	ITU
COMSAT	Communication Satellite Corporation* (now COMSAT Corp.)	US
CPE	Customer Premises Equipment	US
DELTA	Developing European Learning through Technological Advance	EU
DRIVE	Dedicated Road Infrastructure for Vehicle Safety in Europe	EU

†*Cautionary Note:* Most of these acronyms have become the only official names of the respective organizations or programs. In the case of certain companies, an (*) indicates that the original name has been formally made obsolete.

Acronym or Abbreviation	Definition	Region or Country of Origin
EC	European Community (or Communities)	EU
ECMA	European Computer Manufacturers' Association	EU
ECSA	Exchange Carriers Standards Association	US
ECU	European Currency Unit	EU
	A computed "basket" currency, based on the twelve EC Member countries' currency values. The three-letter acronym has a francophone dictionary meaning. Pronounced *ākü'*, the word is derived from Latin *scutum* = shield; the shape given the first coins minted in France in the reign of Louis IX (Saint-Louis), in the mid-thirteenth century.	
EEC	European Economic Community, a term now generally replaced by EC	EU
EFTA	European Free Trade Association	EU
EIA	Electronic Industry Association	US
EMUG	European Manufacturers' User Group	EU
EN	European Standard (N = *Norm* in German, *Norme* in French)	EU
ESPRIT	European Strategic Program for Research in Information Technologies	EU
ETS	European Telecommunication Standard (*see also* NET)	EU
ETSI	European Telecommunication Standards Institute	EU
EUSIDIC	European Association of Information Services	EU
EVE	European Videoconference Experiment	EU
EWOS	European Workshop for Open Systems	EU
FCC	Federal Communications Commission	US
GATT	General Agreement on Tariffs and Trade	WW
GTE	General Telephone and Electronics Corporation* (now GTE Corp.)	USA
ICC	International Chamber of Commerce	WW
IEC	International Electrotechnical Commission	WW
IEEE	Institute of Electrical and Electronics Engineers	US, WW
IEV	International Electrotechnical Vocabulary	WW
INMARSAT	International Maritime Satellite Consortium	WW
INSIS	Interinstitutional Integrated Services Information System	WW, EU
INTELSAT	International Telecommunication Satellite Consortium	WW
INTUG	International Telecommunications Users Groups	WW
ISDN	Integrated Services Digital Network	ITU
ISO	International Organization for Standardization	WW

Acronym or Abbreviation	Definition	Region or Country of Origin
ITSTC	Information Technology Steering Committee	EU
ITT	International Telephone and Telegraph Corporation* (now ITT Corp.)	US
ITU	International Telecommunication Union	WW
JACUDI	Japan Computer Usage Development Institute	J
JCG	Joint Coordination Group	IEC, ITU
KDD	Kokusai Denshin Denwa Company Ltd. (Japan) (literally translated "International Telegraph and Telephone," Japan's transoceanic carrier)	J
LAN	Local Area Network	US
LATA	Local Access Transport Area	US
MAN	Metropolitan Area Network	US
MCI	Microwave Communications Inc.* (now MCI Communications Corp.)	US
MFJ	Modification of Final Judgment	US
NAPLPS	North American Presentation Level Protocol Standard	US
NEC	Nippon Electric Company	J
NET	European Telecommunication Standard (*see* ETS)	EU
NTT	Nippon Telegraph and Telephone Corporation	J
OECD	Organization for Economic Cooperation and Development	WW
OFTEL	Office of Telecommunications	UK
ONA	Open Network Architecture	US
ONP	Open Network Provision	EU
OSI	Open Systems Interconnection	WW
RACE	Research and Development in Advanced Communications Technologies for Europe	EU
RBHC	Regional Bell Holding Company	US
RPOA	Recognized Private Operating Agency	ITU
SI	International System of Units	WW
SIP	Societá Italiana per l'Esercizio Telefonico	I
SITA	Airlines Worldwide Telecommunications Network	WW
SNA	Systems Network Architecture: company proprietary	IBM
SOG-T	Senior Officials Group on Telecommunications	EU
SPAG	Standards Promotion and Application Group	EU
STAR	Special Telecommunications Action for Regional Development	EU

Acronym or Abbreviation	Definition	Region or Country of Origin
SWIFT	Society for Worldwide Interbank Financial Telecommunications	WW
PCM	Pulse Code Modulation (in Digital Systems)	WW
T1	North American Digital (PCM) Carrier System	US, Canada
T1	Telecommunications Standards Committee of the ECSA	US
TA	Technical Advisory	US
TAT-8	Transatlantic Telephone Cable Number Eight	US, EU
TEDIS	Trade Electronic Data Interchange Systems	EU
TIA	Telecommunications Industry Association	US
TR	Technical Reference	US
TRAC	Technical Recommendations Application Committee	EU
TRIF	Technology Requirements Industry Forum	US

Legend of country and regional codes:

EU = Europe
I = Italy
ITU = terminology used by ITU
J = Japan
UK = United Kingdom
US = United States
WW = worldwide application

Select Bibliography

This concise bibliography is arranged by major subjects covered in this book.

(a) ITU (International Telecommunication Union) and its Standards-Making Committees CCIR and CCITT:

1. ITU's publications are available by order from Geneva headquarters, as follows:
   General Secretariat—Publication Sales
   ITU
   Place des Nations
   Geneva, Switzerland
   A *List of Publications* will be mailed upon request.
2. Codding, George C. Jr., and Rutkowski, Anthony M., *The International Telecommunication Union in a Changing World,* Norwood, MA: Artech House, 1982.
3. Wallenstein, Gerd, *International Telecommunication Agreements,* Three-volume set of loose-leaf service, periodically updated documentation of ITU and its committees. Dobbs Ferry, NY: Oceana Publications, 1976–1986.

(b) International, Regional, and US National Standards Organizations, other than ITU:

1. *IEEE Communications Magazine,* v. 23, n. 1 (January 1985). Entire issue devoted to this subject.
2. *ETSI—European Telecommunications Standards Institute,* Director: Diodato Gagliardi. Mail address:
   BP 52
   F-06561
   Valbonne Cedex, France
3. *Standards Committee T1 Telecommunications.* Current chairman is Ivor Knight. The committee's parent organization, ECSA (Exchange Carriers Standards Association), provides the mail address:
   ECSA
   5430 Grosvenor Lane
   Bethesda, MD 20814-2122, USA
   O. Gusella is Executive Director of ECSA.

(c) Deregulation, Divestiture, and Restructuring:

1. In the European Community (EC),
   Ungerer, Herbert, and Costello, Nicholas, *Telecommunications in Europe,* Free Choice for the User in Europe's 1992 Market, Brussels: The European Perspectives Series, 1988.
2. In Germany,
   Reform of the Postal and Telecommunications System in the Federal Republic of Germany, Concept of the Federal Government for the Restructuring of the Telecommunications Market, Prepared by the Ministry of Posts and Telecommunications, Heidelberg: R. V. Decker–G. Schenck, 1988.
   Witte, Eberhard, chairman of commission, *Restructuring of the Telecommunications System,* Report of the Government Commission for Telecommunications, Heidelberg: R. V. Decker–G. Schenck, 1988.
3. In the United Kingdom,
   Hamilton, R. N. D., ed., *Telecommunications Act of 1984,* London: Surveyors Publications, 1984.
4. In the United States,
   Brotman, Stuart N., ed., *The Telecommunications Deregulation Sourcebook,* Norwood, MA: Artech House, 1987.
   Hubert, Peter, *The Geodesic Network,* 1987 Report on Competition in the Telephone Industry, Washington DC: US Government Printing Office, 1987. *IEEE Communications Magazine,* Special issues: v. 23, n. 12 (December 1985) "Divestiture: Two Years Later"; v. 25, n. 1 (January 1987) "Special Issue on Telecommunications Regulation"; v. 27, n. 1 (January 1989) "Telecommunications Deregulation."

(d) ISDN (Integrated Services Digital Network):

1. Kahl, Peter, *ISDN: The Future Telecommunication Network of the Deutsche Bundespost,* Heidelberg: R. V. Decker–G. Schenck, 1986.
2. Pepper, Robert, *Through the Looking Glass: Integrated Broadband Networks, Regulatory Policies, and Institutional Change.* Washington, DC: FCC, Office of Plans and Policy, 1988. OPP Working Paper No. 24. This paper deals with questions regarding the future of broadband ISDN in the United States.
3. Stallings, William, *ISDN: An Introduction,* New York: Macmillan, 1989. Decidedly the most complete and up-to-date engineering textbook, based on the 1989 vintage CCITT Recommendations.

(e) French Original Contributions to the Concept and Marketing of Telematics:

1. Marchand, Marie, *The Minitel Saga: A French Success Story,* Paris: Larousse, 1988.
2. Nora, Simon, and Minc, Alain, *The Computerization of Society,* A Report to the President of France. (Translated from original French edition titled, "L'informatisation de la société.") Cambridge, MA: MIT Press, 1980.
   This seminal study introduced the concept as well as the new term of *telematics*. Unfortunately for the reader of this English translation, the title word "computerization" utterly fails to do justice to the book's scope.
3. *Teletel Newsletter,* English Edition of *La Lettre de Teletel,* Published by France Telecom, Paris, Direction Générale. International mail address:
   >France Télécom, DAII-SAI
   >Immeuble Périsud
   >7, Blvd Romain-Rolland
   >92128 Montrouge Cedex, France,

Index